The Ancien Régime

the text of this book is printed
on 100% recycled paper

The Ancien Régime
FRENCH SOCIETY 1600–1750

Pierre Goubert

TRANSLATED BY STEVE COX

HARPER TORCHBOOKS
Harper & Row, Publishers
New York, Hagerstown, San Francisco, London

Contents

Documents and lists of books for further reading appear at the end
of chapters.

Documents

Foreword to this edition

It is always an honour for a French historian to see one of his books translated into English – an honour that tempts the author to venture a few introductory English words of his own. One cannot deny that French historians have for their English colleagues complex feelings of superficial differences and yet of deep brotherhood; mainly because England has never destroyed her ancien régime, though she has painfully suppressed the penny, the old denarius once used in France and in such an important part of Roman Europe.

This book may surprise the reader, since it bears little resemblance to so many others published under the same title. In a way, it is a testament written before its time. It results from fifteen years of teaching in French universities (and some others). The aim is to understand, to explain and to simplify facts; therefore the text is necessarily schematic. This book also results from twenty-five years spent reading old documents written between 1600 and 1750 – reading, but also reflecting. These long hours of study have led the author to represent ancien régime society as it seems to have been. This vision may appear rather intricate, but the reader must remember that ancien régime French society was the opposite of simplicity and rigour. The author must confess that he has depicted it as he saw it. If he is wrong, others will doubtless prove it; he knows they will be up to the task, since they have never breathed the dusty air of French archives.

The author can be reproached for not supporting a theory or obeying a system in this book. But no theory or system will exactly account for the subject. May the author add that most of the theories and systems are, in his opinion, the very negation of historical endeavour and even of intelligence?

A second volume, setting this society against the ancien régime State, is nearly completed in French. If the history of the opposition between the two, which was never so violent in England as in France, should interest the English, they will be able to read it soon.

The author wishes to acknowledge Steve Cox who successfully translated his too French style into English, and his London publishers, especially Susan Phillpott, whose patience and kindness have been constant.

P.G. *(July 1972)*

Foreword to
the original French edition

It was René Redmond who had the idea for this book and asked me to write it. That is why it is dedicated to him, as well as to the student groups of all ages at Rennes, Paris and Nanterre who first encountered it in its draft stages and who contributed unwittingly to its development. Only the author, of course, is to be blamed for its weaknesses.

This book does not adopt any theoretical form, since it is not intended to take its place within the spheres – at once related and distinct – of law, political science or sociology. And yet it does aim for a bird's eye view of general characteristics.

Nor does it take the form of a chronological survey. It is difficult to enclose the ancien régime within specific dates. It grew quite naturally out of the Middle Ages, as the mature man grows out of the child, or rather as the old man out of the adult, between the Hundred Years War and the wars of religion. Outwardly, at least, the circumstances of its disappearance are more definite: the basic structure collapsed between 1789 and 1793, although various buttresses and even a few main beams resisted for a long time, and some, perhaps, are still in place.

This work is also intended as a handbook. It is generally accepted that a handbook should offer established, simple, orderly and easily assimilable facts. A tone of certainty and a three-point plan would answer to a part of that definition, given that these were still satisfactory prescriptions. But it is difficult, without resorting to artifice, to give a straightforward account of a régime which had no official birth date, nor even a written constitution, and which positively cultivated confusion. It is impossible, in fact, and perhaps dishonest, to shed light where it has never shone and where it will not enter: in a sense the method of Descartes, that voluntary exile, is probably the antithesis of the ancien régime. It is also hard to give any cut and dried account of a régime whose true workings are still something of an unknown quantity to historians, and for a whole host of not altogether justifiable reasons.

Some of these are sentimental and politico-philosophical; this régime, the would-be destroyer of the Revolution, still gives rise to partisanship and elicits defences and accusations, or at any rate attractions and repulsions, which all too many historians are unable to resist. There are other reasons connected with respectable, necessary, but inadequate concepts of historical research, confined for too long to the juridical texts, acts of government, public figures, institutions and political and religious ideas of the thin upper crust of the literate and cultured. Seen in this light, the ancien régime seemed to have held sway over a desert. Lastly, many historians – a highly traditionalist breed – have for more than a century retailed ready-made formulas all decked out in 'isms' – absolutism, classicism, capitalism, feudalism – whose vagueness leads to confusion; these have to be rejected, or rejuvenated by fresh thinking.

During the last fifty years many worthy studies have been exposed to further, sometimes immoderate, scrutiny. The assault was spearheaded by sociologists, geographers and the Bloch-Febvre group (known as the 'école des Annales'). More recently, traditional history has been shaken up by the demographers, the psychologists, a few philosophers and ethnologists, and most recently by the linguists, who at the same time have also been broadening its horizons. It would be an insult to the reader to fob him off with an 'ancien régime' reduced to kings and ministers, plus a few handsful of jurists, theologians and 'philosophers'.

This handbook is not intended as a cut-price work of condescension, concocted for a quickly satisfied public. While it lays down a few indisputable certainties, it never glosses over the shadowy areas, and sets out to be both a full, which is to say a social, living description, and an exposition. Or is it too ambitious to aim at a straight, broad view, to pose problems, to try to understand and be understood, and to criticize so as to understand still better?

Lastly, this work is based on a threefold gamble. It sets out to examine separately, and in two successive volumes, the entities of Society and State, which are obviously tightly interwoven. Further, its focus is essentially the period 1600–1750, because the previous period is still not well enough known, while the subsequent period seems to me altogether different, and deserving of a separate study. This involves two options, if not two bets, on which opinions may differ. The third gamble is almost antihistorical: I have tried to take in four reigns, three regencies and five generations at one swoop, on the assumption that their common features outweigh their differences, their evolutions, even their contrasts. I can only make up for this by attempting in future to produce closer chronological accounts. I have already covered the time of Louis XIV; I hope to be able to do the same for the fascinating decades in which the two cardinal-ministers strove to dominate. And besides there are other people at work, who will surely get there sooner, and better.

I · EMERGENCE AND DEFINITION OF THE CONCEPT OF THE ANCIEN RÉGIME

At the present time there exist two standard approaches towards defining and therefore explaining the ancien régime: they tend to complement rather than contradict one another.

a) The narrow approach amounts to the analysis of a political and juridical structure. Theory is its point of departure, institutions, and little more than institutions, its objective. It certainly had a long period of ascendancy, and the members of the Constituent Assembly – being lawyers and political theorists themselves – generally regarded their work of demolition and reconstruction as a political and juridical operation, at least to begin with.

b) Most historians adopt a much broader approach. They use the term 'ancien régime' as a blanket expression to cover anything that occurred in France between the first of the Valois and the last of the Bourbons, robbing the term of all significance and reducing it to a mere label.

It seems reasonable to assume that the truth lies somewhere between these two extremes, and more methodical to begin at the beginning and consult the opinions of those best entitled to hold them, the men who defined the ancien régime by the very fact that they tried to put an end to it.

1. THE ANCIEN RÉGIME DEFINED BY THE CONSTITUENT ASSEMBLY

The most outstanding feature of the 'ancien régime', both as an idea and as a term, is its late appearance, its posthumous birth, the fact that it did not emerge until the system it described was extinct and had been recognized and ratified as such both in law and in popular acceptance. The death of the ancien régime, certainly as a phrase, in part as an entity, was also its birth.

But when and how did it die? (We shall shelve for the moment the question why.)

It died very quickly, if the forty months it took to die are compared with two or three centuries of adulthood and a thousand years of gestation and infancy. It died between 1789 and 1793. Yet it has survived, like so many of history's rejects, in people's minds, in nostalgia, and even in the customs of slow-moving, conservative provinces that are out of step with the overall tempo of French evolution – in the museum provinces, the backwoods of the west, and in isolated mountain regions. It persists too wherever various backward-looking social groups survive, but these are no concern of ours.

It is important to have a clear picture of the various stages in that final decline, which are also the prenatal stages of a 'new régime', that asserts itself by seeking to be different from, and thereby defining, its predecessor.

JUNE 1789: EMERGENCE OF THE NATION

Setting: the States-General, meeting at Versailles since 5 May.

After six weeks of growing impatience and royal delaying tactics, the representatives of the Third Estate, soon to be joined by the mass of the parish priests – a decisive and significant shift of allegiance – and by a few 'liberal' aristocrats, declare that they represent 'at least ninety-six hundredths of the Nation', and that they are entitled to the designation of 'National Assembly' (17 June).

On the same day, the same assembly declares invalid those royal taxes it has not approved but cannily authorizes their continued collection, for *raison d'État*. The opening sentence of its declaration invokes 'the power whose exercise the Nation is now resuming under the auspices of a Monarch...' whose cooperation is hoped for.

Three days later, on the occasion of the tennis-court oath, the National Assembly records its belief that it has been 'called upon in order to decide the constitution of the realm, effect the regeneration of public order, and uphold the true principles of monarchy' (20 June 1789).

These terse, pithy statements elicit a number of comments.

The first is negative. In the thinking of the men who are about to set up a 'new régime' the existence of the monarchy is taken for granted. As all the evidence (including that of the *cahiers de doléances**) tends to show, neither the man nor the institution is under attack; the king's person and monarchy itself still inspire respect, trust and near-adoration. It will take a whole series of disastrous blunders on the part of Louis XVI, typified by and culminating in the escape intercepted at Varennes in June 1791, to precipitate the final split between part of the French people and their king, if not their monarchic system. The notion of the 'ancien régime' is not therefore inseparably bound up with the monarchic character of the central power – as the nineteenth-century experiments in monarchy confirm in any case.

The second comment has to do with 'the nation'. The nation declares itself certainly 'under the aegis', 'under the auspices of the monarch', but distinct and separate from him, although respecting his prerogatives. A long undercurrent of thought and opinion has built up to this astonishing affirmation of a new concept that is to be even more forthrightly expressed two months later, in Article Three of the Declaration of the Rights of Man and of the Citizen (26 August 1789):

> The essential principle of all sovereignty lies in the Nation. No body and no individual can exercise any authority not expressly derived therefrom.

The principle here stated so forcefully is a new one, and needs to be set against its opposite. First, Louis XIV's blunt proclamation: 'In France the nation is not a separate body, it dwells entirely within the person of the King.' A hundred years later, in the session known as the 'flagellation of the Parlement of Paris', Louis XV expressed himself in almost identical terms:

---

* The 'books of grievances' submitted to the States-General by various sections of all three Estates. See pp. 10-12. – Tr.

The rights and interests of the Nation, which you dare to make into a body apart from the Monarch, are of necessity one with my own, and lie in my hands only.

Before going into battle the armies of the ancien régime used to cry *'Vive le roi!'*; those of the Revolution were soon to cry *'Vive la nation!'* (*'Vive la France!'* is a much later arrival). What these slogans and quotations show is that the emergence of the idea of 'the nation' was a prime factor of the Revolution and the régimes that followed it. The idea of the nation is intrinsically alien to the nature of the ancien régime, and where it does occur is merged and absorbed into the person and function of the king. (We pass over the question of whether the 'nation' of the Constituent Assembly included all Frenchmen, or just the élites of wealth and merit.)

The third comment has to do with the constitution. The Constituent Assembly sets itself the task of 'deciding the Constitution of the Realm', appoints a 'Constitutional Committee' from among its own membership (7 July), proclaims itself the 'National Constituent Assembly', and embarks on drafting what is to become the Constitution of 1791, the first great constitutional document of France. This kind of concept and intention presupposes that the ancien régime 'did not possess a constitution', a proposition that can be understood in at least two not necessarily contradictory ways:

a) France had no constitutional document written as a single entity, or no accumulation of separate instruments (after the English manner) which because of their continuity and consistency might be taken as having constitutional status. The early jurists, and a great many historians in their wake, conducted a long debate as to whether the realm might not at least be held to possess an 'unwritten' constitution, and made claims for widely varying numbers of 'fundamental laws'. The obvious disagreement of these 'authorities' is sufficient indication that France (like the United States before her) needed a single comprehensive instrument drawn up by the nation or its representatives, and with the definitive title of 'constitution'.

b) The second meaning harks back to Montesquieu and others. A true 'constitution' must be clear, firmly based and beyond dispute; that is, it must comply with a set of principles approved in advance by a majority of the delegates to the Constituent Assembly. These principles are popular sovereignty, natural rights, equality of birth and separation of powers.

Whatever else may be thought of the jumble of individual documents, unwritten conventions and disputed customs that jurists and historians have dignified with the name of 'constitution', it is obvious that it did not comply with these simple principles that were accepted by enlightened opinion and had already been partially embodied in the American constitution of 1787.

AUGUST–SEPTEMBER 1789: THE COMPLETE DESTRUCTION OF THE FEUDAL RÉGIME

After the utterly unexpected rural and urban uprisings in July, the National Constituent Assembly, as it was now called, took another of the steps that negatively define the régime it was rapidly demolishing; by the decrees of 4 to 11 August 1789, it 'completely destroys' the 'feudal régime'.

Fierce controversies have raged between historians and historical theorists over the term 'feudal régime', but these have to be discarded, since to the members of the Assembly it was clearly a common term with a clear meaning: in abolishing it, except for a few second thoughts, as an integral part of the dying régime, they showed that this 'feudal régime' constituted one of the pillars of the ancien régime.

But what was this régime that they called feudal? Analysis of the decrees discussed, accepted and promulgated on and after 4 August produces a precise answer. The Constituent Assembly counted the following as integral elements of the 'feudal régime' and therefore of the ancien régime:

1. All traces of personal servitude, the remains of medieval serfdom, usually designated by the name of *mainmorte*.

2. All feudal (or seigneurial) rights, and primarily those of keeping pigeons and doves, game reserves, and exclusive hunting-rights – which may seem strange in the twentieth century, but brooked no argument in the late eighteenth, as the *cahiers de doléances* amply prove.

3. All seigneurial courts – the 'village tribunals' – held by the seigneur and his agents.

4. All types of tithe. The inclusion of what is strictly speaking an ecclesiastical institution may seem odd to us, but it corresponds to the spirit of the times and of the Assembly: the tithe was one of the pillars of the ancien régime.

This condemnation of tithes goes hand in hand with that of the *casuels* (the parish priests' perquisites) and the multitude of contributions levied on behalf of the Holy See. These methods of paying parish priests and subsidizing Rome are thus seen as integral parts of the 'feudal' and so of the ancien régime.

5. All judicial or municipal venal offices. The system of buying and bequeathing administrative office is therefore equally inherent in the nature of the 'feudal régime' – which will surprise only the historians of the twentieth century – and so of the ancien régime – which will surprise nobody.

6. All 'pecuniary privileges . . . in the matter of subsidies', which means taxes and dues. A wide range of privileges (by no means exclusive to the nobility and the clergy) constituted one of the fundamental principles of the ancien régime, perhaps the most central of all. From now onward, lip-service at least was to be paid to equality of taxation, which was to fall upon 'all citizens and all property in the same manner and in the same form' (Article Nine of the decree of 11 August).

7. Inequality of birth and of access to employment. A cardinal point, as well as being the springboard for the great onslaught on the nobility (which did not yet stand condemned as such, however). Nevertheless, the opening sentence of Article One of the Declaration of the Rights of Man and the Citizen (26 August) clearly stated that 'Men are born and remain free and equal in their rights'.

Neither the feudal nor the ancien régime had ever accepted this principle.

8. In the little-noticed Articles Seventeen and Eighteen of the decree of 4 August, the Assembly proclaims the king 'restorer of French liberty' – which neatly forces his hand – and decides to go to His Majesty in a body to present its decree, 'to bear him the homage of its most respectful gratitude and beseech him to permit the Te Deum to be sung in his chapel, and to attend it in person . . .'

Quite obviously then, there is no attack on the Christian, Catholic nature of the pre-1789 régime, which is seen as no more fundamental or abhorrent than the monarchy. What singles it out and condemns it in the eyes of the Constituent Assembly is its seigneurial character, tithes, marketing of offices, and the inequality in its taxation, law and concept of man.

THE DEATH-KNELL OF THE ANCIEN RÉGIME AND ITS POSTHUMOUS DEFINITION: THE PREAMBLE TO THE CONSTITUTION OF 1791

The strenuous efforts and impassioned discussions that occupied the period between August 1789 and September 1791 culminated in the constitution 'sworn' by the King on 14 September 1791. We shall excerpt the preamble to this lengthy document for close examination and analysis:

The National Assembly . . . irrevocably abolishes the institutions that offended against liberty and equal rights. There is no longer either nobility, peerage, hereditary distinctions, class distinctions, feudal rule, patrimonial courts, or any of the titles, denominations and prerogatives derived therefrom, or any order of chivalry, or any of the guilds or decorations for which proofs of nobility used to be required, or which presupposed distinctions of birth, or any other superiority than that of public functionaries in the exercise of their duties. There is no longer either venality or heredity of any public office. There is no longer, for any part of the Nation or for any individual, any privilege or exception from the common law of all Frenchmen.

There are no longer either guild-masterships or guilds of any trade, craft or profession. The law recognizes neither religious vows nor any other commitment that would be contrary to natural rights or to the Constitution.

In this solemn, thrilling proclamation of both death and victory, the Constituent Assembly epitomizes its idea of the régime it has destroyed. It was a feudal régime, yet they conserve its respect for property and monarchy; an ecclesiastical or Church-bound régime, yet its respect for religion survives; a régime of venality and administrative heredity – this they totally reject; and a régime of inequality of birthright and all kinds of privilege – again rejected. But all these decisions had been practically in force since the autumn of 1789. Two years later, the previous emphases and condemnations were extended to include at least three further elements held to be part of the condemned régime:

a) The 'guild-masterships and guilds of professions, crafts and trades', trespassing on common law, individual liberty and freedom of employment, are classed among the 'privileged bodies' rejected by the new régime;

b) The second addition – the ban on religious vows – is evidence of a serious attack on an important aspect of Catholicism. Such vows are now deemed contrary to 'natural law'. Irrespective of principles, this move expressed the low esteem in which the regular clergy were held now and had been held for some time past, for instance by Colbert and even by Louis XIV, whose memoirs complain of 'that great number of priests, most of whom, being of no use to the Church, were a burden on the State';

c) The crucial point, however, is the new, angry, insistent condemnation of all nobility, which is absent from the 1789 documents but reiterated here in the most precise and forceful form. The members of the Assembly concluded by specifying the fact of nobility as one of the fundamental characteristics of the régime that they were taking apart.

Thus, the men of the Constituent Assembly defined the ancien régime in terms of its social, juridical and psychological far more than its political and religious characteristics. They condemned a society, laws, practices and customs. They were not condemning either monarchy or a religious faith, as Tocqueville saw, except in those outward forms which in their eyes were not part of the old régime.

It only remained for them to give a name to the society whose death-knell they were sounding, and it was not long before they did so.

THE ANCIEN RÉGIME: THE POSTHUMOUS BIRTH OF THE TERM IN 1790

The philologist Ferdinand Brunot let very little escape him, and he did not overlook the little problem of the origins of such a long-lived and widespread term. In volume nine of his *Histoire de la langue française* he wrote:

A régime was an order, a rule, a rule of health, for example; it was also a method of administration . . . That the term should be applied to the age-old system of governing France was only natural. The daring stroke lay in coupling it with the epithet *ancien* . . . Groping towards it, the decrees of the Constituent Assembly often refer to the 'preceding régime'. *Régime ancien* and *vieux régime* also occur, but *ancien régime* soon prevailed, and became an expression in its own right.

'Soon' – but when? Close scrutiny of the immense legislative output of the Constituent Assembly would pin down the date of birth, but it would have to be combined with analysis of the vocabulary of journalism, letters, everyday speech, etc. Do we need to go to such lengths, when Tocqueville, quoting Mirabeau, provides an answer?

Less than a year after the start of the Revolution, Mirabeau wrote to the King: 'Compare the new state of affairs with the Ancien Régime. . . .'
(Tocqueville, *The Ancien Régime and the Revolution,*
Book I, Ch. 2.)

After making its appearance in the course of the year 1790*, the expression was very quickly adopted, continually and commonly used, and exported to foreign countries, where it still survives. A comparative study of its distribution, travels, extensions and distortions would be well worth while.

From our own point of view, however, the main objective is to grasp its meaning at the moment when it appears and spreads. Here again we must go back to Tocqueville:

The aim of the French Revolution was not only to change a previous way of government but also to abolish the previous form of society.
(Tocqueville, I, 2.)

Tocqueville makes the essential point: the ancien régime is first and foremost a form of society. And he goes on: in order to abolish this society, the Revolution had to

attack every established power simultaneously, destroy every acknow-

---

* But a pamphlet originating from the nobility of the Beaujolais area, dated 1788, contains the term 'Ancien Régime'. It is contrasted with the magnificent new régime that the States-General are sure to inaugurate (information from M. Daviet); the same sense crops up in some parish priests' *cahiers de doléances* (F. Furet).

ledged influence, eradicate traditions, renew customs and morals, and in some sense strip the human spirit of every idea on which respect and obedience had hitherto been based.

The ancien régime is a whole society, with its powers, traditions, customs, morals and therefore mentalities, as well as its institutions. Its bases, closely linked, are social, legal and intellectual. It is for this reason that they die so hard and slowly, even after being condemned and legally abolished.

The élites have given their evidence. Is it possible to consult the masses?

2. THE ANCIEN RÉGIME DEFINED BY THE PEASANTS

During the 1920s, in country areas still almost untouched by the modern world, it was not unusual to meet old men born under the Second Empire, or even earlier, who had been in living contact, via their own grandparents, with the Revolution and what came before the Revolution. The term that sprang most readily to their lips for the pre-1789 régime was 'the time of the seigneurs', an expression often taken up by the history textbooks of the Third Republic.

'The time of the seigneurs', a phrase often heard by the present author and many of his contemporaries in their youth, does quite well in this rural environment (but with exceptions) to characterize what the Constituent Assembly had baptized the 'ancien régime'. Under 'the seigneurs' – and they spoke the word with a mixture of hatred, relief, fear and a certain respect – the rural patriarchs of the 1920s lumped together everything which had once dominated the countryside and collected 'feudal rights', including tithes: great and lesser noblemen, bishops, monks, canons, bourgeois and their agents, tax-gatherers, millers and lawyers. Two categories of documents are contemporary with the decisive facts and enable us to confirm and elucidate the version preserved in the collective memory.

THE PEASANT GRIEVANCES IN MARCH 1789

Any number of writers have drawn upon the thousands of *cahiers de doléances*. For our purposes in particular, they have two major drawbacks.

On the one hand, and in accordance with their stated purpose, they are collections of 'grievances', and often amount to little more than a hotchpotch of recriminations. At the same time, almost all of them teem with sincere expressions of loyalty and love of the king, and moreover the 'moderate' *cahiers* are in the majority.

On the other hand, it is an undoubted fact that the poor peasants who made up the most numerous group were almost always prevented from making their voices heard in the *cahiers*, because of their illiteracy, or the composition of the parish assembly (dominated by the wealthy), or because they accepted or had imposed on them the influence of some 'progressive mind', usually a bourgeois, a notary, a *curé* or a tax-gatherer, who took up the pen on behalf of the country people.

In spite of these two obstacles, systematic analysis of the contents of the *cahiers* (at present being investigated by research teams using semantic and statistical methods) leads to a number of incontrovertible conclusions:

a) The king and kingship inspire loyalty and love;

b) But there is deep-seated resentment of the financial methods of the monarchy, although it is hoped that the good king and the States-General will reform them;

c) The majority protest against various feudal rights, or against all of them, or against the principle of them (the word 'feudal' is continually used, and so has to be used here);

d) There is an at least equally powerful resentment, not of the principle of tithes but of the way they are collected, their unfairness, exorbitance and inconsistencies, and above all of the fact that they have been diverted from their original aim (hardly any of the *cahiers* are hostile to religion itself);

e) In a large minority of cases, and perhaps echoing 'bourgeois' complaints, there are bitter protests against the contempt shown towards commoners and 'peasants' by the entire nobility, among them the higher clergy, who rarely come off unscathed. This extract from an Angevin *cahier* gives the usual tone, which tends to be dignified rather than truly bitter:

It would be desirable for some seigneurial rights to be abolished. The seigneurs regard the tenant farmers who work their property as veritable servants, the labourer who feeds them as a slave; if a day-labourer in their employ succumbs under the load, they are less grieved than by the death of one of the horses in their stable. The contempt of the nobility for the commonalty is beyond belief.

(GASTINES, *Bas-Anjou.*)

This moderate document calmly underlines one of the basic cleavages of the ancien régime, the one that separates commoner from nobleman. It also exemplifies the frequent and significant inability of the ordinary people to distinguish between nobles and seigneurs.

For the peasants, who were unaware that they were bearing witness to a régime on the point of death, it is only too clear that neither kingship, religion, nor property are at issue, which means that these are not basic attributes of the system and society that they are generally condemning, although in varying degrees. What are at issue are the injustices of the fiscal system, seigneurial rights, tithes, most privileges and the habitual conduct of all the nobility.

But the peasants – at least three quarters of the French people – had better means of expression than these not altogether reliable black books. They also took outright revolutionary action.

THE PEASANT UPRISINGS OF 1788–93
Georges Lefebvre, undoubtedly the greatest historian of the Revolution, described the successive waves of these uprisings.

THE FIRST WAVE: WINTER AND SPRING 1788–9
The rising generation, technological stagnation, the 'feudal reaction', the sudden rise of prices in the winter of 1788–9, and old traditions all came together to produce 'agitation' and localized or incipient revolt on the part of scattered groups of peasants throughout most of the country. The convocation of the States-General (29 January), then the meetings of the assemblies appointed to elect delegates and draw up the *cahiers,* gave rise to a kind of happy surprise in the countryside that touched off the wildest expectations:

The king wanted to hear the authentic voice of his people and obtain accurate knowledge of their suffering, needs and wants, obviously in order to right all wrongs. What a surprising new development! The king was the anointed of the Church, the lieutenant of God: he was all-powerful – therefore hardship must be about to end. But simultaneously with the birth of hope, hatred of the nobility intensified: certain of their prince's support, the peasants chewed over the day's sufferings with growing bitterness now that they were invited to speak out, and dredged up from deep in their minds the suppressed memory of past injuries . . . 'God be thanked, we have no noblemen in our parish,' says the village of Villaine-la-Juhel, in the Maine. 'They have four seigneurs everlastingly sucking their blood', state the peasants of Aillevans, in Franche-Comté . . .

(G. LEFEBVRE, *La Grande Peur de 1789*, p. 44)

Going beyond the *cahiers*, where their voices are unheard, many of the peasants find other ways of demonstrating their hope of a new age and hatred of the age they take to be condemned. Around Paris, they begin to kill game; in Alsace, they believe that taxation has been abolished; in the heart of pious Brittany, the *subdélégué* of Ploërmel anticipates tithe-riots, and writes:

All the peasants in our neighbourhood and in my department are making ready to refuse the tithe-gatherers their sheaves, and flatly stating that nothing will be taken without bloodshed.

From March 1789 onward, the people of the bailiwick of Saumur are convinced that they are no longer liable for either seigneurial dues or tithes, and that they are entitled to hunt. With the onset of spring, the peasant revolt spreads to whole cantons in the Paris region, Picardy, Hainault, Dauphiné and the Midi. In Provence alone, there are assaults first on the higher clergy and the wealthier monasteries, then on noble seigneurs and their servants. The episcopal palace at Toulon is pillaged, the Ursuline convent at Barjols held to ransom, the châteaux of Solliès and Besse devastated, the mills* of Pertuis destroyed, and notice served on the bishop of Riez and several notaries and seigneurial agents to surrender their papers, destroy their manorial rolls (*terriers*) and pay back extortionate fines. Some nobles take flight; M. de Montferrat is murdered when he puts up resistance at Aups (26 March). Some weeks later,

---

* By a right known as the *banalité du moulin*, the inhabitants of a seigneurie could be obliged to have their corn ground in the seigneur's mill. This right was often farmed out to the miller in return for a lump sum payment. – Tr.

the powerful canons of Saint-Victor de Marseille, like the great noblemen of the Parlement of nearby Dauphiné, express both their bewilderment and resignation:

> Since the popular insurrection that came at the end of March, tithes and other feudal rights are no longer thought of as anything but voluntary obligations that may freely be cast off . . . the greater part of the shepherds have refused their tithes; as for the *droit du four** almost every country-dweller has cast it off by having bread baked in private ovens . . . There is daily talk of destructive plots against the nobility and setting fire to châteaux so as to burn all the title-deeds . . .
>
> (Documents quoted in G. LEFEBVRE, ibid., p. 50.)

The first wave of rural uprisings was therefore aimed mainly at tithes, feudal rights and the men who received them, generally the nobility of sword or robe, tonsured or otherwise, although by a stroke at once clever and naïve it is their archives and 'feudal' title-deeds that suffer, rather than their châteaux and their persons. It is quite obvious that to the peasants the ancien régime was synonymous with seigneurs and feudalism. The ensuing uprisings show this more clearly still.

THE SECOND WAVE: JULY 1789

Now that the States-General were assembled but slow in responding to these expectations of liberty, the great mass of the peasantry reached a simple, spontaneous decision. The harvest was over. They would stop paying the tithe-gatherers, the seigneurs, and even the royal tax-collectors. Angry minorities assailed charter-rooms and châteaux with pitchforks and firebrands. The majority adopted the wiser and more effective course of passive resistance, and refused to pay up. Even in the clerical heartland of Léon, the prince-bishop in person announces in July that his flock have agreed among themselves not to pay their tithes, at least at the usual, albeit moderate, rate. Peasants almost everywhere 'anticipated the coming new law' in the words of the *curé* of Moreille, in Beauce. The night of 4 August put on its own spectacular performance, but the sacrifices then offered up with out-

* Obligation to bake bread in the seigneur's ovens. – Tr.

ward enthusiasm had lost their purpose. The future decrees were already being applied by the peasants themselves.

After the events of the famous night of 4 August, the delegates tried to recoup what a little generosity and a great deal of fear had lost them. They came to their senses and, being in the main jurists, receivers, feudists and seigneurs, fell to hairsplitting and temporizing. Some few 'feudal' rights would remain rescinded; the great majority would have to be 'bought out', by the peasants, of course; meanwhile the peasants were ordered to go on paying.

This touched off the far less violent but decisive third wave. With various local exceptions, the peasants did not buy anything out, and did not pay. In this manner they broke the backbone of the ancien régime – feudalism – by forgetting and ignoring it. What could be done against passive resistance, the most effective of all methods?

Meanwhile the Revolution was taking its course and coming to grips first with the aristocracy, then with Europe, the king, and the faint-hearted. After 10 August 1792 it decided that 'feudal' dues to which the seigneur could not show title were to be cancelled; since the original deeds had been lost or burnt, or their holders had fled, peasant obstinacy had its reward three times out of four. The Montagnard Convention did the rest: by the law of 17 July 1793, abolition became total and unconditional.

Even the Restoration never officially revoked these death certificates of an age-old régime, dispatched by the peasants themselves long before the jurists performed their usual function of ratification after the event.

3. THE ANCIEN RÉGIME DEFINED BY THE HISTORIANS

A régime – which is to say a society, a law, institutions, methods of government, mental attitudes, almost a 'civilization' (if the word still has meaning today) – all this cannot be defined only by the voices and actions of those who have rejected, then replaced it. At a remove of two centuries the historian has a wider perspective. Monographs have accumulated, research has flourished, and so have interpretative approaches and attempts at syntheses. Without levelling any kind of reproach against the men of 1789 – an absurdly antihistorical attitude in any case – the historian can pick out confusions and anachronisms in their concepts, both of these explicable in terms of the more or less distant origins of the condemned régime.

ANCIENT ORIGINS

The incorporation of the tithe, a more than millennial institution, and ecclesiastical by nature, into feudalism, a civil and younger institution, might count as a fundamental error. Its gravity diminishes when we take account of the fact that the Church infiltrated feudalism (and vice versa) and that their methods of collection, like the very identity of the collectors, were often closely related. All the same, while it may be economically, socially and above all psychologically justified to equate tithes with feudal rights, it is playing ducks and drakes with the nature of things.

It is true that the preamble to the Constitution of 1791 is a rhetorical document. Nevertheless, when it seems to lump together heredity of offices, a fairly late (1604) royal institution, with the 'patrimonial courts' (very ancient feudal institutions) and with the peerage, which is both an ancient and a modern institution, redolent at once of medieval supernaturalism and up-to-the-minute controversies, then we are dealing with evidence that throws light on the mentality of an influential group of men in the late eighteenth century, but not on the nature of the régime they were condemning.

A brand-new 'common law for all Frenchmen' is systematically contrasted with a varied range of privileges, some of which stem from sacred unction (the clergy), others from ancestry (the various orders of nobility), some from ancient treaties concluded between a king and a province (the marriage contract of Queen Anne, in the case of Brittany) or even a town, others from 'franchises' granted, sold, resold and confirmed for cash down on behalf of such and such a category of official, guild, craft, village or line of descent. It is a motley yet utterly characteristic asssortment.

'Seigneurial' and 'feudal' rights are continually put on the same footing, with a marked preference for the latter expression: does this not involve confusing 'feudality', a mere relic if we take Marc Bloch's definition of a pattern of ties between man and man in a military society, with 'seigneury', more alive although undoubtedly older, and defined simply as a method of exploiting the land? Twentieth-century historians have fought heroic battles (actually with philosophic and political objectives) over the nature of 'feudalism' (a system which in Marxist terminology is said to precede 'capitalism'), and have introduced formal distinctions where contemporaries saw none. These terms will require clarification.

Finally, when 'noblemen' are often identified by the peasants with 'seigneurs', and in particular when 'nobility', a concept of blood, is identified with 'seigneury', primarily a territorial concept, how far are we to go in accepting or rejecting these equations?

In reality, the ancien régime stands out only by contrast with what came after it. It becomes a distinctive entity only by its legal death, which defines and names it. The quintessence of the ancien régime is confusion, and the Constituent Assembly reacted against this confusion. Moreover, they believed that they were destroying it in the name of that Reason and Enlightenment it never possessed.

The confusion which is the hallmark of the ancien régime derives from its nature. It is a conglomeration of mostly centuries-old, sometimes thousand-year-old elements, none of which was ever discarded. Its profound conservativism often protected the obsolete, creating museum-pieces that were simultaneously respected, venerated, distorted, forgotten, revived and fossilized. The precision of its death-certificate and posthumous definition has an obvious counterpart in the absence of its birth-certificate. Its constituent parts have a wide range of real or suppositious ages. The systematic heredity of official posts is hardly two centuries old; the rights of *cens* and *champart* (see p. 83) are three to eight centuries old; tithes go back more than a thousand years, the peerage further still, or so it claims, and the nobility may date from any period. The ancien régime is like an immense, turbid river carrying dead hulks of trees, rank weeds torn from its banks, and living organisms of all ages and sizes; without any significant loss, it has collected the great rivers of the Middle Ages and the streams of barbarian times and even of the Roman Empire (whose laws it constantly invokes). The triple division of the 'orders' of the state may derive from an even more distant Indo-European source, as Georges Dumézil has come close to proving. When this huge river suddenly drains into the ocean of the 'new régimes' it leaves its traces, colouring and sediments in them for a long time.

But whether the 'new régimes' are dated from 1789 or 1815, are they enough in themselves to account for the end of the ancien régime? Civilizations do not die violently, because of a single document or a single blow – not in those days at least. Certainly the ancien régime was not established (some time between Louis XI and Henry IV) by a series of clean breaks, but by gradual shifts. The breaks came late in the day, and although the Revolution was swift and sudden the breaks were successive, spaced out over almost a century. We shall take the opportunity of examining them in the last chapters of this work.* It may be useful, or convenient, to observe and enumerate them at this point.

A SLOW DEATH, BY SUCCESSIVE BREAKS
(ROUGHLY 1750–1850)
We must venture further afield than the Tennis-court Oath and the Night of 4 August, which are essential stages but not the only ones. It will simplify matters to consider nine slow or sudden breaks that gradually tore the ancien régime apart:

a) Accelerated transportation: in a single century, between Trudaine and Guizot, from the first great royal highways to the national railway network, trade became easier, the cost of transportation decreased, whole provinces were rescued from their isolation, and the economy and the country finally unified.

b) Industrialization: launched in the late eighteenth century, then shaken by two decades of revolutionary and imperial wars, it came into its own in the mid-nineteenth century, perhaps even a little later, taking over the hitherto predominant role of agricultural production and its work force and especially the rentiers of the land. The 'harbingers' of industry were steam and iron-working, previously quite unimportant.

c) The foundation of a reliable banking system, present in outline but little known before 1789, dismantled by the Revolution, resumed with the Bank of France, an incipient national bank (a century

---

* See volume 2.

after England, two after Holland!), and fully-fledged half a century later.

d) The linguistic unification of the country: in the old kingdom of France the language of the north – Touraine and Paris – was a minority tongue. François 1 made it compulsory for written documents, later kings slowly followed his design, the Revolution accelerated it, and Guizot's primary schools initiated its completion.

e) The introduction and acceptance of military service. The royal militia, introduced by Louvois and resumed in the eighteenth century, was unpopular and detested, and disabled by the high rate of desertion. The Revolution gave the army common cause with one section of the nation by the first conscription measures, ratified by the Jourdan Law of 1798, and by a real but short-lived enthusiasm. The problem of desertion and recruitment continued for a long time, and national service was only slowly accepted.

f) The juridical unification of the country was a slow process. Louis xiv touched upon it, but it was a true creation of the Revolution, crowned by that superb instrument of national unity, the Code Napoléon, which replaced dozens of provincial codes.

g) What several French kings had striven to achieve, in particular with the institution of the *intendants*, was the rationalization and unification of the administrative system. The work was done first by the Constituent Assembly, then by the Consulate and the Empire. Its success is symbolized by the first prefects.

h) What has been called the 'demographic revolution' – a gradual fall in the death-rate and a rapid fall in the birth-rate – had been no more than hinted at prior to 1789; only after that date did France become the first nation in the world to control its birth-rate systematically, for reasons not yet apparent, but which put a very early brake on her demographic expansion.

i) The decline in religious belief, and the onset among a probable majority not of atheism but of a vague religious indifference, seems likely to have made its appearance in the early eighteenth century in the towns, wine-growing areas, and even in some provinces. But little is yet known about the phenomenon, and its effects were not felt much before the latter half of the nineteenth century.

The origins and overlappings of these nine partly related factors do not always stand out sharply. To point them out and stress them is helpful in understanding, delimiting and perhaps defining the ancien régime: it is the exact converse of this series of slow and decisive new developments, even if some of them are already present in outline before 1789. Economically, it is characterized by slow communications, the predominance of agriculture, the low status of iron-working in industry, itself of minor importance, and an almost non-existent banking system. For some time it remained demographically medieval (and this term will keep recurring like a leitmotiv) because of the high rates of birth, marriage and death, together with the persistence of great epidemics and famines. Politically, it remained the régime of juridical, linguistic and administrative diversity, and of complication and privilege, in spite of great efforts to redress imbalances. Mentally, it is distinguished by a blend of supernaturalism and Christian fervour, widespread illiteracy, a very blinkered provincial and local way of life, and a uniformly weak, sometimes non-existent concept of state, nation and fatherland, except for the worship of the monarch or the physical presence of danger. This is the age of patois and witches, shepherds and millers, seigneurs and tithe-gatherers, salt-tax collectors and tipstaffs, barter and small transactions, moving at the speed of mule and wayfarer, of the seasons and the signs of the Zodiac, with a distant King and God who are the ultimate judges and the last resort and consolation. Even a blurred sense of these ancient, ponderous presences is a step closer to penetrating a way of life and a pervasive traditional atmosphere that was only gradually destroyed by the deep rifts that appeared at scattered intervals in the late eighteenth, but mainly in the nineteenth, century.

It is with the aim of bringing this ancient, complex, consistently chaotic universe into focus that this book has been written.

Its first objective is to dig down to the foundations, which will necessitate delving far back into the past, even if only to describe the society with which the mainstream of the ancien régime seems to be identified.

Secondly, it will describe the State into which the ancien régime crystallized, dealing in the main with what has been misleadingly dubbed its 'classical' period, between Richelieu and Fleury.

Finally it will try to elucidate how the ancien régime grew old, how Society and State came gradually into conflict within it, and how it found itself in some sense out of step with new conditions in the half-century preceding the only Revolution that matters, the Revolution of 1789.

DOCUMENTS

1 THE REVOLUTION AND THE ANCIEN RÉGIME: TOCQUEVILLE'S THESIS

The revolution was not made, as has been thought, in order to destroy the rule of religious belief; it was in essence, despite appearances, a social and political revolution; and within the sphere of institutions of that kind it tended not to perpetuate disorder . . . but rather to increase the power and rights of public authority. . . . When it is separated from all the accidents that have momentarily changed its aspect in different eras and in different lands, and viewed strictly in itself, it may clearly be seen that this revolution had the effect only of doing away with those political institutions that had reigned unrivalled among most of the peoples of Europe for several centuries, and which are commonly referred to under the heading of feudal institutions, in order to replace them with a simple and more uniform political order, based on equality of conditions.

That was enough to make an immense revolution, for irrespective of the fact that the old institutions were still mingled and so to speak intertwined with almost all the religious and political laws of Europe, they had in addition given rise to a host of ideas, feelings, habits and manners that were like loyal followers to them. It needed a terrible convulsion to destroy and completely extirpate from the body social a part so bound up with all its organs. This made the Revolution appear even greater than it was . . .

. . . What can truly be said of it is that it utterly destroyed everything in the old society that derived from aristocratic or feudal institutions, anything connected with them in any way, and anything that bore their slightest impress . . . [The Revolution] took the world unawares, and yet it was no more than the complement of the longer haul, the sudden, violent culmination of a task at which ten generations of men had laboured. Had it not taken place, the old social structure would still have crumbled, earlier in one place, later in another, only it would have gone on crumbling a piece at a time, instead of collapsing all at once . . .

A. de TOCQUEVILLE, *L'Ancien Régime et la Révolution,*
book I, ch. 5.

2 A DUALIST CONCEPT OF THE ANCIEN RÉGIME:
STATE AGAINST SOCIETY

The monarchy of the ancien régime was the offspring of the civil wars that had ravaged France during the second half of the sixteenth century. It carried out a sizeable task . . . [with Henri IV . . . with Louis XIII and Richelieu . . . with Louis XIV . . .]. The period of ancien régime monarchy is one of the most brilliant in our history.

But although it fulfilled a national task, it was unable to give its authority a national base, and remained a prisoner of the past. It retained the ancient character of an individual monarchy, and developed only by sapping the vitality of those institutions that might have acted as supports. It made the irreparable mistake of believing that it is enough for a government to be strong. At the end of the seventeenth century – to borrow Lavisse's own borrowing from Lemontey – 'the pillars on which the monarchy rests are hollow'. The administrative institutions created by Louis XIV and Colbert did not help matters: they increased the powers of the central authority still further, and gave the nation no feeling of being part of it. The monarchy of the ancien régime stood isolated against a changing society and became incapable of changing with it. Hence its death-sentence.

Georges PAGÈS, *La Monarchie d'Ancien Régime* (A. Colin, 1928), final pages.

3 A DUALIST CONCEPT OF THE ANCIEN RÉGIME:
SOCIETY AGAINST STATE

Struck by the vicissitudes of the political régimes that have appeared in France during the last century and a half, their titles serving to designate the basic divisions of her history, many Frenchmen have grown used to the notion that the form of the political régime . . . is the basic question upon which everything else depends. It is true that, whatever its form, the State exerts enormous influence over the destiny of a country; often it may even pride itself on reshaping society in its own image; but it is also certain that the State and its policy did not create society.

Of the two mainsprings of historical evolution, Society and State, it is quite clear that the old historians laid stress only on the latter, which was so powerful in their own times. Perhaps modern historians, emulating the Ancients, living as they do in centralized, even despotic states, have been more prepared to study the institutions superimposed by the State than the structure, even the development, of modern societies . . . Yet in France, society was always very much alive. A few historians have barely scratched the surface of an account of society for modern, contemporary

France ... It is our concern to follow [its] evolution over two great centuries, a stage at a time, by pointing out the extent to which society acted
on the State, and the State on society, under the rule of absolute monarchy.

Philippe SAGNAC, *La Formation de la société française moderne*
(P.U.F., 1945), i, preface, vii–viii.

4 THE ANCIEN RÉGIME IN OUR MIDST

France is much more than two hundred years old. Anybody so taken in by
the brilliant paradoxes of some journalists as to doubt this assertion may
reflect on the authentic features of ancien régime society that modern
historiography has unearthed ... In many regions the most unpopular forms
of the traditional social hierarchy have survived the Great Fear and the
resentment of the peasants, under different names and different descriptions. Even in the mid-twentieth century, some areas where share-cropping
(*métayage*) once flourished, such as the Bourbonnais, have seen the continuance of statutory labour for the château, and a statute for sharing out
the fruits of the earth which was a faithful replica of the dues paid prior
to 1789. Not to mention the public gestures of respect retained in
addressing the tenant of the château, whoever the owner may be, and all
the more if the Restoration returned the titled family of former times to its
lands. More, we can discover modes of behaviour that express relationships bound up with the social hierarchy of the ancien régime and that constitute the most glaring anachronisms in a supposedly democratic society.
The finest example is undoubtedly provided by the obsession with hierarchy
that activates all social relationships, codifies the structure of every profession, constitutes the driving force of education, and is universally to be
found on the verge of becoming a fundamental social reflex utterly opposed
to the stated aspirations of contemporary society ... It might seem that
the rise in standards of living and the decline of outward shows of distinction come nearer to realizing the equality of conditions, if not of opportunities, of which the men of 1789 dreamed, talked and legislated. Yet these
appearances are more than deceptive; they have disguised – they have
been cultivated in order to disguise – the persistence of the overall social
conditionings for which the ancien régime had provided the blueprint.
The political importance of this continuity into our own times is obvious.

In the still largely uncharted province of mental attitudes, the conditionings inherited from an older France are just as strongly felt. The
single example of popular culture will suffice as an illustration. Some
remarkably permanent features have survived within it to this day, with
no profound discontinuity: the practice of astrology in the form of weekly,

monthly or annual horoscopes; the predilection for gossip news (and its judicial sequels), told, discussed, illustrated and rounded off with a moral, just as the old-time broadsheets used to serve it up; the biographical sob-story or scandal, shifted from its previous subjects – princes, swordsmen, saints – onto film stars and '*la vie parisienne*'. While the mass-communications of the twentieth century are technically capable of profound new developments in cultural content, it is noticeable that whole sections of our heritage have come down to us with no real alteration . . .

Robert MANDROU, *La France aux* XVIIe *et* XVIIIe *siècles*
(Nouvelle Clio no. 33, P.U.F., 1967), 301–2.

FURTHER READING

ON THE CONCEPTION OF THE ANCIEN RÉGIME

Of the innumerable books devoted to this subject, we omit:

1. Polemical works devoted to the glorification or execration of the ancien régime; their connection with history is strictly accidental even when they are written by Academicians.

2. Works aimed at the 'general public', whose only purpose is to chronicle the heroic or amorous adventures of famous people, from Diane de Poitiers to Madame de Pompadour; there is precious little difference between this kind of literature and the fodder that maintains the circulations of the scandal-sheets and romantic weeklies of the mid-twentieth century.

3. Most of the foreign studies of the ancien régime derive from *a priori* ideas, and are based on the most cursory inspection of French archives. Thus we are unable to accept R. R. PALMER'S ideas, taken up by J. GODECHOT, when they make the French Revolution a mere episode in an 'Atlantic revolution' supposed to have occurred between 1770 and 1850, with all that this implies about the conception of the ancien régime. Similarly, the much more subtle analysis of C. B. A. BEHRENS in *The Ancien Régime* (Thames and Hudson, 1967) puts itself out of court when its author begins the ancien régime in 1748, a schoolboy misconception.

Six books at most may be recommended. The first two are by great nineteenth-century writers whose insights go too deep to be superseded; the next two are painstaking works by precise, traditional, if a little short-sighted historians; the last two are thoroughly contemporary.

TOCQUEVILLE, Alexis de, *L'Ancien Régime et la Révolution* (1856). Despite its age, omissions and biases, one of those rare books that bear the stamp of genius.

TAINE, Hippolyte, *Les Origines de la France contemporaine,* vol. 1, *L'Ancien Régime* (1875). Systematic, arguable, and anti-Tocqueville, but strikingly intelligent.

PAGÈS, Georges, *La Monarchie d'Ancien Régime en France, de Henri IV à Louis XIV* (A. Colin, 1928). Concise, penetrating, well-organized, but over-chronological, partly superseded, and stopping short at the curious date of 1715.

SAGNAC, Philippe, *La Formation de la société française moderne* (2 vols. P.U.F. 1945-6). Long, detailed, always useful, but over-compartmented (five periods for less than 130 years); often short-sighted, factually dated.

MÉTHIVIER, Hubert, *L'Ancien Régime* (Collection 'Que sais-je?', P.U.F., 1961). A dense, remarkably well-documented outline, and an indispensable introduction.

MANDROU, Robert, *La France aux XVIIᵉ et XVIIIᵉ siècles* (Collection Nouvelle Clio, P.U.F., 1967). Fresh, individual, exceptionally intelligent, but unhappily too brief, and assuming a great deal of previous knowledge in its readership (impressive range of allusion); chapter 2 of Part Three (socio-cultural) and the whole of Part Four (lines of research) are particularly recommended.

ON THE CHRONOLOGICAL HISTORY OF
ANCIEN RÉGIME FRANCE
AND THE BEGINNING OF THE REVOLUTION

Among the most important works out of a copious literary and historical output:

1. For the Revolution, everything by Georges LEFEBVRE, beginning with his handbook in the 'Peuples et Civilisations' series (vol. XIII, *La Révolution française,* P.U.F., post-1950 editions);

2. For the previous period, the *Histoire de France,* edited by Ernest LAVISSE (vol. VI et seq., 1903-8) remains the most reliable point of departure.

3. Of the innumerable series devoted to general history founded

between the two world wars, the following are still in use, for want of anything better:

'Peuples et Civilisations' series (P.U.F.) vols VIII and IX (the best) and vols X–XII;

Collection Clio (P.U.F.), the volumes dealing with the sixteenth, seventeenth and eighteenth centuries (the reader is referred to their useful bibliographies).

4. Of the more recent works based on fresh research, the following must suffice:

LAPEYRE, Henri, *Les Monarchies européennes du* XVIe *siècle* (Nouvelle Clio, 384 pp., P.U.F., 1967).

TAPIÉ, Victor-L., *La France de Louis* XIII *et de Richelieu* (Flammarion, 561 pp., 1952, new edition, 1967).

MÉTHIVIER, Hubert, *Le Siècle de Louis* XIII (P.U.F., 'Que sais-je?', 128 pp., 1964).

LEBRUN, François, *Le* XVIIe *Siècle* (A. Colin, Collection 'U', 378 pp., 1967).

GOUBERT, Pierre, *Louis* XIV *et vingt millions de Français* (Fayard, 252 pp., 1964).

MÉTHIVIER, Hubert, *Le Siècle de Louis* XV (P.U.F., 'Que sais-je?', 128 pp., 1966).

Lastly, it is advisable to consult any new publications in the two main French series devoted to new material: the 'Nouvelle Clio' series (P.U.F.) and the 'U-histoire moderne' series (A. Colin); and the excellent series published in English by O.U.P. and particularly by C.U.P., including the *Cambridge Economic History*.

5. A number of reviews keep abreast of recent research. The principal French reviews are:

Annales (Économies, Sociétés, Civilisations) (A. Colin)

Revue Historique (P.U.F.)

Revue d'Histoire moderne et contemporaine (A. Colin).

Plus numerous regional reviews.

A number of foreign reviews now deal with French topics, and will be of interest to specialists; they include the *Revue belge de philologie et d'histoire* (excellent and comprehensive book-reviews) and *The Economic History Review,* probably the best of the lot.

DOCUMENTS CONCERNING THE PRELUDE AND THE
EARLY YEARS OF THE REVOLUTION

A number of documents have been quoted in the text of the preceding
chapter (contrary to what will be the standard procedure of this book)
because they seemed appropriate there. They will be found, together
with numerous others, in at least three volumes of the 'U' series:

VOILLIARD, CABOURDIN, DREYFUS and MARX, *Documents
d'Histoire,* vol. 1, 1776–1850 (A. Colin, 1964, pp. 20–65).

DUPEUX, G., *La Société française, 1789–1860* (A. Colin, 4th
edition 1968, documents appended to chapter 1, pp. 89–102).

RÉMOND, R., *La Vie politique en France,* vol. 1, 1789–1848 (A.
Colin, 1965, documents appended to the early chapters).

As regards the *cahiers de doléances,* a selection is provided in
GOUBERT, P. and DENIS, M., *1789, Les Français ont la parole* ('Archives' series, Julliard, 270 pp., 1964).

SOCIETY

To analyse a society does not mean measuring it against
prefabricated 'models' expressed in abstruse jargons
deriving from ancient or modern systems conceived in a
different context. Ancien régime society needs no additional
complications, and the historian does not deal in pre-
established systems. He looks, describes, and tries to
understand and explain.

Our account of this society is not timed for the eve of
its death: for the moment we shall forget the year 1789
and the preceding two or three decades, in an effort to
capture ancien régime society in its heyday, roughly between
1600 and 1750.

All classifications, whether scholastic, juridical or
material, must give way to the essential point that this
is a primarily rural society, organized in terms of land.
It has long ago developed demographic, economic, juridical
and psychological patterns that are a guide to understanding
it. We are beginning to be familiar with the first two,
which take pride of place in our examination; the rest
will follow in good time.

II · THE DEMOGRAPHIC SETTING

The ancien régime was firmly entrenched in a territory that covered something in the region of two hundred thousand square miles in 1700, when it could support some twenty million inhabitants, at least four-fifths peasant. These geographical and human resources warrant a more than cursory description, because they condition everything else and because we are beginning to piece together a reliable picture of them.

1   THE BIGGEST, DENSEST POPULATION IN EUROPE

OUR SOURCES OF INFORMATION: THE PRELIMINARY CRITICAL PROCESS

Except in a few towns and bailiwicks, there was no nationwide census before 1789, as was pointed out by a number of responsible men in the course of the eighteenth century, the last of them being Necker himself. Here France lagged far behind better administered countries such as Spain and Sweden (where the first censuses date from 1717 and 1720), and even most of the Italian and some of the central European states.

Consequently we only have rough estimates, none of them prior to 1697. All figures concocted and published for previous periods amount to pure guesswork.

These rough estimates are of two kinds:

a) The oldest and most numerous are obtained by collating tax-rolls used by collectors of the *tailles*, various *capitations, dixièmes*

and *vingtièmes,* and even the salt-tax. These lists give the names
and number of family-heads liable for taxation, and are consequently
incomplete, since the wealthiest and the poorest usually escape.
Furthermore they are not consistent, since the legislation differs
from one tax to another, and worse still, from one province to
another for any given tax. In particular, we shall observe what
a difference there could be between the *taille* of the Midi, levied
on the amount of land owned, and that of the North, which embraces
the landless but often overlooks the biggest landowners.

These incomplete and ill-assorted documents were collated at the
time in order to extrapolate from the number of taxable family-heads
the actual number of inhabitants – the thorny problem of the
'coefficient'. The administrators usually put it at between 4 and 5,
although they rarely inform us how and why they choose, or
even which!

Vauban, the earliest, in his *Project d'une dixme royale* (1707),
collated his speculative estimates and came to the conclusion that
in the years following 1700, France (minus Corsica and Lorraine,
and of course Savoy and Nice) had a population of slightly more
than nineteen million. Without embarking on a thoroughgoing
study of the document (genuine work for the historian, nevertheless),
we shall confine ourselves to underlining three facts.

First: in the course of adding about thirty figures Vauban made
two arithmetical errors and allowed them to be published. Fortunately they only affect the thousands, but they are disturbing. Errors
of this type abound in the book-keeping of the time, so that one
wonders about the reliability of calculations made at the lower levels
of bailiwick, *élection, subdélégation,* and even at the level of the *généralité.**

Second: Vauban quite simply forgot one *généralité,* that of Bourges; seventy-five years later, Necker noted that the Clermontois† had
always been left out of population 'researches'; this is bound to

---

* The *généralités* were the major administrative sub-divisions of France, each supervised by a royal *intendant.* There were 23 by the time of Louis XIV, 33 in 1789. Bailiwick
(seneschalcy in the Midi), *éléction* and *subdélégation* were lesser subdivisions that often
overlapped, and were supervised by bailiffs, *élus* and *subdélégués.* – Tr.

† A region of Clermont-en-Argonne, belonging to the Condé family, with several
thousand inhabitants.

arouse suspicions about the competence of cross-checking methods even at local level.

Third: we know that the estimates provided by some *intendants* are second-rate or worse. Vauban himself realized that Paris could not possibly contain 720,000 inhabitants in 1694 (it was fewer than half a million, in fact). It has been shown that the estimate for Brittany (1,655,000) is a good twenty-five per cent too low, because it relied on the tax-rolls of the first capitation of 1695. It will soon be proved that the *intendant* Bâville overestimated the population of Languedoc by consistently using the inflated coefficient of 5.

These few comments are enough. Pending further corrections, we can only hope that the administrators' mistakes may cancel each other out. Since no better is available, Vauban's estimate will have to do, with a margin of error of plus or minus (probably minus) as many as two million.

b) The estimates made at the end of the eighteenth century are more solidly based, and rely on the fairly accurate statistics of the 'registry office' and of a small number of dependable surveys.

Thanks to Terray*, it has been possible to work out the total number of births, marriages and deaths from about 1770 onwards. Except for deaths, where they remain incomplete (mainly in the Midi), these statistics hold good after about 1774, and constitute a well-known primary source.

In addition, a few towns and *bourgs* and a number of rural areas were the object of a detailed house-by-house and person-by-person census. For the regions tested it was a simple matter to determine the relationship between the overall population and the average number of births and marriages celebrated. Extrapolation from these local figures then produces quite reliable overall estimates, most of which hover around the twenty-six million mark for the last years of the ancien régime. There is no valid reason for doubting this estimate: it should be accurate to within two per cent or thereabouts.

The critical appraisal outlined above is more than an academic exercise. It underlines the need for caution, and shows what difficul-

---

* Joseph-Marie Terray, Louis xv's finance minister (1715–78). – Tr.

ties must be faced by the historian when he tries to branch out into demography. All the same, it does enable us to claim certain things as matters of fact.

A MATTER OF FACT: THE DEMOGRAPHIC STRENGTH
OF ANCIEN RÉGIME FRANCE

With the exception of far-off Russia, ancien régime France was by far the heaviest-populated country in Europe. At the time when Vauban was compiling his statistics England had a population of from five to six million, Spain six to eight million, and the entire possessions of the Austrian Habsburgs perhaps eight million. So France had two or three times as many people as any other state around 1700! But this overwhelming advantage decreased in the course of the eighteenth century, when the European population grew faster than the French, and disappeared altogether in the nineteenth century.

With such a massive population France could have achieved a considerable military superiority, given the same technical resources, if conscription had been the basis of army recruitment. When something like it was introduced by the Jourdan Law of 1798, Europe learnt its lesson the hard way.

In fact, the substantial material advantages that the French monarchy derived from its host of subjects was the envy of foreign kings. Around twenty million people, twelve million of them productive and almost as many taxable, are an invaluable power base. It was enough for these subjects not to be positively destitute, and for them to agree to pay their taxes, to ensure that both the undertakings of government (war included) and the future of the country should give no serious cause for concern. Now the fiscal system, which from our point of view was crushing, unfair and inefficient, was eventually accepted, after considerable resistance which will be illustrated at a later point in this book. And except in certain social strata, certain regions and certain years, the people went on living, working and paying. On the basis of close local analyses that cannot be gone into here, it is even held that inside the same frontiers the realm maintained this level of around twenty million inhabitants roughly between 1550 and 1750, despite alternating, complex fluctuations in either direction. Which would indicate that the superiority was still more marked before than after 1700.

And the constancy of this figure gives grounds for maintaining that in spite of so many grievous outward appearances and tragic episodes, the relative prosperity of the realm was a major factor in its strength. The simplest explanation of this extraordinary prosperity – for its time, that is, and allowing for all provincial variations – is undoubtedly the best. Some credit may go to the variety and advantages of climate, soil and water, as well as the bravery and ingenuity of the individual Frenchman, but much more incisive is the notion of population density.

In a realm the size of France an average density of more than a hundred inhabitants per square mile was remarkably high, although it may seem unimpressive in twentieth-century terms. Apart from a few small, atypical areas – coasts, valleys, polders and urban areas – it was the highest in the world before 1750. The wealthiest regions in Europe – in particular Flanders and the Low Countries, but also including the London basin, Rhineland Germany, and Paduan and Florentine Italy – barely exceed this figure, over far smaller areas. The level of French development is evidence of the combined qualities of nature and human beings, but what it indicates above all is that a fundamental balance has been achieved.

This optimal balance is that between the economy and the population, and it must have altered very little in the two centuries from 1550 to 1750. A hundred people per square mile is what France was able to support, given its type of production, technological level, kinds of consumption and physical and mental usages. It is adapted to an economy in which nothing basic has changed (cf. Chapter Three), and to demographic conditions that have been difficult to uncover but are starting to emerge with some clarity.

These demographic conditions could, with slight variations, be those of the white, Catholic populations of the temperate zone: late marriage (at twenty-five or over, for women), infrequent celibacy (rarer than in the nineteenth century), a close to 'natural'* fertility-rate

---

* This 'natural' character of early demography is being increasingly disputed by advanced research.

(forty births per thousand of population, one pregnancy every two years, a very low illegitimacy-rate) and a more fluctuating death-rate, heavy among the young (one child in two did not reach adulthood) but often a few points lower than the birth-rate. This involves an obvious danger: in 'favourable' times – no wars, epidemics or famines – the population tends to rise above the physiological threshold, but the economy and in particular the food-supply do not expand with it. Malthus, following in the footsteps of various administrators, expressed this pattern clearly, but a little late in the day. Catastrophes strike suddenly and violently, reducing the population to the level demanded by its material circumstances, and sometimes well below.

These catastrophes and this level of subsistence may not constitute the primary characteristics of the ancien régime, which shares them with the greater part of the Middle Ages, but they do constitute the environment, almost the 'plasma' in which it existed, at least until 1710, and often much later. For this reason it is necessary to dwell upon them at greater length.

2 THE MACHINERY OF THE DEMOGRAPHIC CRISES

Long unknown or misunderstood, the intermittent and drastic falls in population – the 'demographic crises' – are now fairly well documented and understood, thanks to the labours of the latest generation of demographic historians and demographers turned historian.

DESCRIPTION

What stuck most in people's minds before 1750 was the regular occurrence – several times in a single lifetime – of what was commonly known as 'mortality'. For several months, sometimes a year, occasionally longer, the number of funeral processions in a parish, bailiwick or one or more provinces would double, triple, or worse. From ten to twenty per cent of the population (sometimes more) went to their graves. Nobody really understood what was happening, and there would be allegations of divine wrath, punishment for accumulated sins, demonic vengeance, or the horrible effect of some dreadful 'omen' or of some 'spell' that had been cast.

More careful observation shows that the increase in burials was usually accompanied by an easily explicable almost total falling-off of marriages, and by a heavy fall in 'conceptions', as if the fertility of married couples had suddenly dropped. In addition, the afflicted areas were characterized by exceptionally high mobility, as the poor, the panic-stricken, the unemployed and great numbers of children scattered along the highways and byways in search of help, which usually meant bread.

After a few months or a year, the reverse phenomena emerged, apparently in compensation. The funeral processions ceased now that the weak had been eliminated; the marriage-rate shot up, and then the birth-rate, both among newlyweds and among those not separated by 'mortality'.

This repeated phenomenon has been the subject of any number of inquiries. The current conclusions are roughly as follows:

THE PROBLEM OF CAUSES

For hundreds, perhaps thousands of years, three distinct causes have been traditionally ascribed to these crises: war, plague and famine.

The problem of the real effect of wars on the French population has been obscured by literature and sensationalism. The actual year-by-year balance-sheet of provinces spared, provinces ravaged and provinces crossed by armies was never drawn up. With the exception of a very few provinces such as Languedoc and Burgundy, the real effects of the wars of religion are unknown, and the opinion of historians is completely divided on this subject. More is known about the effects of the Thirty Years War, but the horrors that have been described so often (and illustrated in the engravings of Callot) were strictly confined to the northern and in particular the eastern provinces of the realm; all the rest, which is to say the great majority, were spared. After the Frondes, which require further study, and which devastated only a few quite restricted areas, war seldom encroached inside the frontiers of France, while armies were reorganized and better disciplined. In any case, it became more and more exceptional for wars to set in motion the typical demographic crises that we have described, and they tended instead to produce temporary exoduses.

Plague, bubonic or pneumonic, was endemic throughout France

until about 1650, occasionally springing to life here and there in brief, appalling outbreaks. In the course of a few weeks, always in summertime (the rat-fleas that harbour the virus cannot survive in cold conditions), a clear-cut group of parishes, in rare cases a whole province, might lose a quarter, a third, sometimes half of its population. After 1650 the plague retreated and disappeared throughout most of the country, and its last incursions, from the North (1667) and the Orient (Marseille, 1720), were contained by efficient and commendable administrative action. Yet even when it had been defeated and perhaps naturally diluted by what may have been a mutation in the rat-population, the plague lived on in men's minds and in their fears and imaginings, so that any serious epidemic would be labelled 'plague'. And in fact it does seem to have been replaced by other serious epidemics, which appeared under Louis xiv and often persisted well into the eighteenth century. There are indications of probable smallpox, diphtheria, typhus and typhoid fever preceding the cholera of the nineteenth century. But these epidemics do not follow the well-known sequence of the classical demographic crisis: they are short-lived, attack specific age-groups (mainly children and young people), and naturally do not reduce fertility.

The true demographic crisis, as studied principally in northern, eastern and central France, where the population is densest and grain is the standard crop, stems from a series of climatic accidents (usually high summer rainfall) in a given socio-economic context. Successive harvests have been poor and have not stored well; provisions have given out; the price of grain, and therefore of bread – the basic foodstuffs – has gone on rising, generally doubling, often tripling and quadrupling. Owing far more to the high cost than to the scarcity of food, the shortage seems to trigger off 'mortality' and its companion phenomena, so that these seem to derive from rocketing prices, and do in fact derive from them to a great extent. Most people's incomes have not followed prices – quite the contrary – and the common people have turned hungrily to inferior or contaminated foodstuffs (dubious kinds of flour, rotten meat, grass, etc.). Epidemic diseases of the digestive system break out and are spread by beggars, pedlars, soldiers and vermin. The incidence of starvation pure and simple is far higher than was once thought. Hopes of a better crop, the harvest, the first threshing and finally the onset of winter prevail both over the famine and the chain of epidemics it has abetted or caused . . . Just as in Biblical times, the 'fat kine' appear again. These mechanisms are so far-reaching as to enable them to be considered as a pointer to economic and social structures and even mental attitudes.

THE SEVERAL 'MEANINGS' OF THE DEMOGRAPHIC CRISES

The vulnerability of most provinces to these fatal outbreaks up to and after the beginning of the eighteenth century does in fact point to quite a number of basic features of the ancien régime (and of the preceding periods). These include:

a) Inadequate transportation. When a number of provinces are suffering from famine, an appeal for extra grain will move too slowly, be answered too slowly, and the grain will tend to be delivered spoiled and at too high a price. Slow, dear transportation, even by water, is obviously one of the basic features of the economy of the time. We shall return to it in the following chapter.

b) Rapid, disproportionate price-rises are characteristic of markets that are too localized, badly supplied, inelastic and subject to speculation (prices go up before the harvest). Various features of collective psychology are partly instrumental here, but in addition panic fear of shortages and starvation, fed by collective and often exaggerated memories of former famines, is nevertheless encouraged by the tactics of cunning *monopoleurs* (the word dates from these times), who were occasionally identified, more often blindly denounced. Panics are one of the basic features of the ancien régime, and they partly outlived it.

c) The fact that a shortage virtually of nothing but grain could give rise to under-nourishment, malnutrition and 'mortality' demonstrates the excessive extent to which grain is the exclusive diet of the majority of the population, and how deficient, inadequate and precarious their diet is (except in those rare regions that possess more varied resources, such as the coastal areas, Brittany, which has other deficiencies, and the Midi). The supremacy of flour, whatever its colour (usually grey or black), constitutes a serious weakness, and the great plains that grow cereals and little else are most at risk.

d) The fact that one or two hard years could quickly reduce the greater part of the population to sickness and starvation points straight at the essential failings of this economy and society:

– The pattern of rural development gives most of the peasants no safe guarantee either of growing or buying their daily bread; a large number of peasants do not therefore enjoy economic independence. We shall come back to this point in Chapter Five.

– Those common people who are neither landowners nor peasants do not have steady enough resources or sufficient savings to keep them going. The absence or paucity of popular treasuries, like the incapacity of available resources to deal with the sudden periods of high prices, points both to the inefficiency of the economic mechanisms and to the extreme inequality of social conditions.

– In spite of a few efforts, mainly after 1650, private relief and disorganized public relief were practically incapable of providing assistance during these crises, which were beyond their means.

e) It is surprising even today to note that shortage and high price of grain usually produced a slump in other products, in particular a fall in the price and production of cloth, which gives rise to unemployment (contemporary documents talk of 'the silent looms'), and thus aggravates the demographic crisis. This indicates that the non-agricultural sectors of the economy are dependent upon the agricultural and especially upon the grain-producing sector – another long-lived basic feature of the economy (until the early nineteenth century), and one that we shall encounter again and again.

Suggestive though this analysis is, it must not lead us to suppose that these crises always follow a final procedure without variation in time or place. The pattern shifts continually.

GEOGRAPHY AND CHRONOLOGY OF THE
DEMOGRAPHIC CRISES

Until about 1710 the big demographic crises, like the plagues, seem to have occurred roughly in thirty-year 'cycles': those of 1597, 1630, 1662 and 1694 stand out particularly sharply; others appear during the intervals in this chronology, in accordance with a similar rhythm – 1584, 1618, 1649, 1677, 1710, 1741, even 1771. All sorts of climatic, astronomic and economic hypotheses have been put forward to account for this quasi regularity, but none of them rings really true.

One thing is certain, however: these catastrophes strike at geographical areas of different size, with different central points. Some of them must have affected the whole of Europe (1597, 1630). The great famine of 1662, which brought Bossuet's eloquent indictment, mainly affected the Loire and Paris basin areas, and bypassed Brittany and the Midi. The famous crisis of 1693–4 spared the Mediterranean south, which tended to benefit from the rainy summers that elsewhere prevented the corn from ripening or rotted it where it stood. Even the *'grand hyver'* of 1709 spared Brittany, with its extensive coastline. Thus plagues and epidemics were always localized.

Yet in the course of the eighteenth century these basic mechanisms gradually began to break down, clearly proving that general conditions were inexorably changing.

After 1710 grain shortages became less acute, and it was exceptional for the price of bread to double. At the same time, the improvement which had begun in better-off regions such as Brittany, Normandy and the whole of the Midi slowly spread to the rest of the country. The almost automatic progression from 'dearth' to 'mortality' was halted; the crises never developed and administrative attention turned from the now diminished problem of hunger to epidemics, with attempts to isolate, treat and sometimes prevent them. The turning-point lies somewhere in the decade between 1740 and 1750. One last 'great crisis' flared up violently in a few provinces (1741–2), slightly in others, and not at all elsewhere. The dreaded old periodic curse reared its head again here and there in feeble or vigorous outbreaks around 1770, under the Revolution and Empire, and sometimes later still, but it was no longer the great scourge of ages past.

Something had changed, whether in the nature, level, yield or cost of production, the speed or cost of transportation, the resources of the consumer or perhaps in government policy. True, there was still a direct and much-criticized connection between agricultural crisis, however mild, and slump in industry, particularly in textiles, but already these were relics of the past. Events that are symptomatic of a society's basic material processes do not vanish overnight. But

with the decline of the great demographic crises, a centuries-old world
was fading, giving way to a new world in which the ancien régime
would falter and finally collapse. After 1750 at least, the regular
succession of large-scale purges began to tail off, and the French
population began to change and grow. Now that the brakes were
off, France managed at last to take off from its twenty-million plateau.
Its stagnant economy followed suit, and not before time. These two
new drives combined to propel the ageing realm along a trajectory
of expansion, but this was not until late in the eighteenth century,
when the ancien régime was nearing its end.

3   A ROOTED, SEDENTARY, STABLE POPULATION

Historians, who are only too much aware of superficial catastrophes,
changes and disturbances, have nevertheless eventually succeeded in
focusing some attention on the deeper, more stable forces and structures. Unchanging elements, so obvious as to be no longer noticed,
are as much a part of the ancien régime's landscape as the insects that
fly around it. And the ancien régime is undoubtedly typified by
stability more than by movement – again, that is, before 1750.

THE FRENCH LANDSCAPE, A PERENNIAL FIXTURE

The towns and villages of France stood on or close to sites carved
out of forest or steppe many centuries previously, whether in remote
Celtic times or at the height of the Middle Ages. The losses and set-
backs of the fourteenth and fifteenth centuries had been made good
from the early sixteenth century onward, and there were to be no
more 'deserted villages' except in out-of-the-way marches. The precise pattern of *quartier,* messuage, garden, field, grazing- and even
waste-land remained essentially the same; all the elements in a
meticulously laid-out landscape held fast. There was no real change
until the great urban explosion and rural redistribution of the
nineteenth and twentieth centuries. The principal alterations to this
landscape have been lengthily described by historians, but add up
to nothing more ambitious than the drainage of marshes and lakes,
a task performed mainly by the Dutchmen called in by Henri IV; the
slow retreat of the forest (compensated by reafforestation and con-

servation measures, thanks to the efforts of efficient forestry-workers and to Colbert); changes of fashion in landscaping and the Mediterranean *garrigues* and a few clearance projects that were unimportant or short-lived even in the time of the physiocrats. With the exception of Le Havre, Richelieu and Versailles, no new towns were built. During the two or three centuries of the ancien régime, the delicate architecture of the French landscape was a permanent fixture, an immense, age-old tapestry retouched only with a few stitches here and there.

STABILITY OF HUMAN GROUPS

It is of course by no means difficult to accumulate a thousand and one vivid details to show that the French people apparently moved, wandered and emigrated a great deal. Emigration is wholly accounted for by twenty or thirty thousand southerners in Spain (exactly 2,243 in Catalonia in 1637), a few thousand adventurers in the first colonies, a far greater number of Protestants scattered almost everywhere (100,000, perhaps 200,000?), plus a glamorous sprinkling of great travellers. Inside France there was a small annual movement of servant-girls, apprentices and once more adventurers from country to town, the migrations of some tens of thousands of beggars, and a smaller number of soldiers (except after Louvois, to whom we shall return later), and the hill-dwellers who came and went but generally returned to their native villages. Yet it is doubtful whether vagrants, seasonal travellers and people moving to settle in a different area ever amounted to more than half a million at any one time throughout the realm[*].

Nineteen and a half out of twenty million people remained bound to the land, plot, hut, cottage or *quartier* where they grew up. Old France is characterized not by unrest, social mobility and popular migration, but by sedentariness. Except for the perennial adventurers, people only became mobile when driven by necessity, which usually meant destitution.

This is strikingly demonstrated by the several million marriage certificates preserved since the seventeenth century, and may be

[*] Cf. Chapter Five, section 2.

illustrated by taking a rural parish of some substance – a good thousand inhabitants. In this parish at least three quarters of the newlyweds were born and lived in the place where they were joined in marriage; of the other quarter, half come from next-door villages, and even the most intrepid travellers have come less than ten miles to be wed. Such powerful and predominant stability often lasted until the early twentieth century (although to a diminishing extent, of course): the names on many village war-memorials are the same that appear on the parish-registers of the *grand siècle*.

Stability and sedentariness are not always the rule, and naturally it is the towns and ports – and of course Paris, always a special case – that provide the exceptions to an essentially peasant trait. No peasant will voluntarily leave his land, be it only half a furrow, and we know that France was more than eighty per cent peasant, and that relatively few were completely landless.

The fierce peasant deep-rootedness of the French people probably explains their habitual hostility both towards naval enterprise and military service, even in the embryonic form of the militia, which they found perplexing and disturbing. This rootedness nevertheless begins to loosen in the later eighteenth century (an unusual era in every respect), and the very same study of marriage contracts, together with other sources, now reveals increased mobility and a greater frequency, distance and number of population-shifts, although these are still in the minority. The catchment area for marriages expands slightly, and parish 'endogamy' decreases by a few points. There are more newcomers to the towns, and from further away, and the same goes for prostitutes, domestic servants and foundlings, often provincial 'imports', whose numbers swell from two to six thousand in Paris alone. Yet this is still a far cry from the military or other migrations under the Revolution and the Empire, and from the great industrial migrations of the following century.

Granted the countless little ebbs and flows of parish and district life, stability of landscape, habitats, inhabitants and probably of numbers of inhabitants is a paramount aspect of ancien régime France between the early seventeenth and the mid-eighteenth century. From then onward, the tremors begin.

DOCUMENTS

5 'ABSTRACT OF THE CENSUS OF THE PEOPLE OF THE REALM' PRODUCED BY VAUBAN IN 1707

Généralité	Population
Town of Paris, 1694	720,000
Généralité of Paris, 1700	856,938
Généralité of Orleans, 1699	607,165
Généralité of Tours, 1698	1,069,616
Brittany, 1698	1,655,000
3 *généralités* of Normandy, 1698	1,540,000
Picardy, 1698	519,500
Artois, 1698	214,869
Flemish Flanders	158,836
Walloon Flanders, 1698	337,956
Hainaut, 1698	85,449
Trois-Evêchés	156,599
Champagne, 1698 (includes Sedan and part of Luxembourg)	693,244
Généralité of Soissons, 1698	611,004
Burgundy, 1700 (includes Bresse, Bugey and Gex)	1,266,359
Lyonnais	363,000
Alsace, 1697	245,000
Dauphiné, 1698	543,585
Provence, 1700	639,895
Languedoc, 1698	1,441,000
Roussillon	80,369
Auvergne, 1697	557,068
Généralité of Bordeaux, 1698 (includes Bigorre, Labour and Soule)	1,482,304
Béarn and Basse-Navarre, 1698	241,094
Généralité of Montauban, 1699	788,600
Généralité of Limoges, 1698	585,000
Généralité of La Rochelle, 1698	860,000
Généralité of Poitiers	612,621
Généralité of Moulins	324,332
Total according to Vauban	19,094,146

From the Coornaert edition of the *Project d'une dixme royale* (Alcan, 1933), 157–9

6 TABLE OF BAPTISMS, BURIALS AND MARRIAGES IN FRANCE, 1770–84

(in thousands)

	Baptisms	Burials	Marriages		Baptisms	Burials	Marriages
1770	950	710	185	1778	933	744	204
1771	913	770	173	1779	957	967	232
1772	906	865	186	1780	989	914	241
1773	901	841	204	1781	970	881	237
1774	940	775	216	1782	976	949	225
1775	934	817	215	1783	948	952	229
1776	939	741	235	1784	966	887	230
1777	998	752	233				

Average, 1770–84

948	836	216

Taken from P. VINCENT, 'French demography in the eighteenth century', in *Population Studies,* vol. I, 1947, p. 69.

N.B. these official figures are too low because:

1. The data for 1770 and 1771 are incomplete;
2. Some non-Catholics and small *pays,* such as the county of Clermont-en-Argonne, slip through the administrative net;
3. Many child-burials probably remained unregistered throughout the Midi.

7 THE DEMOGRAPHIC CRISES: TWO DOCUMENTS

1. *The parish register of La Croix-du-Perche (Eure-et-Loire)*

... Buried 4 March 1662, the child of the late Bignon, dead of actual starvation.

Buried 2 January 1662, in our church, the child of the late Jean Vedys, died of starvation in a cowshed.

Buried in our cemetery 20 January 1662, a man named David and his wife, died of starvation at Les Charnois, together with a man named La Gravière, died of starvation.

Buried in our cemetery on the first day of March 1662, Jacques Drouin, died of starvation.

Buried in our cemetery in March 1662, Anne Rochette, who died of starvation with her two children.

Buried in our cemetery 28 April 1662, the son of the late Jacques Drouin, died of starvation, like his father.

Buried in our cemetery 1 May 1662, the wife of the late Jacques Drouin, who died of starvation like her husband and son.

Buried in our cemetery 30 April 1662, Jean Peleleu, called le Cles, who died of starvation.

Buried in our cemetery 2 May 1662, the daughter of La Pelaude, dead of starvation like her sister and brother.

From the researches of Marcel COUTURIER, maître-assistant at
the École Pratique des Hautes Etudes.

2. *Journal of the* curé *of Rumegies (near Saint-Amand-les-Eaux, Nord)* (1693) . . . the final misfortune was the utter failure of the ensuing harvest, which caused grain to reach a tremendous price. And since the poor people were exhausted in like measure by the frequent demands of His Majesty and by these exorbitant taxes [the reference is to wartime levies], they fell into such poverty as might just as well be called famine. Happy the man who could lay hands on a measure of rye to mix with oats, peas and beans and make bread to half fill his belly. I speak of two thirds of this village, if not more . . .

Throughout this time, the talk was all of thieves, murders and people dying of starvation. I do not know if it is to the credit of the *curé* of Rumegies to refer here to a death which occurred in his parish during that time: a man named Pierre du Gauquier, who lived by the statue of the Virgin, towards la Howardries. This poor fellow was a widower; people thought that he was not as poor as he was; he was burdened with three children. He fell ill, or rather he grew worn-out and feeble, but nobody informed the *curé*, until one Sunday, upon the final bell for mass, one of his sisters came and told the *curé* that her brother was dying of starvation, and that was all she said. The pastor gave her some bread to take to him forthwith, but perhaps the sister had need of it for herself, as seems likely to be the case. She did not take it to him, and at the second bell for vespers the poor man died of starvation. He was the only one to drop dead for want of bread, but several others died of that cause a little at a time, both here and in other villages, for that year saw a great mortality. In our parish alone, more people died than in several ordinary years . . . Truly men wearied of being of this world. Men of goodwill had their hearts wrung at the sight of the poor people's sufferings, poor people, without money while a measure of corn cost nine to ten *livres* at the end of the year, with peas and beans corresponding . . .

The ordinance made by His Majesty for the relief of his poor people [20 October 1693] cannot be forgotten here . . . Every community *had to* feed its poor. The pastors, mayors and men of law taxed the wealthiest and the middling, each according to his capability, in order to succour the poor, whom it was also their duty to seek out. It was the right way to keep everybody provided . . . In this village, where there is no court and everybody is his own master, the *curé* read out and re-read that ordinance to no avail. The *mayeurs* and men of law, who were the richest and would therefore have to be taxed most, fought it with all their might. With much hardship, August was finally reached. A fortnight beforehand, people were harvesting the rye when it was still green, and putting it in ovens to dry it, and because this grain was unripe and unhealthy it caused several serious illnesses. May the Lord in his fatherly Providence vouchsafe us to be preserved henceforward from a like dearth . . .

Henri PLATELLE, *Journal d'un curé de campagne au* XVIIe *siècle*
(Editions du Cerf, 1965), 90–4.

8 FROM 'MORTAL' TO 'STILLBORN' CRISES

'Through the various inquiries that have been made, it has been proved that the years when the corn was dearest were also those when mortality was highest and disease most common.' This is how a major problem is stated, as early as 1766, in a memorandum entitled *Réflexions sur la valeur du blé tant en France qu'en Angleterre depuis 1674 jusqu'en 1764* and subsequently published in Messance's *Recherches sur la population*. The problem is that of the effects of food shortages on the demography of ancien régime France.

How are we to isolate mortality due to food shortages? The thoroughly scientific caution of the author of the *Réflexions* will be remarked. He begins with a statement of fact, the coincidence of the maxima of grain prices with the annual maxima of the death-rate, but rounds it off by adding that these years also show the highest rate of disease. It would therefore be a thankless task to attempt statistically to locate a specific distinction among facts so closely linked as those of death through actual starvation, through illness attributable to under-nourishment and lastly through contagion, when this contagion is itself inseparable from the state of famine that was instrumental not only in inducing but also in spreading diseases by way of the shifting population of beggars. . . .

We can . . . precisely determine those years with exceptionally high death-rates for which the extra casualties can be related to a food shortage. These years are easy to single out. The order of magnitude of the phenomena concerned is such that there is any amount of corroborative testimony, and even historians who pay slight attention to the study of economic and social realities can hardly overlook events such as those of 1693 and 1709. In any case, there is a quite considerable number of monographs that leave no doubt as to the cause-and-effect relationship between rising prices, hardship and mortality . . .

. . . The age of Louis XIV saw the onset of a type of widespread food shortage whose character is so exceptionally clear-cut that it would suffice by itself to differentiate it. Similarly, the ratio of deaths to births shows an increase . . . of comparable and no less exceptional intensity. There can be no doubt as to the nation-wide character of the crisis . . .

In the age of Louis XV, and still more of Louis XVI, everything changes. Gone are the obvious correlations between the price-maxima and the demographic indices. If there is still a demographic problem of food-supply, it is of an altogether different magnitude, and this quantitative difference is of itself a qualitative one. Between the age of mortal and of stillborn crises, a revolution has occurred.

Jean MEUVRET, 'Les Crises de subsistances et la démographie de la France d'Ancien Régime', in *Population,* 1947, 643–7.

FURTHER READING
The problems of population have received keen attention, mostly since 1945.

1. First, the basic books (most of these have gone through several editions, and the most recent is therefore recommended).
SAUVY, Alfred, *La Population* (P.U.F., 'Que Sais-je?' No. 148, several eds.).

LANDRY, Adolphe, *Manuel de démographie* (Payot, several eds.).

ARMENGAUD, André, DUPÂQUIER, Jacques and REINHARD, Marcel, *Histoire générale de la population mondiale* (Montchrestien, 3rd ed., 1968).

ARMENGAUD, André, *Démographie et Sociétés* (Stock, 1966).

HUBER, BUNLÉ and BOVERAT, *La Population de la France* (Hachette, several eds.).

2. The following works are first-rate, but less easily obtainable:
SAUVY, Alfred, *Théorie générale de la population* (P.U.F., 2 vols, several eds.)

PRESSAT, Roland, *L'Analyse démographique* (P.U.F., 1961).

FLEURY, Michel, and HENRY, Louis, *Nouveau manuel de dépouillement et d'exploitation de l'État-civil ancien* (I.N.E.D., 1965).

GLASS, D. V. and EVERSLEY, D. E. C., *Population in History* (London, Arnold, 1965). Contains several first-rate articles on French subjects.

3. For keeping abreast of new developments:

First, the numerous publications of the I.N.E.D. (Institut National d'Études Démographiques), and in particular the outstanding review *Population* and its collection of *Cahiers*, which contain the best monographs;

The annual of the Société de Démographie Historique, which first appeared in 1964 and took the title of *Annales de Démographie Historique* the following year;

Lastly, the great English-language reviews such as *Population Studies* and *Population Index*.

4. Over the last ten years or so, a fair number of doctoral theses devoted to ancien régime France have included one or more chapters of historical demography. (See Chapter Three, Further Reading, section 2.)

III · THE ECONOMIC BASE

It has sometimes been suggested that the ancien régime – in the restricted sense of a juridical and political system – may have been 'determined' by the economy within which it had developed. This problem looks like yet another rhetorical exercise, but it was indeed at the time when economic structures were beginning to take off into expansion and industrialization, after the mid-eighteenth century, that the ageing political and social system started to crumble. Similarly, it is clear that the medieval economy was transformed into a 'modern' one by slow transitions during the same period that finds the politico-social régime progressively acquiring new characteristics. The problem does therefore warrant examination. Certainly there are links between the politico-social ancien régime and its economic 'wrapping' – it would be surprising if it were otherwise – but the nature and significance of these links remains to be seen, if they can be discovered. The prospect is open-ended, and unlikely to provide any easy solutions.

The historian's task is more straightforward, and consists of keeping an open mind while he analyses the economic data, which he will do by isolating them from the rest, perhaps somewhat artificially. Three methods have been suggested for achieving this objective.

The first is of very long standing, and amounts to putting oneself in the shoes of the theoreticians and administrators and registering and reproducing the systems of the former and the declarations of intent of the latter. This involves talking in terms of mercantilism, physiocracy, 'bullionism', balance of trade and so on, standpoints that held pride of place for some time and are always useful, but which break down in the long run. Theory is primarily evidence about the theoreticians and their followers; legislative documents, like administrative papers, are mostly evidence about their host-environment, and consequently run the risk of presenting a picture of millions of Frenchmen that is slanted and partial.

J. Marczewski and his adherents have recently put forward a second method in a daring effort to bring to bear on the past techniques of statistics and economic analysis belonging to the later twentieth century. Unfortunately it so happens that the basic data for periods prior to 1770–80 are either absent or do not stand up to criticism; hence the efforts to estimate the 'national income' towards 1700 yield next to nothing, even when backed by the most refined mathematical techniques, and only blind the reader with figures. 'Quantitative economic history' has nothing to show for the ancien régime, at least before the later eighteenth century.

The last method is humbler, slower, but reliable. It is microscopic investigation, within the compass of a small region, over a span of roughly a hundred years' duration, undertaken with the aid of the most derelict archives of that region and century. Thanks to a number of first-rate account ledgers, mainly ecclesiastical in origin, whose preservation was luckily institutionalized by confiscation at the time of the Revolution, it is possible in this case to use the quantitative method, and with real exactitude, at the level of the parish or group of parishes. In other words, the patient historian gains in reliability what he loses in scope and ambitiousness, and since his objective is to seek out the truth, he is now performing his proper task. A series of such micro-analyses over the last ten years or so have gradually assembled an image of the old French economy well-grounded enough for him to put forward the ensuing provisional and elementary synthesis. Provisional, because it is always open to expansion or correction by current or future research; elementary in the deliberately scholarly sense of the word, because it is mainly addressed to young people in the later twentieth century, who must learn to put themselves into an unfamiliar context.

1   OVERWHELMING DOMINANCE OF THE AGRICULTURAL ECONOMY

Obvious though it is, this dominance must never be lost sight of. Here are just a few of the most elementary data:

a) At least eighty-five per cent of the population is rural both in its habitat and employment.

With the exception of Paris, which never accounts for more than two per cent of the realm, France does not number more than a score of towns with populations in the tens of thousands, together with numerous good-sized *bourgs* promoted to 'town' rank only by their walls and their ancient privileges; even then, the towns abound with gardens, meadows, cowsheds and rural revenues, and they generally flow into the countryside in August for the big operations which require extra manpower. In the same way, the countryside usually buzzes with crafts and 'manufactures': half of the workers of the ancien régime are actually country-dwellers or peasants. Cloth, one of the great staples of French trade abroad, derives almost exclusively from rural 'industry' plied by weavers who are at the same time peasants.

b) The material environment of everyday life, like most of the tools and equipment used, is made up of vegetable or animal products, culled, collected and hand-worked in the heart of the countryside. Wood and wicker predominate; leather is rarer, and is often found in the form of harness for the horse, a frail, expensive animal; iron is quite exceptional, and is of poor quality if manufactured inside the realm. Except among the wealthy, meals are prepared and eaten off earthenware and wood. Again except among the wealthy, or in provinces with their own supply of stone, houses are of wood or a mixture of clay and straw, the basic building material even in the towns. Farm implements, including swing-ploughs and carts, and many of the craftsman's tools are cobbled together in farm or workshop out of wood chosen for the purpose, seasoned and rough-hewn. Spades, rakes, rollers, harrows and even large ploughs (apart from the ploughshare) are made of wood, which is also the only fuel, barring localized variations like coal, peat or dried cow-dung. These are commonplace observations, but their significance is far-reaching.

The products of iron- and steel-working are the preserve of restricted, wealthy sections of the population, and not least of the military.

c) The composition of private fortunes is copiously documented (wills, marriage contracts) and gives rise to similar observations. After sifting out a few thousand celebrated exceptions (bankers, big merchants, ship-owners), these fortunes are almost always composed of an overwhelming majority of stored rural products, rural assets and various kinds of rural revenue. The State budget itself is mainly replenished by direct or indirect levies on rural or agricultural production, taken at source or while in circulation.

d) In the structure of French foreign trade, as known to us through the medium of a few great works on 'economics' of the time and meagre statistical information, five main products are generally paramount: grain, wine (and spirits), salt, woollens, and hempen and linen cloth. With the exception of a section of the woollen industry and the 'finishing' of fabrics, all this comes out of the rural world and from peasant hands.

e) Lastly, the reader will recall what has been said in the preceding chapter on the subject of the periods of falling population or of the demographic form of a type of 'brief' economic crisis, generally arising out of a series of bad harvests. And it is always agricultural crisis (under-production, maldistribution, soaring prices) that leads to 'industrial crisis' (falling demand, production and employment, and little relief for the unemployed), and never the reverse. This sequence holds true at least until the Revolution, and it is only after the mid-nineteenth century or thereabouts (the exact timing is still disputed) that the chain of consequences and dependent effects is reversed: crises now originate in industry (particularly in metal-working) but also in the financial sector (which seems rarely to have been the case under the ancien régime, even at the time of the Law affair).

This overwhelming predominance of agriculture expresses itself primarily in the near-frantic pursuit of the basic staples of life – usually grain – as well as in the necessity of bartering or selling in order to 'buy' coinage, which is indispensable, if only to meet the demands of the tax-collectors. These obvious but essential distinctions will keep recurring in this and the following chapters.

2 INDUSTRY: IN SECOND PLACE BUT NOT OF SECOND-RATE IMPORTANCE; DOMINATED BY TEXTILES

The word 'industry' is convenient, but was hardly ever used in its present sense before 1750. The contemporary term was 'manufacture', which seldom meant a concentration of buildings and workers but referred rather to local scatterings of artisans, although these would be relatively specialized in processing natural raw materials such as wool.

It used to be fashionable to make much of *'la grande industrie'* and the 'corporations' – thoroughly anachronistic expressions as they are – but it is still worth emphasizing the subsidiary, dependent nature of all French 'industrial' output under the ancien régime. The foregoing pages illustrating the predominance of the agricultural world make it quite clear that in terms of value of output, numbers of producers, the structure of the economic 'crises' themselves and many other features, the industrial sector occupies a subordinate position.

At the same time, it is worth repeating and analysing to some degree the concomitant statement that most of the producers in this sector were country-dwellers, in fact peasants whose main employment was agricultural. Even in Picardy, the number of wool-workers dotted about the countryside undoubtedly tended more and more to exceed those who clustered around the urban workshops, while numerous detailed studies have shown that the weavers of hemp and linen, from Flanders to the Vendée, were nearly all peasants, and quite lowly ones at that. Even the labour-force of the metal-working sector consisted for the most part of seasonal, migrant workers of rural origin, not only as providers of labour for the forges and furnaces (these include the essential and longer-established charcoal-burners), but also as specialists – in the manufacture of Normandy pins, for instance. The operations of bleaching, dyeing, finishing and stockpiling the finished article prior to marketing were more often carried out in the towns. There were even a number of manufacturing towns (often big trading centres too, but not always), such as Lille, Amiens, Beauvais, Rouen, Rheims and Lyons, in which there was a genuine worker proletariat, well-documented from this time onward. These conditions foreshadow those which become the norm in the factories of the nineteenth century, although the total number of wage-earners may not have amounted to more than a hundred thousand before 1750.

VARIABLE STATUS OF INDUSTRY

French coal-mining is almost nonexistent before the later eighteenth century, with some local exceptions such as the Saint-Étienne region, whereas English coal brought about a preliminary 'industrial revolution' from 1600 onward and by 1789 was being mined in at least ten times the quantity of French output. In spite of the isolated trials stimulated mainly by military demand in the sixteenth century and later under Colbert, French metal-working remains slight, scattered, of poor quality and very expensive. It does not modernize until after 1780, when it begins to copy English techniques, never manages to produce genuine steel (except perhaps at Rives, in Dauphiné), and depends on foreign countries even for scythes, which are imported from Styria.

Not counting building, a seasonal, fluctuating, mainly urban industry, particularly active before the Fronde and after the Regency – or in the construction of royal show-pieces – it is the textile industry which is easily the most important sector. Its comparative predominance is the result of various factors: the size of its labour-force, the value of its output both for domestic and foreign consumption, the supplementary income it provides for hundreds of thousands of country-dwellers, and the beginnings of centralization, commercial at first, then properly-speaking industrial (with the manufacture of printed fabrics, but again not until the second half of the eighteenth century). We must not be misled by the existence of a few institutions of great prestige, but not very great profitability, such as the great royal tapestry workshops of Gobelins or Beauvais. The French textile industry concentrates on 'coarse' textiles, turning out moderately-priced fabrics for very large markets: it was here that its real strength lay, as its English competitors had good reason to realize and deplore. Over a million men, women and children worked either full- or part-time, and whole towns hummed to the rhythm of the loom, particularly in the North, where Amiens is the best-known and best-documented example. In rainier regions from the Lys to the Vendée, '*murquiniers*' and '*texiers*' processed the flax, which was bleached and dressed by big specialized firms at Valenciennes, Saint-Quentin, Beauvais, Laval in particular, and Vitré in the sixteenth century. As for coarse linen, it was woven in every village, just as practically every garden gave room to its hemp-patch. Making their own clothes was one aspect of 'subsistence' for the common people, and this ability to make a few *écus* from sales to merchant middlemen coincided with the general, national interest; which explains the attention paid to every branch of the textile trade by royal legislation before and after Colbert. Cloth, and particularly the hempen and linen cloth in which Blacks and Indians were dressed, was the country's foremost export, taking pride of place even over grain and wine, and enabling France to obtain the precious metals which she herself did not produce, or the American *piastres* which filled the same function.

For all these reasons, the dispersed yet massive strength of the textile industry played a far more important role than its output (apparently not even five per cent of the GNP) and working force (probably not much more than five per cent of the population) would suggest.

Lastly, it was by centralizing, improving and gradually modernizing its industry that the French economy was able to prepare for 'take-off'. Progress was slow at first, especially in the traditional sectors, but the overall rate of expansion must still have worked out at around sixty per cent for the eighteenth century as a whole. The English model and the superior performance of a few expanding key-sectors (cotton, printed fabrics, iron-working, paper and the beginnings of the chemical industry) were to elicit and sustain this decisive leap forward, which seemed bound finally to signalize the last years of the outgoing century at the very moment when, politically and socially, the ancien régime was digging in its heels, not believing that it was on the verge of collapse. In fact, this collapse must have at least partially retarded the move towards industrialization, if the Revolution and the Empire really were economic 'national disasters', as recent work by men such as M. Lévy-Leboyer tends to indicate . . .

Once again, we have noticed the contrast between the last decades (and here even the dynamic last years) of the eighteenth century and the quasi static or slowly fluctuating patterns which had typified well-nigh all the ancien régime – a leitmotiv that appears again in our next area of study.

3 SLOW, INCONVENIENT, COSTLY TRANSPORT

It would not have been at all illogical to lay the main stress of an introductory chapter on the often crucial problem of transport, were it not for the amount of work and manpower represented by the agricultural world, where subsistence farming and therefore the absence of transport were the rule.

The first thing that strikes someone living in the last third of the twentienth century is how slowly things move, rarely averaging more than two or three miles an hour for any kind of journey before 1760. Going by horse 'post haste' (that is, at the gallop, theoretically the preserve of the king's service only) the giddy speed of twelve miles an hour may be achieved, but even so there have to be fresh horses waiting at each stage . . . Whatever the emergency, the fastest journeys rarely cover more than twenty-five miles a day. Going by stage-coach and waterway, Lyons is ten days from Paris in the time of Louis XIV, but Bordeaux is a fortnight's journey, and Rouen three days! Goods move even more sluggishly: wine takes four days to reach Paris from Orléans; at the height of the eighteenth century, textiles from Laval trundle along for two weeks before reaching Rouen, and Rouen textiles for a month to get to Lyons. The tempo of life in ancien régime France was not markedly faster than in the Middle Ages, and went at the pace of man, mule or plodding horse. The canals (three in 1700: the Briare, the Orléans and the Midi) and the achievements of the Trudaines and Perronet in road-building brought only moderate improvements, which once again did not really begin to come into play until after 1750 (even in 1789, the highway network planned around 1750 is a long way from completion and speeds up only some local transport). The real and unmistakeable 'revolution' came with the railways, which broke down barriers, shrank distances and unified the nation.

LOCAL HIGHWAYS

The busiest and certainly the most useful roads in the circumstances of the time were the now disused multitudes of footpaths, mulepaths and local roads whose origins are lost in time, the straightest being generously credited to the Romans. No village was without its links with the neighbouring *bourg* and market, whether by *sentier* (single-file footpath), *carrière* (eight feet wide in Clermont; according to local custom, open to carts in single file and roped animals) or sometimes even a true *voye,* theoretically sixteen feet wide. Some of these routes had special names and functions: 'fish-cart roads' (*chemins de chasse-marée*), winding down from the northern Channel to Paris, carried more pack-animals than carts, laden with fish to meet the demand arising out of the Church's imposition of upwards of 150 'fast-days' a year. Here and there are 'potter's paths'; everywhere vineyard tracks, narrowest of all, and especially 'green paths', enclosed by hedges, along which the cattle could go from stall to communal pasture without straying on to ploughland. The *drailles* (sheep trails) of the Cévennes, transhumance paths, portages, salt (and contraband) paths ... the list is long: there is no need to look beyond the old ordnance survey maps, or those drawn up by Cassini in the eighteenth century. This superb network was perfectly adapted to the life and needs of the majority of Frenchmen, peasants tied to the soil, striving to be self-supporting and seldom venturing beyond a circle of four or five miles' radius, within which lay the family, the weekly market, the notary and the local seigneurial or royal court.

THE 'MAIN ROADS'

Like the rivers and river-banks, the 'king's highways', some of which became 'post roads' from the end of the sixteenth century (galloping permitted, regular travel-connections, and a royal courier and packet service), were the preserve of an altogether different type of regional, inter-regional and even international traffic, carrying costly products dispatched not by peasants but by merchants and government departments. However, the volume of this traffic was certainly much less than the above-mentioned: in any domain the local always takes precedence over the national in the centuries before 1750.

Apart from the *pavé du Roy* and a few urban paved surfaces (the Orléans road, château avenues, entrances to towns), the roads are little more than somewhat wider dirt pathways, with their usual drawbacks – dust or mud according to the time of year, wooden bridges, often broken down, or even just fords, innumerable road-tolls (but heavily reduced in the course of the eighteenth century), and frequent danger for the traveller, as much in the forest of Fontainebleau as in remote mountain areas. The numerous bodies responsible for their upkeep are continually quarrelling among themselves and habitually inefficient, so that it is by no means unusual to break an axle or to lose horses and baggage. No produce or merchandise, no matter how light, will stand the cost of transport over a distance greater than fifteen miles or so; this applies to building materials, wines (even Burgundian), and especially to grain and timber: their bulk and low prices consign them to waterways, where these are available. The main roads mostly carry small expensive articles, well-to-do travellers, and letters and packets for which the Royal Mail has held the monopoly since the time of Louis XIII – a monopoly exploited by wily businessmen and even by some ministers, Louvois among them.

ASCENDANCE OF THE WATERWAYS

Maximum use was made of any river that could accommodate boats (whose average tonnage varied between ten and fifty), if only for a few weeks per year; even minor rivers such as the Clain and the Orb. The reason was simple, and here Vauban expounds it: 'A boat of reasonable size, in good water, can by itself, with six men and four [tow] horses . . . take the load that 200 men and 400 horses would have the utmost difficulty in hauling over ordinary roads.' It is for this reason that the favoured regions and nearly all the towns were those with maritime or river ports surrounded by a hinterland that could produce with an eye to the export trade. Thus it has been clearly shown by Roger Dion that the only vineyards of any account at the time were those which had easy access to the sea, a good river – or a thirsty town, like Paris.

Yet these favoured connections are on a fairly moderate scale. At Orléans, a road and river junction situated on what was at the time one of the busiest rivers in France, an average of about four hundred boats a year passed through in the time of Louis XIV: one a day – really two or three, allowing for the interruptions raised by floods, drops in the water-level and freezing. And most of these boats go downstream never to return, being broken up and sold as lumber or firewood when they reach the estuary. The French ports that have attracted so much favourable mention from historians counted themselves 'great' when they managed to fit out fifty or more ships of 100 tons. In 1664, this modest figure was approached only by Saint-Malo, and exceeded only by Le Havre; in 1686, only the same two ports fitted out a hundred or so 'great vessels'. True, a few big shipowners – Danycan at Saint-Malo, Montaudoin at Nantes – amass legendary fortunes of millions (of *livres*), but these are only exceptions: as a rule the transport business is conducted on a much smaller scale, by a host of medium or small carriers by land or water, often working part-time and with more than one occupation. Nevertheless, ships grow bigger and trade expands in the course of the eighteenth century, and the big shipowners (and small companies of their enthusiastic financial backers) begin to play an economic and sometimes a political role that is no longer out of the ordinary. The difference is one of degree far more than of structure, and is due principally to the slave-trade and to sugar from the West Indies, particularly from San Domingo, pearl of the French economy and mainstay of its prosperity. Once again, however, it is a declining régime that lights its way to death with the riches of the Caribbean.

Transport under the ancien régime is small-scale, irregular, expensive, unsafe and unevenly distributed: it is these characteristics that combine to give a picture of ancien régime life throughout its centuries of existence (except towards the end) as localized, dispersed, and poorly served by communications. They foster the fragmentation and the semi-isolation of the great peasant, provincial, uneven, uncoordinated mosaic that France then was. Taken together, they are also a conclusive explanation of the difficulty that besets the ruler of the nation, who needs to ensure that decisions made at the centre are known and observed. In spite of the royal mail and express couriers, the villages of France are days and weeks away from Paris and Versailles; travelling in either direction is often a chancy business. The taste for provincial independence and individual conservatism was well protected.

4 A COMPLICATED, OLD-FASHIONED MONETARY SYSTEM

Seen from a twentieth-century standpoint, money and credit present such a scene of confusion and creaking antiquity that there is little choice but to offer an almost scandalously simplified account.

THE COINAGE

The French coins struck from the sixteenth to the eighteenth century were made of either gold (the *écu soleil,* succeeded by the *louis* in 1640), silver, or *billon* (an alloy of silver and copper). The monetary unit was the *livre tournois* (minted at Tours), which supplanted the *livre parisis* (minted in Paris) in the sixteenth century. The value of the *livre* is often expressed in grams of silver: it contained 18 grams towards 1500, 11 towards 1600, 8 from Richelieu to Colbert, and 4.5 after 1726, when it was finally stabilized for almost two centuries (the '*franc de germinal*' under the Consulate and the *franc-or* prior to 1914 contained much the same weight of pure silver). The first observation to be made, then, is that the ancien régime quite readily practised frequent devaluations until 1726. We must now list a few of the factors that complicate this oversimplified picture.

a) The coinage carried no face value: it would bear the stamp of the king's head, some Latin, and a few decorative details (such as the sun that gave the *écus soleil* their name until 1640). The value of each coin was fixed by royal ordinance, a convenient method of devaluation, since it was only necessary to ordain that such and such an *écu* would henceforward count as four *livres* instead of three. This 'augmentation', as it was called, was actually a devaluation: one *livre tournois* now counted as worth a quarter of the metal in the coin, instead of a third!

b) Until about 1640 the coins were poorly minted, and a skilled worker could 'clip' or 'dip' them (in acid) to remove some of the precious metal; hence the accurate scales of the merchants, made familiar by contemporary paintings. But real improvements in the minting process took place towards the mid-seventeenth century.

c) There was a long period during which various more or less independent princelings went on striking their own coinage (as was their right) and in fact imitating the French coinage, which bordered on counterfeiting. Mints of this type were operating at Sedan, Charleville, Orange and the Dombes well into the seventeenth century.

d) Foreign coinage was in general circulation – mainly Spanish, but also English, Imperial, Italian, etc. This circulation was legally valid, and every foreign coin was assigned an official (and often also a black-market) exchange-rate.

e) Gold, silver and copper were all imported, their production frequently varied, in changing and conflicting proportions, and none of the types of coinage in circulation was of the same composition. Wholesale speculation had the end-result of driving good money out of circulation and of giving rise to complicated speculative processes that were not always to the advantage of the economy.

f) The exchange-rates set by royal ordinance for the various types of coinage often lagged behind international economic events, reciprocal variations in metal-prices, the state of the money-market and so on, to such a degree that a 'parallel' exchange-rate for currency often existed side by side with the official quotation. International-class merchants in particular had their own rates, which were not necessarily identical with the king's. A kind of imaginary *écu* of three *livres* represented French coinage on the foreign markets, particularly in Amsterdam. It was usually quoted below the official domestic rate, notably throughout most of the seventeenth century.

g) Lastly, an abundance of small coins of no real value, such as the *liard**, were in common circulation, and were sometimes refus-

---

* A copper coin worth 3 *deniers*, or a quarter of a *sou*. When the *livre tournois* succeeded the *livre parisis*, the coinage worked as in pre-decimal England: 1 *livre (l.)* = 20 *sols/sous (s.)* = 240 *deniers (d.)*. – Tr.

ed in payment among the more enlightened (but fobbed off onto the common people, an occasional cause of uprisings).

In other words, the day-to-day handling of coinage in old France took the kind of expertise that probably not two men in a hundred possessed. Here again the position clarified after 1726, but the truth is that for most Frenchmen the problem was always quite simple: it was the absence of money that plagued them, rather than its complications.

MONEY IN SOCIETY: CIRCULATION, HOARDING, SUBSTITUTION

Economic analyses remain somewhat abstract when taken out of their social context. Monetary phenomena become intelligible only when they are put back into their social frameworks, which have not yet been defined. However, it is neither rash nor premature to assert that within the extremes of affluence which then existed, money posed quite different sets of problems.

a) The mass of the people consists of small peasants who are hard-pressed to harvest enough to live on. For them, wealth equals crops, in all their forms; they make up for what they lack by means of barter or extra work. Money is only a supplement to barter and is often not used at all. The 'wage' earned (by day- or piece-work) – 'recompense', as it was then called – is not necessarily monetary: many payments take the form of food, kind (harvesters get a percentage), other services (such as the loan of a plough-team), or the remission of debts. In the last case, it is enough to tear up or alter the bits of scribbled paper which are the small peasants' IOUs to their creditors. These existed in considerable numbers, and often changed hands, thereby constituting a kind of local currency – real currency expressed in *livres* and *sols tournois* – which makes them more reliable than the second-rate metal coins whose value was open to debate. In the lowly rural settings that contained the majority of the population, barter, the exchange of services and the circulation and withdrawal of private IOUs certainly played a more prominent part than did the *écu* or the *louis;* the *billon* would often take care of any differences.

But all these small peasants were liable to various fiscal obligations. Whereas the tithe-owner and often the seigneur were happy with payments in kind and direct appropriations from the harvest, the king could hardly cart loads of sheaves all over the realm, and required hard cash. Steps had to be taken to obtain it, therefore, which meant 'buying' it by the sale either of produce from the domestic small-holding (cheese, honey, calves, piglets, fleeces, capons . . .); products in short supply (wheat, wine), so that the peasant had to go short of them; whatever could be spun, woven or otherwise manufactured by cottage industry at evening-time or in winter; or by the sale of labour.

To sum up, among the rural masses, the backbone of the realm, a sort of barter-economy, dependent on subsistence farming and a primitive credit-system, still played an important part, although a slowly declining one, especially in the manufacturing regions along coast and river which were the most 'open' of all. Money was used, partly for fiscal reasons, in the lowly unreliable form of the *billon* and minor silver coins. *Écus* and *louis d'or* must have been treasure, to be brought out and displayed as the family sat up in the evening, and jealously guarded so as to make up a dowry, or buy a field. In popular settings, money was distinguished by its rarity, low quality and poor circulation.

After 1760 or thereabouts a pronounced change set in. Even fairly modest peasants turned up in some numbers to bid for farmholdings whose soaring prices easily doubled in one generation. Better coinage was consequently circulating more freely and its distribution was broader and quicker. The new Brazilian mines, a four-fold increase in trade, rising prices, an indeterminate improvement in the growth-rate (anything from twenty to sixty per cent, according to the experts), and greater general prosperity – these were the probable factors behind a kind of resurgence which, yet again, does not make its appearance until the latter half of the eighteenth century.

b) Switching from the mass of the general population to the well-to-do, we find an altogether different set of monetary problems. Scarcity still exists, although in an altered form, but the main problems are those of disorganization.

Merchants and Ministers in the era of Louis XIV complained a great deal about the scarcity of currency, particularly of sound currency. These grumbles were fairly well-founded, if difficult to interpret, and hinge upon the fall in production and frequent devaluations. A number of deeper causes relating to the poor circulation of currency and organization of credit are often overlooked. From this point of view, France lagged well behind those countries which were in the forefront of modern trading and financial techniques (first Italy, then the Low Countries and England), for reasons which are hard to diagnose.

As far back as the Middle Ages, the businessmen of the great Italian city-states had perfected a system of compensatory credit payments among merchants in far-removed localities with different monetary systems. This was the bill of exchange, which quickly turned into an instrument of credit and a means of speculation. The practice of endorsement very soon made it into a type of currency with an international circulation among merchants and even among states, and capable of yielding interest to anybody with the skill to manipulate exchange-rate variations in time and place. French merchants were slow to adopt this system and slower still to practise systematic endorsement: they did not catch up before the mid-seventeenth century. In the time of Louis XIII it was not unusual to find big cloth-merchants – those of Amiens for instance – still using a kind of rudimentary IOU, a primitive book-keeping system (not even double-entry), and setting off on real *tours de France* with horses, coffers and armed retainers to collect the *écus* owing to them from Troyes to Lyons and from Limoges to Toulouse! – an outlandish procedure whose archaic character can only be explained in terms of psychological traits such as profound traditionalism and suspicion. Religious scruples also play their part, since the stricter theologians, reinforced by the Jansenists, roundly condemned anything that smacked of 'usury' and even went so far as to lump the simple, moderate interest drawn on capital together with almost all the '*trafics d'argent*' under this heading (cf. Document 10).

c). More striking still is the absence of any reliable banking organization, and above all of any state bank, although not for want of assiduous efforts, all unsuccessful.

Certainly the realm possessed its '*financiers*' and 'bankers'. For some time, the former were Italians, then Germans, often working in semi-familial association: they collected the royal taxes, at no small profit to themselves, and advanced large sums to the king at equally profitable rates. The latter were relatively numerous (about a hundred in eighteenth-century Paris, which is too many, and testifies to the small scale of their activities). More often than not they were merchants who changed money and, increasingly, discounted bills of exchange. They also tried to horn in on the international circulation of bills of exchange, sometimes at a profit, sometimes at a loss, so that bankruptcy was not uncommon. We shall encounter the former again, in the guise of '*partisans*', financial officials and finally farmers-general, 'the leeches of the people', detested, reviled, but practically indispensable. As for the latter, they are of necessity connected with the international banking circuit, whose main strength lay outside France, in London, Amsterdam, Hamburg and Geneva, to mention only these few instances. Independent of the realm and yet bound to the king, who drew on them for loans in wartime, they are often Protestants, with extensive, competent connections and surprising affiliations. In spite of some good recent studies, not much is yet known about them. It is certain only that their activities did not stop at the borders of the realm. They extricated themselves successfully at the time of the Revolution, only to return after the holocaust, when they helped to found the Bank of France.

In addition to these influential figures, but coming from outside France, were the companies of wealthy individuals who dabbled in banking and rediscounting, but remained basically traders. Their usual objective was to fit out a few vessels for the Indies or China. They might go into partnership with a few others, often with relatives, to risk some of their assets on long expeditions or to engage in marine insurance or brokerage, making arrangements for reinsurance in Amsterdam or London even (indeed especially) in war-time. Their lack of specialization, restricted, short-term associations and partial subservience to international high finance point towards the defects in technique and organization that were a brake on the French economy for many years.

Be it said that the state provided precious few good examples. It lived from hand to mouth, kept going by the *financiers* then by bankers such as Necker. Despite Colbert and his nephew Desmarets, and despite John Law and abortive projects for a *Caisse d'escompte* (discount bank) in 1767 and again in 1776, it proved impossible to create a state bank. Yet city-states like Genoa, Venice and Valencia had had theirs by the sixteenth century; in 1609, Amsterdam led the world with the Wisselbank, which Hamburg and Sweden strove to imitate; the Bank of England arrived on the scene later still (1694). There can be no doubt that the unfortunate collapse of Law's 'system' (1719-20) contributed to the French loathing of any kind of paper money, and state-backed paper in particular. Barring a few big business circles, the eighteenth century believed only in '*espèces sonnantes et trébuchantes*' (hard cash), a belief echoed in all contracts, even in run-of-the-mill rural farm-leases. And again, how was anybody to have confidence in a state which was such a chronic debtor and a potential and often partial bankrupt?

With no state bank, no really independent private bank, nothing worth calling a stock exchange and not a single great, permanent, non-familial capitalist company, France was a museum-piece among far more 'contemporary' states. It is surprising to find her so well off, until we recall her wealth in manpower, agricultural output and exportable commodities. What then, in the final analysis, is the key, the inmost core of the French economy?

5   A STURDY TRADITIONAL ECONOMY

Except for a few limited and late-developing sectors which were almost nonexistent before 1750, ancien régime France is characterized not by banking, the money market, the machine, large-scale manufacture, or concentration of capital, business or manpower. She remains a patchwork of rural provinces with traditional attitudes, archaic techniques, chronic shortage of currency and poor communications, where the struggle for daily bread remains the over-riding consideration and every human grouping strives to be self-supporting.

The '*bon ménager*', the good husbandman self-sufficient on his own land, was the collective traditional ideal kept alive not only in popular almanacs but also in the aristocratic *Théâtre d'agriculture et ménage des champs* (1600) by Olivier de Serres, which went on reprinting until the time of the Consulate. *'Oeconomie Domestique'* and the *'Bon Mesnager'* are recurrent themes among serious writers, and those unconscious traditionalists, the physiocrats, were only to attempt to bring image and concept up to date. Even the king himself, ensconced in his palaces in the bosom of his 'family' of relations, great vassals and retainers, is readily envisaged as ruling his *'mesnage'* – the realm – like a good, wise paterfamilias living off his estates . . . which ought to suffice him.

The vast majority still see the perfect state of affairs as a kind of localized autarky relieved by a little 'commerce'. The basis of the economy is 'subsistence' in the broad sense of essential food-stuffs – the various types of grain, plus sweet chestnuts or fish here and there – clothing, a roof over one's head, and lastly fuel, the ideal being to produce everything on one's own land, supplementing it where necessary with shrewd deals. To feed the spirit, since 'man does not live by bread alone', there are the priests, story-tellers and witches: only the first have any semblance of legality, and the usual thing is to help provide them with a living, since they provide the prayers. The arrangements for the other two are more discreet. For hundreds of years, the safeguard against enemies, brigands, thieves and neighbours was a powerful warrior-class with its fort-ress-refuges. It too had to be provisioned because it offered secur-ity, order and a modicum of justice. The king ranks high above: he is protector, guarantor and supreme judge under God, who anoints him in the rite of coronation. And since he is unable to live off his own estates, there is nothing for it but to give him 'aid', an old feudal term*. For his sake, and all the others', cash now has to be obtained, by judicious sales or by piece-work. If there is any left over, the money will see the family through bad years, set up the children or buy a little more land. Thus the money-economy has been infiltrating the barter-economy for centuries, by dint of work and intelligence, and because it was not in conflict with at-tachment to the land. The original preoccupation with subsistence has been coupled with the pursuit of 'commerce' and 'manufacture'

---

* The *'aides'*, originally subventions due to the sovereign, became indirect taxes on commodities in the fourteenth century, and applied mainly to consumer goods – fish, meat, snuff and particularly wine – by the seventeenth. – Tr.

as means of acquiring the all-important cash. These are the explanations and justifications offered by simple traditional souls for the basic social divisions (king, warrior, priest, worker) and for the fundamental economic dichotomy (subsistence and commerce).

These simplistic but deep-rooted and enduring conceptions do not amount to much of an explanation. The state has grown. Governed first by seigneur, then by count or duke, finally by the king himself, it has revelled in its three passions – ruling, building, and fighting, especially fighting, both for prestige and for power. Vast new resources have become necessary, over and above what the royal estates and the traditional 'aid' could provide: taxation and credit systems are needed. When the businessmen of the realm (a Jacques Coeur, an Ango) prove neither numerous nor strong enough, the vacuum is filled by foreigners, mainly Italians from towns where money-management had achieved a long unequalled degree of expertise. These high-living 'colonists' helped the kings and their servants to collect money, start commercial enterprises, exploit resources, modernize, and also to squeeze the people. They left disciples. Those who did not return to Florence, Siena, Genoa or Lucca converted their enormous profits into land, stone, position, benefices and power; two of their Medici descendants became queens of France. Germans and Dutchmen followed in their footsteps, with the Swiss not far behind.

These modern, efficient, imported methods wrought no profound changes in the old rural realm, which went on subsisting, trading and providing for its ever more numerous priests, warriors, judges and administrators. What they did was to perfect the exploitation of its resources, and make a finer, wider, more burdensome art of the large-scale collection of revenue from land and workshop, thereby giving rise to murmurs, conspiracies and uprisings. But not one uprising yielded positive results, and the increase in the tax-load and proliferation of the various collectors never actually ruined the country. The strength of the realm lay in its having remained a populous, productive rural society. A tiny élite of noblemen, priests, wealthy commoners and the state itself fed off the substance of the peasants, which was tapped in part by an ingenious and diversified system of impositions.

The ancien régime was a teeming and, in its time, fertile rural society, dominated by rentiers.

DOCUMENTS

9 ON THE PROSPERITY AND SUPERIORITY OF THE REALM OF FRANCE

... Your Majesties possess a great Estate, pleasing in situation, abundant in riches, teeming with people, strong in good solid towns, invincible in arms and triumphant in glory. Its territory is spacious enough to contain its boundless number of inhabitants, its fertility to nourish them, its wealth in livestock to clothe them ...

Only France can do without all her neighbouring lands, and none of them can do without her ... The least of the provinces of France supplies Your Majesties its grain, wine, salt, cloth, wool, iron, oil and woad, which make it richer than all the Perus in the world ...

As for the abundance of trade and of those who ply it, there are more traders in France, and more trade-products, than there are men in any other realm whatsoever ... As for the industry of the arts, it is from us that all others have it ...

[As for forges and metal-working] there are in your State more than five hundred thousand persons who live like salamanders in the midst of that fire, which also applies to so many crafts that it would take several pages to list them ... Our neighbours have learnt them from ourselves and ... the pupils do not excel their teachers. A good enough example is England, which ... has been so well taught by the ability of our men ... What I say of England applies equally to Flanders and especially Holland. For in this same matter, she owes more to ourselves than to the Germans ...

In sooth, Germany prides herself on her iron-working, but what we make with it has been and is worth as much as theirs, and, if I say worth more, the proof will not belie me ...

> Antoine de MONTCHRÉTIEN, *Traicté de l'Œconomie politique dédié au Roy et à la Reine mère du Roy,* 1615 (Funck-Brentano edition, n.d.), 23–50 passim.

N.B: This document is printed only as an example of the more or less 'political' literature of the time; the general drift is a very common one; the examples, strongly ingrained with national vanity, are all untrue.

10 ARCHAIC COMMERCIAL TECHNIQUES: THE EXAMPLE OF AMIENS

[Upon] examining the minutes of notaries and posthumous inventories ...

what strikes us is first of all the archaism of these practices at the beginning of the seventeenth century, and how dated they are compared with what could be observed in great international centres such as Lyons or Antwerp.

Domestic trade retains its individual character, and continues to rely on a vast network of personal contacts and reciprocal trust kept alive from one fair to the next. Periodic voyages and sometimes even matrimonial alliances contribute to the upkeep of regular contacts from province to province.

Trading companies seem extremely rare in Picard commerce, while the law and the Church continue to ban the financing of one partner by another . . . [The] occasional companies set up for textile trading usually involved members of the same family – thus, two brothers, a widow and her son, and two cousins, one resident in Amiens, the other in Rouen. These associations enabled each individual to cut down on his travel to fairs. With greater numbers and better organization they would have enabled the merchants of Amiens to keep themselves informed about market conditions and to assess competition abroad more reliably.

The same archaism appears in book-keeping . . . To judge by the inventories, many of the merchants of Amiens in the early seventeenth century did not yet keep a ledger, but simply bundled together debts and notes of hand. The prevailing negligence in the recording of accounts owed and owing is a source of perpetual surprise to the researcher . . . Heirs . . . seem incapable of reckoning up the liabilities on the estate: 'there is a reckoning due with so-and-so, merchant of Paris, Rouen, Lyons . . .' or again: 'The aforesaid Morgan has stated that he could not yet make a statement of the company liabilities, as he still has to work out debts owed to his suppliers.'

This negligence was fostered by the delay allowed in settling bills. The first payments often took six months, and sizeable credits would remain outstanding after a year or more . . . An early eighteenth-century report on Spanish commerce points out that the Spanish 'prefer to send their wool to England and Holland rather than to France, because settlement falls due there within three or four months, whereas in France, by a most pernicious practice, settlement falls due after twenty or twenty-two months'.

. . . Another remarkable feature of the early seventeenth-century French economy is its backwardness in banking and exchange. In Amiens, the *échevins** and burghers seem to have gone out of their way . . . to obstruct

---

* Municipal magistrates; as a body (the *échevinage*), the highest municipal authority – the 'town council'. – Tr.

the organization of any kind of credit system. In 1559 and 1560, the Town Hall repeatedly rejected proposals by several Piedmontese merchants who wanted to settle in the town as bankers. Yet a number of craftsmen and manufacturers had intervened in favour of the granting of their petition: presumably they had personal experience of the exorbitant conditions of illicit moneylenders. Whatever the real reasons may have been for these bans – religious scruples or the greed of the usurers and moneylenders – Amiens, the capital of a great province, remained devoid of any kind of credit institution.

This deficiency explains the slow spread of the general use of bills and notes of exchange ... Ecclesiastical doctrine and royal legislation prohibited their use in domestic trade, preventing them from functioning like present-day discountable bills ...

It was only in the last quarter of the century that economic necessity gradually prevailed over religious and legal scruples. Examination of posthumous inventories reveals the greater frequency of bills of exchange and promissory notes bearing successive endorsements ...

> Pierre DEYON, *Amiens, capitale provinciale, étude sur la société urbaine au* XVIIe *siècle* (Mouton, Paris-The Hague, 1967) 98–102.

N.B: Amiens, a town of some thirty to forty thousand inhabitants, was the foremost producer of woollen fabrics in France throughout the duration of the ancien régime.

11 PRICES OF THE *MUID* (660 LITRES) OF NEW WINE ON THE BÉZIERS MARKET

(in *livres tournois*, prices for September–October, after the grape harvest)

1613	25	1625	18	1637	50	1649	22
1614	36	1626	18	1638	48	1650	36
1615	8	1627	30	1639	54	. . .	. . .
1616	30	1628	30	1640	34	1680	30
1617	57	1629	?	1641	20	1681	23
1618	30	1630	24	1642	39	1682	15
1619	15	1631	36	1643	66	1683	21
1620	20	1632	50	1644	16	1684	22
1621	8	1633	24	1645	12	1685	18
1622	30	1634	23	1646	16	1686	13
1623	18	1635	30	1647	22	1687	10
1624	15	1636	24	1648	30	1688	15

1689	17	1696	72	1703	48	1710	56
1690	18	1697	32	1704	30	1711	45
1691	33	1698	50	1705	16	1712	36
1692	21	1699	50	1706	9	1713	53
1693	45	1700	24	1707	23	1714	60
1694	56	1701	23	1708	46	1715	38
1695	46	1702	56	1709	95	1716	13

From Emmanuel Le Roy-Ladurie, *Les Paysans de Languedoc* (S.E.V.P.E.N., 2 vols, 1966), 823–4.

12 MEAN ANNUAL PRICES OF THE *SETIER* (156 LITRES; ABOUT 4.3 BUSHELS) OF RYE IN PARIS

(prices after the harvest, expressed as decimals of the *livre tournois*)

1635	7.4	1651	20.8				
1636	8.1	1652	13.6	1667	4.9	1682	6.3
1637	6.4	1653	7	1668	5	1683	7.1
1638	5.2	1654	5.9	1669	4.7	1684	11
1639	5.1	1655	7	1670	4.9	1685	6.1
1640	7.9	1656	6.2	1671	4.8	1686	5.7
1641	7.9	1657	7.1	1672	4.7	1687	4.4
1642	10.3	1658	10	1673	5.1	1688	6.7
1643	12.3	1659	9	1674	9.1	1689	6.7
1644	8.7	1660	12	1675	7.1	1690	5.4
1645	4.6	1661	20.6	1676	6.4	1691	7.5
1646	6.4	1662	14.4	1677	9.3	1692	12.1
1647	8.4	1663	10.4	1678	8.7	1693	26.5
1648	10.5	1664	7.5	1679	9.8	1694	9.8
1649	18	1665	8.4	1680	6	1695	5.4
1650	13.9	1666	5.5	1681	8		

From Micheline Baulant and Jean Meuvret, *Prix des céréales extraits de la mercuriale de Paris* (S.E.V.P.E.N., 2 vols, 1962), 136.

13 VALUE OF THE *LIVRE TOURNOIS* IN GRAMS OF PURE SILVER

1513	17.96	1652	7.56
1521	17.19	1653	4 variations from 7.16 to 7.92
1533	16.38	1654	8.33
1541	16.07	1666	8.60
1543	15.62		then back to 8.33
1549	15.57	1690	7.56
1550	15.12	1693	6.93
1561	14.27	1700	7.02
1573	13.19	1715	5.60
1575	11.79	1726	4.45
1602	10.98		(then stable until
1636	8.69		the Revolution)
1641	8.33		

Simplified and augmented table based on Micheline BAULANT and Jean MEUVRET, *Prix des céréales extraits de la mercuriale de Paris* (S.E.V.P.E.N., 2 vols, 1962), 157.

FURTHER READING

1. Volume 2 (1660–1789) of the *Histoire économique et sociale de la France moderne* by Ernest LABROUSSE, Pierre LÉON, Pierre GOUBERT *et al.*, published in 1970 by P.U.F., supersedes practically all the previous textbooks and contains an extensive selective bibliography.

It is still worth while referring to the latest edition of Henri SÉE, *Histoire économique de la France* (A. Colin, 2 vols, 1948 and 1954), with bibliographies updated by R. SCHWERB.

2. The works (occasionally review articles) which have produced decisive advances in the economic history of ancien régime France include a fair number of doctoral theses dealing with regions. They are indicated by an asterisk in the following brief selection:

BAEHREL, René,* *Une Croissance, la basse Provence rurale (fin du XVIᵉ siècle–1789)* (S.E.V.P.E.N., 1 vol., 1961), 842 pp., with maps.

DELUMEAU, Jean, *L'Alun de Rome* xve–xixe *siècle* (S.E.V.P.E.N., 1962), 347 pp.

DERMIGNY, Louis, 'Circuits de l'argent et milieux d'affaires au xviii^c siècle', in *Revue Historique*, Oct.–Dec. 1954, pp. 239–78.

DEYON, Pierre,* *Amiens, capitale provinciale, étude sur la société urbaine au* xviie *siècle* (Mouton, Paris and The Hague, 1967), 606 pp.

DION, Roger, *Histoire de la vigne et du vin en France des origines au* xixe *siècle* (Paris, 1959), 768 pp.

FRECHE, Georges,* *La Ville de Puylaurens et le diocèse de Lavaur, 1598–1815, étude d'histoire économique et sociale* (Nanterre thesis, unpublished), 538 pp. with maps, typewritten.

GOUBERT, Pierre,* *Beauvais et le Beauvaisis de 1600 à 1730, contribution à l'histoire sociale de la France du* xviie *siècle* (S.E.V.P.E.N., 1960), 1 vol. + maps, 653 + 120 pp. (abridged edition, 1968, collection 'Science', Flammarion, under the title of *Cent Mille Provinciaux au* xviie *siècle*).

LABROUSSE, Ernest,* *Esquisse du mouvement des prix et des revenus en France au* xviiie *siècle* (Dalloz, 2 vols, 1933), 698 pp.

LABROUSSE, Ernest,* *La Crise de l'économie francaise à la fin de l'Ancien Régime et au début de la Révolution* (P.U.F., 1944), 664 pp.

LEFEBVRE, Georges,* *Les Paysans du Nord pendant la Révolution française* (Lille, 1924, reissued Laterza, Bari, 1959).

LÉON, Pierre,* *La Naissance de la grande industrie en Dauphiné, fin du* xviie *siècle–1869* (P.U.F., 2 vols, 1953), 968 pp.

LE ROY-LADURIE, Emmanuel,* *Les Paysans de Languedoc* (S.E.V.P.E.N., 2 vols, 1966), 1,035 pp.

LUTHY, Herbert, *La Banque protestante en France* (S.E.V.P.E.N., 1959), 2 vols, 454 and 860 pp.

MEUVRET, Jean, 'Les Mouvements des prix de 1661 à 1715 et leurs repercussions', in *Bulletin de la Société de Statistique de Paris*, 1944; 'Circulation monétaire et utilisation économique de la monnaie dans la France du* xvie *et du* xviie *siècle', in *Etudes d'histoire moderne et contemporaine*, vol. 1, 1947, pp. 15–28; 'Manuels et traités à l'usage des négociants aux premières époques de l'âge moderne', ibid., vol. 5, pp. 1–29.

POITRINEAU, Abel,* *La Vie rurale en Basse-Auvergne au* XVIIIe *siècle (1726–1789)* (P.U.F., 1965), 2 vols, 780 and 149 pp.

SAINT-JACOB, Pierre de*, *Les Paysans de la Bourgogne du Nord au dernier siècle de L'Ancien Régime* (Les Belles-Lettres, 1960), 643 pp.

'Aspects de l'économie française au XVIIe siècle' No. 70–1 of the review XVIIe *siècle* (1966), with contributions from MEUVRET, JACQUART, DEYON, DELUMEAU and others.

IV · THE RURAL SETTING

In spite of the difference in climate, language and customs between Flanders and the Pyrenees, Brittany and Provence, rural society – the essential society, the society of the majority – is the heir to an enduring past which has moulded it, etched it into the soil and set it within solid boundaries. It is no easy job to uncover these ancient, consecutive, complex and resilient structures, and we shall simplify matters considerably by examining in their turn the agricultural unit (the *terroir*) and the seigneurial, religious and fiscal/familial units.

1 THE *TERROIR*

Putting it very simply, the *terroir* is the sum of all the types of land cultivated or exploited by a group of men either centred on a big village or around several hamlets or else dispersed over a patchwork of scattered holdings. The unity of the *terroir* is always sanctioned and embodied by a communal body, the 'assembly of inhabitants', which abides by traditional rulings and occasionally makes new ones to ensure that where the exploitation of the land is the concern of the community it operates in the common interest. There is an obvious need, for instance, to control the grazing of livestock so as to prevent it from trampling seedbeds or browsing on growing corn.

The *terroir* is quite often synonymous with the parish (the religious unit), particularly in regions where the population comes in tight clusters, like most of the great cereal-bearing plains; this is not the case in areas where residence is semi-dispersed (occupying several hamlets, as in the West) and several *terroirs* may make up a parish. What usually complicates (or perhaps simplifies) matters is that the parish 'religious' assembly often became identified in the long run with the 'agricultural' assembly of inhabitants, where concurrent debates tackled material problems to do with the church, agrarian problems to do with the *terroir* and even fiscal problems, principally those raised by the collection of the royal taxation.

The extraordinary variety of the *terroirs* is enough to discourage (or fascinate) the historian, and yet in the footsteps of Roger Dion and Marc Bloch it is mainly geographers who have dealt with the question, possibly focusing too closely on the open-/enclosed-field contrast which takes pride of place in the textbooks but is not of fundamental importance.

Whatever its area, shape or contours, a rural *terroir* almost always combines three distinct but complementary elements:

THE *MANSE**
The *manse,* to adopt a medieval term that survives in many provincial dialects (*mas* in the Midi, *meix* in Burgundy, *mazure* in Normandy), a holding which is legally one and indivisible, includes house, yard, buildings for livestock, and garden. A great many villages and hamlets are made up of holdings carefully demarcated by hedges, walls or paths, rigorously equal in area (but liable to subdivision or combination), and enjoying important privileges – enclosure itself, immunity from the tithe, and the payment of what were frequently very light seigneurial dues (low *cens,* or quitrent – see p. 83). In addition, the holder ('owner' would be misleading, as we shall see) enjoys a broad degree of freedom, and in particular may cultivate his garden exactly as he wishes. Here he might grow roots and herbs (today's 'vegetables'), as well as hemp and flax, high-grade fodder-crops (clover and sainfoin were developed in this manner) and experimental crops like the new grains which came from Italy, the Near East and Iberia by way of the gardens of the Basque country and especially of Languedoc and the county of Avignon before going on to invade the North. Here artichokes and melons had

---

* The English equivalent is 'messuage': these lesser holdings within the domain, seigneury etc. are what many historians, cutting through terminological complications, refer to as 'tenures'. – Tr.

preceded them, as had American tomatoes and *gros millet* (maize), to be followed by the potato, long familiar and despised or dismissed as cattle-food.

The *manse* is at once the nucleus of life and the seed of the future.

THE ARABLE

Whether it is enclosed by living hedgerows, drystone walls or simply by deep furrows marked off by boundary-posts, the field has the function of providing the basic food-crop, grain, often more grey than white, the staple of the material life of a society of consumers of bread, soups, biscuit and porridge. It also provides horse-fodder (oats) and the rich man's grain (wheat), which is sold off to serve the dual purpose of supporting subsistence and trade. Whether the fields lie fallow every other year (biennial rotation, mainly practised towards the Mediterranean), or every three or four, or much oftener if the soil is poor, depends upon adaptation to natural conditions and local customs; whether they are in the forms of strips, quadrangles, curved lines or terraces; whether they come in vast expanses with not a tree or enclosure in sight, or in tiny plots adjoining the farm buildings in a jigsaw of scrub and grazing-land, whatever their shape and form, the fields always help to solve one and the same problem, the production of sufficient grain to feed the rural community in general and each family in particular.

THE 'SALTUS'

This term borrowed from the Latin agronomists is a shorthand way of referring to the aggregation of rich meadows, poor grazing-land, scrub, copses, heath and forest without which a rural community is hard-pressed to survive. Not only does the saltus enable the livestock to graze, it also provides the timber, branches, leaves and fruits which are staples of rural existence and are used for building, fuel, animal litter, beverages (berries), tools and even food (chestnuts are practically the 'bread' of some provinces). Yet these tracts which are neither ploughed nor dug set serious problems to the community, which has to organize their protection (against excessive and destructive use), exploitation (fair shares of the grazing and timber) and defence against those who covet and even lay claim to them, which usually means the seigneurs. This task falls to the heads of the *manses,* who join in assembly after Sunday mass to deliberate on communal affairs.

The very uneven distribution of these three basic elements provides the key to the diversity of the French countryside. The great plains of the North, with tiny *courtils* (gardens) and often completely devoid of 'saltus', are nothing more than cornfields, with all their monotony and vulnerability: here the land cannot support cattle and it has been necessary to devise the system of *vaine pâture* – common grazing rights on all land between harvest and sowing – in order to feed the herds of thin, yellowish sheep tended by the communal shepherd; it has also been necessary to enact strict written or (more usually) unwritten laws to control cultivation, fix the date for harvesting and the closure of fields to grazing, and maintain communal shepherds and harvest-wardens (*messiers*). Then there are the great *bocages* of the West, breeding grounds of individualism, where each little hamlet is the focus of concentric rings of gardens and hemp-patches, *terres chaudes*, constantly manured, cropped and enclosed, and *terres froides*, sown every so often, then fallowed and grazed, not forgetting the great stretches of common land which are systematically exploited even down to the production of forage for horses. Normandy has its vast *manses* or *mazures* where livestock thrive. In the mountain regions, the careful collective exploitation of woods and pastures usually staves off cold and hunger where ploughlands and gardens are scarce and meagre. The vineyards of the grape-growing regions have to be guarded against every kind of two- and four-legged predator, and harvested at the same date. Across the infinite variety of this tapestry, the need for some kind of organization, discipline and law enforcement is everywhere apparent, although in varying degrees.

The requisite control and continuity are ably and resolutely provided by the undoubtedly ancestral institution known as the 'community of inhabitants', although we are still ill-informed about this sturdy forerunner of today's municipal councils, whose uneven growth from one province to the next is probably related to the uneven power of the seigneurs. It also deals with some parishional religious matters, and devotes much of its time to financial questions, being responsible for the distribution of the tax-load. The breadth

or narrowness of its authority from one area to another bears witness to the complexity of the ancient or recent ties that bound up
the rural setting. Among these is the seigneurial tie, whose origins are
remote and uncertain, its evolution more complex still.

2　THE SEIGNEURY

It would take a whole book to study the seigneury in France alone
between the sixteenth and eighteenth centuries, and that book
would inevitably be prefaced by a lengthy catalogue of common
misconceptions some of which we shall mention in passing.

A seigneury is a group of estates, carefully delimited long ago,
which constitute the pre-eminent property and zone of jurisdiction
of an individual or corporate entity called the seigneur.

The territorial dimensions of a seigneury may be minute – a few
ares – or may extend over several thousands of hectares, with all
the gradations in between, so that the limits of a seigneury can be
contiguous with those of a *terroir* or parish; it often happens that
they are completely different and that a *terroir* or parish is dependent
upon two or several seigneurs, with their territory split up among
several seigneuries or portions of seigneuries, large or small.

Despite the popular belief, the seigneur is not necessarily a nobleman, although this was the strongest likelihood, especially in traditional provinces prolific in noble houses, such as Brittany, Burgundy
or Beaujolais. The seigneur can be a layman or a churchman, individual or collective, a nobleman or a commoner (*roturier*). The women's
abbeys represent a type of seigneury which is neither individual nor
masculine, not necessarily noble, and obviously not lay. Anybody
can buy a seigneury, as long as he is rich: in addition to its revenues
it will confer upon him a measure of dignity which will help him
gradually to project the illusion of nobility in the eyes of the naive,
the apathetic and the forgetful.

As a rule, the seigneury is divided into two parts. The *domaine*
(English 'demesne'), the site of the seigneurial dwelling (not necessarily a château) and the seigneurial court, usually comprises a park
around the manor, a big nearby farm (the '*basse-cour*'), often a chapel
and a mill, and almost always a compact grouping of lands and woods
directly subordinate to the seigneur, who may work them with the

aid of servants or day-labourers or farm them out. Often too, the seigneur's own preserve benefits from the practically unpaid services of the *'censitaires'* – statutory providers of labour, horses and transport – who occupy the 'tenures'.

The second and usually by far the most sizeable part of the seigneury is made up of the *censives*, or tenures. These are the *manses* and lands which the seigneur formerly entrusted – or claims to have entrusted – to the care of common peasants (*manants*), who received a more or less free hand in their exploitation in return for a hotchpotch of extremely varied dues, the most important being the *cens*, often a fairly small sum payable at a fixed annual date which is indefeasible and constitutes due 'recognition' of the seigneurial authority. Hence the name *'censives'* frequently applied to these lands, and that of *'censitaires'* applied to the peasants who 'hold' them (the *'tenanciers'*) and who retain the hereditary usufruct (hereditary, that is, subject to other obligations), not the full ownership of the property. This outline is blurred by any number of more or less widespread complications. The seigneur often has a monopoly (the *'ban'*) of mill, wine-press or oven* and charges for their use. When the *censitaire* sells, exchanges or bequeaths, the seigneur nearly always collects various kinds of transfer dues (*saisine, relief, lods et ventes*†), which net between a tenth and a third of the value of the property changing hands. A part of the lands granted to the *censitaires*, probably those most recently brought into cultivation, owes a *'champart'*, in practice a kind of seigneurial tithe generally amounting to between a ninth and a third of every crop, an exorbitant and unpopular charge. Lastly, the seigneur usually has a monopoly on hunting, fishing, the use of rivers, pigeon-rearing and on the sale and even the harvesting of his own produce: for example, he gathers his grapes first and

---

* These seigneurial rights are the *banalités du moulin, du pressoir et du four*. The seigneur often leased his monopolies, especially that of milling flour, and the lessee s profit came out of the peasants. – Tr.

† *Saisine* and *relief* are rights which allow the seigneur to make a levy on the assets of the *censitaire* upon his death, and exact a payment from the heir – different names for much the same process. The *droit des lods et ventes* authorized the seigneur to charge 'purchase tax' on property sold, exchanged or bartered within his seigneury, payable in cash. – Tr.

sells his wine first (the *droit de banvin*). He also – and sometimes quite properly – lays first claim to ownership of the various pastures and woodlands to which the community of inhabitants also lays outright claim. In nearly every legal dispute, the seigneur is judge and jury of his own tenants, whom he tends to call his 'vassals' in significant abuse of the old feudal term which properly applies only to fief-holding noblemen. Whereas he has often renounced his criminal jurisdiction (too expensive, so fobbed off onto the royal courts), he still has a tight hold on the civil, through his bailiff, serjeant, tax officer, clerks and even notaries. According to the custom of the area, often an accretion of local 'usage', he judges peasant disputes over boundaries and grazing, or arising out of drunken brawling, and also presides over the useful *juridiction gracieuse* which rules on matters of inheritance, minority and guardianship. Best, or perhaps worst of all, the seigneurial court sits in judgement over all the different kinds of dispute which are bound to occur between seigneur and tenant, notably in the matter of lands claimed as 'common'. This manifestly inequitable system must not be allowed to obscure the considerable and often beneficial role of the twenty or thirty thousand seigneurial courts, which continued until the end of the ancien régime and may be compared with that of the future justices of the peace.

It would be foreign to the spirit of the ancien régime for seigneuries to be evenly distributed and equally powerful throughout the realm.

One particular type of land-holding has escaped feudal subjection during the Middle Ages and occupies sizeable areas mainly in central France and the Midi: these are the *allodia,* which enjoy a fair degree of freedom and where property is quasi '*quiritaire*' (*quirites* = citizens of ancient Rome), harking back to the Romans and forward to the Code Napoléon. The jurists laboured to abolish them, and Louis XIV often asserted his own claim to be sovereign lord of all the allodia in the realm, notably by an edict of August 1692, but the allodia survived this assault, and historians find them clinging to existence in south-west, west and central France well into the eighteenth century. In Basse-Auvergne, for instance, a total of eight hundred notarized contracts has revealed the existence of something like thirty per cent of allodial lands not subject to seigneurial sway: in localities like Lempdes and Manson, the allodia constitute a majority! This is because Auvergne belongs juridically and linguistically to the Midi, that ample third of the country which has been starved of historical attention. In this land of all the liberties the régime of the seigneurs has no prior legal status. Whereas in 'French' France (the northern half) the well-known saying runs 'No land without lord', the converse saying prevails in the Midi, reflecting the contrast in law – 'No lord without title', boldly commemorated by the Languedoc jurist Caseneuve in 1645 when he proclaimed: 'It is much more glorious for a prince to command free men than slaves'. Recent historical studies of the Midi have been unanimous in underlining the frailty of the seigneurial ties as well as of purely seigneurial revenue.

Conversely, Brittany and Burgundy have disclosed extremely harsh types of seigneurial rule. Over and above the cultivation of the land, the Breton seigneurs live off 'feudal' rights such as the *corvées,* statutory labour laid down by custom, extremely high *lods et ventes,* and general, swingeing flour-milling rights over the 'vassals'. In Burgundy, the seigneury is referred to as a 'fief', and this contamination of seigneurial by feudal terminology speaks volumes about a system which bears down with unusual force upon a peasantry not noted for its long-suffering nature. Pretentious and humiliating honorific rights (see Document 16) are generally augmented by the notorious '*tierce*', a levy of about a third of the crop-yield, which made tithes seem bearable by comparison. Again it is Burgundy, together with the swathe of ill-favoured provinces running from Marche to Franche-Comté, that holds the peculiar distinction of (barely) supporting considerable numbers of the last serfs of the realm, the *mainmortables.*

In the manner of the old serfs, the *mainmortables* are tied to their land, the land of their seigneur, and may quit it only by relinquishing their belongings and rights. Even flight does not rescue them from the jurisdiction of the seigneur, whose *droit de suite* (right of pursuit) still obtained at the height of the eighteenth century. The old right of *formariage* prevents them from marrying without the seigneur's consent, and the wife becomes a *mainmortable* even if she is free by birth. They may bequeath their house and fields only to their children, if any, and provided these children are resident with them: otherwise the inheritance reverts to the seigneur by the right of *échute*. They also owe the seigneur special *tailles* (sometimes 'at will') and *corvées* regulated by statute but still more extensive than anywhere else, particularly in cartage obligations. There were powerful Burgundians – jurists like Bouhier, noblemen like the marquis de Branges, and even the royal intendant Joly de Fleury – prepared to vindicate and even boast of a means of subjection that yielded huge revenues and appeared to the physiocrats and the most moderate philosophers as the last relic of 'barbarism'.

Of all the seigneurial pressure weighing on the greater part of France, the lands of *mainmorte* represent the most grinding example. At the same time they demonstrate the almost familial strength of the links that still related the thriving seigneurial system to a 'feudal' system whose decadence in mind, word and deed was perhaps more apparent than real, as the revolutionaries and the peasants fully realized.

In the places where he is powerful, the seigneur asserts a natural claim as 'first inhabitant' of the village to convoke, preside over and control the rural community, if not in person then through his bailiff or occasionally his receiver. Now the chances of conflict with the community are legion. They may hinge on the level or collection of the various dues, the grazing of livestock (the seigneur frequently claims a right of *troupeau à part**), damage to crops by the seigneur's pigeons, or the usage and ownership of the precious saltus, the 'commons'. Disputes between seigneur and village community were a perpetual bone of contention in the Burgundian countryside. They have been thoroughly researched, but have not produced a single example of a community winning its case against the seigneur. It is a different matter elsewhere, and particularly in the Midi and some other provinces where victory seems often to have gone to the community, known here by the proud name of *consulat*, relic

---

* By which he is not obliged to put his own livestock to graze with the communal herd during those periods when the ploughlands or commons are available but the number of beasts and their location are strictly controlled by the community. – Tr.

of a brilliant past. In Provence, it assumes outright control of collecting seigneurial dues, and pays the seigneur a fixed annual sum. In Haut-Languedoc, it possesses vital and well-kept archives, so that the seigneur is unable to take a chance on claiming what has never belonged to him, since the burden of proof rests upon himself, and the community has its own evidence.

Nevertheless, no amount of local variations can shake the general conclusion that ancien régime society was deeply stained with the seigneurial dye, found it increasingly unendurable, and got rid of 'feudal barbarism' with no apparent regret, whether it took an active part in its disposal or simply heaved a great sigh of relief upon its temporary and partial (1789) then final suppression (1793). After which, apart from local survivals, the 'time of the seigneurs' was well and truly ended. Since its birth in the Middle Ages it had grown intolerable because it was degrading, often oppressive and generally discredited: noble or otherwise, the seigneurs *qua* seigneurs had long since given up protecting anybody against anything.

3   THE PARISH

The parish is the community of souls and of the faithful much more than of the soil. And yet, seeing that it has its place of worship and assembly, its own institutions and its pastor having the 'cure of souls', these souls are bound to be circumscribed by some kind of territory, and one which has long been known and delimited, sometimes bounded, a subdivision of the subdivisions of the diocese, archdeaconries and deaneries. So venerable and distinct was this territory that it functioned as the elementary unit of the royal administration, the more so when that administration had directly or indirectly infiltrated the entire realm with its exacting fiscal system. Even after the Revolution, most of the rural parishes – seldom corresponding to seigneuries, more often to *terroirs,* almost always to *'collectes'* (see p. 91) – became *'communes'*, and remained unaltered in perhaps nine out of ten cases, with the result that the old Christian geography still lives on.

The parish church has the 'patron saint' in whose name it was founded and who is particularly revered by the faithful, the more so when some relic has been preserved, always by miraculous means.

It also has its temporal 'patron', the distant descendant or representative of the material 'founder' of the parish, sometimes a great lay personage, more often ecclesiastical – bishop, chapter or abbey. In theory, but not always in practice (there are rights of 'presentation' and 'resignation' that cannot be enlarged upon here), this temporal patron, or *'collateur'*, has within his gift the appointment of the priest who ministers to the parish and therefore holds the 'benefice in cure of souls' that it represents. This minister is usually referred to as the *'curé'*, not always his rightful title (some ecclesiastical 'patrons' are called *'curés primitifs'* – which they often were – and in law the resident priest is only the *'vicaire'*). Bypassing some unbelievable complexities in routine, the point worth emphasizing here is that the bishops never chose all the *curés* for their diocese and very seldom appointed as many as half of them.

Whatever his rightful title, this man's parishioners refer to him as the *curé* (in Brittany, *recteur*), and we shall do likewise. His prime function is to discharge the duties of his ministry and 'tend his flock', but he is also responsible for a multitude of functions which do not directly derive from this ministry. Ever since the Council of Trent, one of his prescribed tasks has been to keep a register of baptisms, marriages and burials, but mainly since the civil ordinance of 1667 royal legislation has been trying to foist complicated administrative methods onto the *curés* (duplicate registers, etc.), much to the annoyance of many of them. To make them assume the role of announcer of the royal ordinances, judicial assistant and even 'advertiser' of sales of property seems a far cry from the 'pastoral' office of today, but what other channel was available to the central power and the courts when they wanted to communicate with a largely illiterate rural population whose sole point of regular assembly was the Sunday service?

Each parish possessed and administered assets which were altogether distinct from the 'communal' assets. Apart from the church itself, this moveable or immoveable parish property usually included the cemetery, perhaps an ossuary, the presbytery and garden, quite often a school, and also some goods and chattels here and there: the real estate generally formed a cluster at the centre of the village, sometimes known as the 'parish close'. Piety and fear of hell-fire would contribute further lands, revenues and the occasional house to this nucleus. These were endowments established by the will or notarized deed of apprehensive parishioners affluent enough to choose this method of securing masses for their souls at a fixed date (anniversary masses) and in perpetuity. Old and new assets alike are administered not by the *curé* but by the *fabrique,* a parish council more or less interlocking and sometimes identical with the 'body politic' of the rural community. Its members, the *marguilliers,* keep the buildings in repair, lease the various lands, collect the revenues, pay the priest the often considerable sums accruing from endowed masses, and are also in charge of the lighting, altar furniture, pews and benches, not to mention the selection of visiting preachers (Advent, Lent) at least until 1695. Which means that grounds for dispute between *curé* and council are not far to seek.

Here we must emphasize that the upkeep, repair, decoration and even reconstruction of the church and its outbuildings devolve upon the parish as a whole, as does the maintenance of school and dominie, where they exist. In theory, the big tithe-owners are supposed to contribute; in fact, they quibble, plead, and quite often shy off. And there was nothing, barring piety, to compel the seigneurs or the great families of the parish to fork out more than their share of these heavy expenses. A lot of parishes bled themselves dry and ran up years of debt to rebuild a church, a presbytery or occasionally a school. All this necessitated a parish budget and parish dues which the inhabitants allocated among themselves (strictly supervised by the intendant in the eighteenth century).

The 'tithe of the fruits of the earth' ought to have been enough, or almost enough, to cover these expenses and some others (the *curé's* living, poor relief). In addition to the fact that the tithe-paying 'territories' did not necessarily correspond to the territory of the parish (which may consist of several such '*dimages*' – yet another complication), many of the wealthy beneficiaries (bishops, convents, chapters and even laymen) lived a long way off and cared very little about their obligations towards the parish they 'tithed'. Misappropriation of the tithes is one of the foremost and least popular characteristics of the ancien régime, and will be dealt with later (Chapter 6). At parish level, it amounted to a surcharge on the people, levied in

sizeable if varying amounts, in addition to the necessity of remun-
erating the clergy for most of their proper functions, such as masses,
baptisms, marriages and funerals: the fee paid in these various 'cases'
is the *casuel*, whose revenue was uncertain (the other meaning of
casuel) but rarely inconsiderable.

This tissue of material and spiritual complications and potential
conflicts should not lead us to overlook the centrality of parish and
church activities in rural life. Except in emergencies, every new-
born child must be taken to church often within twenty-four hours,
and the record of his baptism constitutes the sole legal basis of his
existence: not to be baptized is to be non-existent, even in civil law.
Between his twelfth and fifteenth year, communion will transform
the child into a fully-fledged Christian, who from now on will regu-
larly take the Easter sacrament, any abstention being an exceptional
and suspect event, and liable to prosecution. Husband and wife
give one another the sacrament of marriage before 'Holy Mother
Church', which has had the exclusive authority to register the marriage and furnish written proof of it ever since the late sixteenth
century, when the old form of statements by witnesses was disal-
lowed even in the presence of a notary. After having congregated
at mass every Sunday, the parishioners will be laid to rest in the
cemetery, and if they are wealthy or privileged, beneath the actual
flagstones of the sacrarium, according to their rank, pretensions or
fortune.

The church and places of worship that are the centre of spiritual
life are also the centre of material life. The assembly of inhabitants,
often whittled down to a 'body politic' made up of the well-to-do
plus the *curé* and the seigneur's bailiff, meets in a chapel, under the
porch, beneath the trees of the close, and sometimes in a special
room or building (ancestor of the future rural '*mairies*'). Here the
budget, lawsuits, taxes, rulings on land-use and grazing, and the
appointment of crop- and vineyard-wardens, shepherds and village
schoolmasters are debated and decided. When danger threatens,
the church becomes a sanctuary once again and whole families seek
its material and spiritual protection, sometimes bringing a linen-
chest, sheaves, even livestock. Church and peasant still have a strong
familiar relationship – too strong sometimes, for the high-minded.

The parish close is the centre not only of the religious life, but of life *tout court*.

4 THE FISCAL UNIT: '*COLLECTE*' AND '*FEU*'

Whatever its composition, the assembly of inhabitants has always had to deal with the financial problem, whether in the matter of paying the shepherd, administering parish council assets, keeping the church in repair, sustaining a lawsuit or sometimes arranging to pay the seigneur's dues as a lump sum. Consequently it is always being faced with collecting revenue and devising a scale of collection: it has to draw up a list of inhabitants, families or dwellings and distribute the tax-load as equitably as possible, according to exact or approximate information about each man's capacities and means. The old dukedoms or countships, then their successor, the royal administration, naturally made use of these powers, experience or customs to avoid the bureaucratic chore of apportioning the tax-load, which they themselves were not equipped to undertake. For this purpose they usually chose the most venerable and clear-cut rural entity, the parish (although the *terroir* was sometimes preferred), with the result that parishes were generally converted into fiscal units which received the name of '*collecte*' at a fairly late date, mainly in northern France.

The Midi was particularly well equipped for the performance of this ticklish operation. Since the fifteenth century and earlier, the regions south of a line roughly from Bordeaux to Lyon had possessed what were variously known as *compoix, cadastres* or *livres terriers*, readily (and rather superficially) seen as remote descendants of the great Roman institutions, but undoubted focal points of material life for several centuries past. These documents are thick registers containing the description, dimensions and assessment of every plot of land in a *consulat* or *terroir*: vineyards and heathlands, woods and commons, *manses* and fields, all were noted, together with the names of their various 'proprietors'. Only those lands which come under the heading of 'noble' sometimes escape assessment (or 'booking' – *allivrement*), if not measurement, but these are not numerous (less than one tenth). The cadastres are kept up to date and periodically renewed. They ensure a degree of fiscal justice for the proprietor, whether noble or commoner (the nobility is *not* exempt from the taille in the Midi), and great convenience for local administration (Colbert lighted upon them, and would have liked to see them instituted throughout the country). They are also a mine of information for the historian.

But northern France was much less well administered at parish level, and was obliged to allocate the tax-load 'according to the appearances' of income, (less scrupulously, therefore) and by 'fires and families' (*feux et familles*). One of the stumbling blocks for the historian of the ancien régime is the problem of defining the various meanings of 'fire'. Sometimes the 'taxable fire' (*feu d'imposition*) is a simple book-keeping device which no longer bears any relation to domestic reality; we shall side-step this meaning. More often the 'fire' in northern France is a family living around the same 'hearth', 'kindling fire' (*feu allumant*), or family fire – but the rule bristles with exceptions. A parish or *collecte* would be said to have such and such a number of 'fires'.

The fiscal machinery of the rural community has raised the question of the family, which merits lengthier treatment and may be outlined as follows:

a) The conjugal family (husband, wife and children) was the general rule under the ancien régime, although it would often include one or both of the surviving parents of one or the other partner, so that this family could be fairly large.

b) A type of patriarchal family unit still existed in some provinces, known either as the *communauté taisible* or the *frérèche,* and distinguished by a number of common customs. Under the rule of an old male of the preceding generation, a kind of latter-day '*paterfamilias*', a group of brothers and brothers-in-law worked and held in common lands which were taxed as one, lived in a single large communal dwelling, but retained the right for any individual or couple to quit the community at their own risk, thereby relinquishing any claims upon it. This relic of the past still existed in the lands of central France, notably in Nivernais, a kind of museum-province, and has been unearthed in considerable strength in Basse-Auvergne at the height of the eighteenth century. Each community comprised a good score of people, counted as one 'fire', and usually inhabited some out-of-the-way spot, perhaps even a hamlet, which sometimes bore its name.

c) Tradition, together with the small or else the excessively large scale of some farm-holdings, led or prodded related households into forming kinds of living and working associations often known as *'consorties'*. These survived well into the eighteenth century and were widely if sparsely distributed, even in the prosperous Vexin. The related households (often an older and a younger one) committed themselves by notarized contract to take over, often from a seigneurial or urban proprietor, a holding which neither family group would have had the manpower and resources to exploit singly. These associations of 'consorts' (*'sossons'*, or associates, in Vexin) were often torn by domestic quarrels and were liable to break up, but they still constitute a kind of family, even of 'fiscal fire', which crops up in all sorts of different provinces, even in Brittany.

d) Since customary law varies from one province to the next (a basic feature of the ancien régime, as we shall see), celibates' 'fires', curiously known as 'half-fires' (*demi-feux*), make their appearance here and there, and in Champagne in particular. They usually belong to widows, a plentiful species owing to the higher male death-rate after the age of forty. The common regulation setting the age of majority at twenty-five occasionally leads jurists and tax-collectors to hold that inveterate spinsters (sometimes called 'old maids' – *filles anciennes*) could constitute, if not a 'family', then at least a 'fire'. Local curiosities.

e) A touch of local colour is provided by the survival in some provincial noble milieux of true *familiae* in the Roman sense – a well-heeled lineage complete with retinue and even vassals – but these are of passing interest, since the provincial nobility always amounted to well under a hundredth of the total population, and the 'familiae' quickly declined.

On the whole, the juridical/fiscal family of the ancien régime differs very little from that of the nineteenth century. It is in a sense the atom of that basic cell of life, the parish, which is frequently merged with rural community, *terroir* and *collecte*. Yet over and above any juridical, fiscal or sociological considerations, the historian has to insist that the true basic unit was the rural holding, familial or not. Any coherent interpretation of the ancien régime must take account of this unit of production and of life.

DOCUMENTS

14 THE *MANSE*, OR *MEIX*, IN BURGUNDY

In the Late Middle Ages, the unit of exploitation was the *manse* . . . A sturdy unit, in terms both of men and of land, and governed perhaps by a family, but above all by a plough. Its heart was the *meix*, the *mansus* proper, a piece of land consisting of the house and its environs, an area which seems generally to have held steady at about one *journal**. Of variable shape, but abutting upon a road on one side and surrounded by hedges elsewhere, the *meix* represented the area of intensive cultivation, perfectly stable over a lengthy period inside its strict boundaries. It had its own name, derived from its tenants or from its shape, location or some incident in its human occupation . . . it was the essential nucleus, the determining factor . . .

The holder of the *meix* automatically held its offices and rights. Toward 1680 the meix is everywhere a living, recognizable reality. The word recurs obdurately in every region as the token of a fundamental institution . . . It always stood for the homestead, the site destined for the *mansio,* and its primary function was and remained that of supporting the dwelling, which may assume whatever form it pleases, develop and organize, but can never outgrow it. The dwelling may even disappear without the land losing the name of *meix,* so that with no alteration in the customary dues [to the seigneur] it remains capable of being rebuilt and reverting to its original purpose.

Generally speaking, however, the buildings do not completely cover the *meix*. It has yards, '*treiges*' (passages and bypaths), garden and trees. Sometimes crops, a vineyard or a meadow encroach upon it . . . The *meix* was therefore the site of a house, but also a privileged plot of land, thoroughly and diversely exploited.

The second factor in the holding also warrants attention. It is another parcel of land often tacked onto the *meix* itself, an annex, 'wing' or outgrowth . . . This was the patrimonial land *par excellence,* and it is tempting to see it as a development from the primitive '*hereditas*' . . . probably

---

* Theoretically, the amount of land which a man could plough in a day – 33 ares, about 4/5 acre. – Tr.

even the original allodium which belonged to the archaic system of land-ownership before it was transmuted in the formation and evolution of the seigneurial system.* Its permanent or temporary enclosure was a sign of ownership. What we are able to ascertain about its juridical status gives us an inkling of an ancient freedom so deep-seated that tithes and feudal dues had difficulty in breaching it.

This land was a direct dependency of the homestead. Like the *meix* itself, it was earmarked for growing the basic necessities – vegetables, peas and lentils, hemp – but it might also be devoted to the standard cereal crops.

The dependent lands of the *meix* made up the main body of the holding, an arrangement familiar in Carolingian times and not altogether extinct. In those areas where the *meix* remained active, the various lands that adhere to it continue to be regarded as a kind of territorial *mouvance*.† It is not unusual . . . to find documents describing '*mouvant*' parcels of land in conjunction with a *meix*. The feudal vocabulary still lingers in these traditionally-structured regions . . .

But in general the primitive *manse* is well on the way to disintegration . . .

Pierre de SAINT-JACOB, *Les Paysans de la Bourgogne du Nord au dernier siècle de l'Ancien Régime* (Belles-Lettres, 1960), 93–5.

15 THE ALLODIUM IN EIGHTEENTH-CENTURY AUVERGNE

. . . Two categories of land stand out in contrast from the point of view of feudal law: the *censives* which are enmeshed in the seigneury, and the allodia which evade it. The *censives* are listed in the land-registers and are periodically (usually every thirty years) subject to the *aveu*:‡ they are compelled to pay an annual '*cens*' and various '*servitudes*' [bond-services] . . .

Lands which are '*cens*-free' or 'allodial' are not accountable to any

---

* It does not seem possible either to prove or disprove this hypothesis. – P.G.

† The *mouvance*, in feudal terminology, was any piece of land, estate or fief dependent upon ('subinfeudated' to) another fief, or the sum of all these lands. – Tr.

‡ In feudal law, the *aveu* was a written statement recognizing the obligation of the vassal to his lord upon acceptance of a fief. The seigneurial system used the same word for a written inventory of the tenure and its obligations in cash or kind, compiled at the expense of the tenant, and due to the seigneur at the end of a given period, or when the tenure changed hands – Tr.

seigneury; consequently they are not liable to any *cens,* and not subject
to the right of *lods et ventes* or of '*prélation*' [the seigneurial right to re-
possession of his property]. It happens that in Auvergne the juridical
dictum of 'no lord without title' is the rule (as also in the whole of the
Midi and parts of central France), which amounts to saying that in case
of any dispute between a seigneur and a landowner as to the existence
of a *cens,* the burden of proof falls upon the former, since he is the plain-
tiff; this built-in safeguard for the peasant defendant [is] contrary to the
situation prevailing in the greater part of the realm – 'No land without
lord' . . . What is the ratio of *censives* to allodial lands? . . . Our only
access to peasant allodial holdings is by way of examining notarial
records . . .

Notaries of:	censives	allodia	cases in doubt
Manson	24	57	1
Manzat	41	39	5
Beauregard	49	22	7
Besse	17	5	30
Jumeaux	45	3	0
Cunlhat	22	1	1
Vertaison	44	27	0
Thiers	16	3	
Lempdes	25	29	3
Mezel	36	23	2
Ambert	41	3	6
Domaize	36	3	0
Sauxillanges	30	13	15

. . . It follows that allodial status is a common juridical feature of rural
holdings in certain regions of Auvergne, notably in the valley of the
Allier; it seems much less so in the highlands . . .

Abel POITRINEAU, *La Vie rurale en Basse-Auvergne
au* XVIII*ᵉ siècle* (P.U.F., 1965), vol. 1, 341–3.

16 POWER AND PERSISTENCE OF SEIGNEURIAL
RIGHTS: THE 'MANUAL OF RIGHTS' OF
ESSIGEY (ECHIGEY, CÔTE-D'OR, CANTON OF
GENLIS), 1780

ARTICLE ONE: In the event of sales, the seigneur is owed the twelfth
part of the price of each and every acquisition, due upon all goods with-

out exception, with the right of retention or confiscation should the charge remain unpaid after forty days, or of a fine of three *livres* five *sous*.

ART. 2: Those inhabitants of Essigey holding 'fire and place' (*feu et lieu*) each owe a hen on the first day of Lent and a manual *corvée* for each labourer at harvest-time. The aforesaid *corvée* has always been performed, but the hen has never been claimed.

ART. 3: Each plough-owner or others possessing horses or oxen and harness also owes an annual *corvée* of ploughing or cartage at grape-harvesting or seed-time.

ART. 4: To the aforesaid seigneur belongs the right to levy a tithe on all the lands of the seigneury at a rate of one in every fourteen sheaves, whereas the prior of Tart takes one of the fifteen sheaves in each stock [making a grand rate of 2/15 for the two tithes].

ART. 5: To the aforesaid seigneur belongs high, middle and low justice throughout his jurisdiction.*

ART. 6: Each inhabitant owes a duty of watch and ward to the château of the aforesaid place.

ART. 7: The inhabitants must maintain the watercourse supplying the water of the river to the château moats. They are likewise obliged to hedge off the meadow called the Closeau, whose area is nine and two thirds *soitures* [about $7\frac{1}{2}$ acres].

ART. 8: All wine-sellers in the aforesaid Essigey owe the seigneur a pint of wine . . . to be taken to his château within an hour of the cask being broached, on pain of the fine of three *livres* five *sous* . . .

ART. 9: No inhabitant has any right to hunt or fish within the span of the aforesaid Essigey, on pain of confiscation of traps and tackle, and of the fine of three *livres* five *sous,* and the same applies to ponds . . .

ART. 10: At all times, the seigneur may keep his woods private and under ban, nor may anybody collect wood or graze his beasts therein, on pain of the fine of three *livres* and five *sous* . . .

Extract from the Departmental Archives of the Côte-d'Or, series E, No. 2688, printed in *La Bourgogne des Lumières,* archival documents published by the Centre Régional de Documentation Pédagogique, Académie de Dijon, 1968, pp. 78–9.

---

* *La justice haute, moyenne et basse* covers the degrees of legal authority from the right to pronounce sentence of death down to the most trivial cases. – Tr.

17 'DAYS' (SESSIONS) OF A SEIGNEURIAL TRIBUNAL IN THE SAÔNE BASIN

Ordinary days of the bailiwick of the marquisate of La Perrière, held and dispatched at the village of Franxault in the usual place and manner by ourself, Christophe Jean Joliclerc, advocate at Court, bailiff of La Perrière, at the requisition of Maître Jean Boisot, *procureur fiscal* of the aforesaid bailiwick and all the inhabitants.

. . . the following persons summoned to appear before the tribunal: Messrs Denis Gault and Jacques Desportes, oath now duly sworn by the aforesaid gentlemen . . .

By order of the *procureur fiscal,* it is declared forbidden for any inhabitant of the marquisate to hunt or to bear a gun on the lands of this seigneury, or to keep fire-arms in their homes.

. . . It is forbidden . . . to swear or to blaspheme the sacred name of God, on pain of a fine and prosecution . . .

We also order that no drink is to be given to the inhabitants, children and servants during divine service or at any other time, and that the aforesaid inhabitants etc. are not to frequent taverns on pain of a fine of one hundred *livres* payable half to the parish council, half to the seigneur . . .

. . . 50 *livres* fine to the taverner Jacquiot for persistent offences in serving drink . . . 10 *livres* fine to the taverner Fleuret both for serving drink and for grazing his beasts apart from the common herd . . .

The inhabitants are forbidden to keep goats . . . to graze their pigs in the meadows . . . forbidden to permit threshers to have lighted pipes in the barns on pain of ten *livres'* fine for those who permit it, and prison for those who do it . . . Forbidden to smoke or to carry firebrands in the streets . . .

> Departmental Archives of the Côte-d'Or, series B 2 . . . quoted
> in Pierre de SAINT-JACOB, *Documents relatifs à la communauté*
> *villageoise en Bourgogne du milieu du XVIIe siècle à la Révolution*
> (Dijon, Bernigaud et Privat, 1962, 158 pp.), 60–2.

18 ELECTION OF THE 'ORDINARY COUNCIL' AND 'CONSULS' OF THE COMMUNITY OF TRETS

Nomination of the ordinary council

. . . At Christmas, after attending the mass of the Holy Ghost, celebrated at seven in the morning at the parish church, the consuls and the ordinary council proceeded to the communal House in the presence of the [seigneurial] judge or his assistant. The four biggest tax-payers [property-tax based on the *cadastre,* therefore the biggest landowners] were now chosen out of the retiring council, and put in charge of verifying the new election. The clerk then wrote the names of the hundred biggest taxpayers on slips of paper and put them in a box, and a young child would pick out twenty-two of these at random, representing twenty-two councillors. Together with the two consuls and the treasurer, these made up the ordinary council ... [After the] new ruling of 12 May 1768 ... the choice of councillors was made from among a restricted number of inhabitants. The clerk wrote the names of people who possessed at least three cadastral *livres* in Trets on thirty-six slips of paper. All the slips were put in a box, and twenty-two were drawn by lot ... Membership of the hundred then of the thirty-six most highly taxed out of a community of some two thousand people was the outcome of a strict selection process, based upon landownership ...

Nomination of the consuls

The twenty-five slips representing the members of the council were [then] collected in a box ... and three 'nominators of the municipal officers' were drawn. Each of them now proposed candidates for the offices of first and second consul, and these were again chosen by being drawn out of the box. [After 1768] it was the outgoing consul-mayor who proposed three candidates, and the draw which decided.

> Gabriel-Jean SUMEIRE, *La Communauté de Trets à la veille*
> *de la Révolution* (Aix-en-Provence, La Pensée Universitaire,
> duplicated text, 1960, 242 pp.), 24–5 & 34.

19 CONVOCATION AND ORDER OF THE DAY OF AN 'ASSEMBLY OF INHABITANTS' IN BURGUNDY

In the presence of myself, the undersigned François Girardin, notary royal at the residence of the town of Beaune, on this twenty-fourth day of June seventeen hundred and seventy-six at about eight o'clock in the morning at the village of Combertault at the usual place of the assembly of inhabitants ... after the parish mass ... Pierre Devevey, farmer, resident in the aforesaid Combertault, appeared in person to inform me that he had convoked the inhabitants of the aforesaid Combertault by ringing the bell in the manner customary at this present day, place and hour, and advised them of several matters of concern to the aforesaid community upon which measures must be taken.

The first concerns a piece of land belonging to the commonlands of Combertault which has been usurped by Jean Gaudrillet, against whom the aforesaid community has obtained a verdict from the bailiwick of Beaune . . . which verdict has not been withdrawn . . . or if so, they have received no notification.

The second concerns a contribution of eight *bichets** of oats which are being demanded from the community by the tax-farmers of the marquisate of La Borde . . . and upon which they have obtained a verdict against [the community] whereupon the inhabitants, having consulted [two Dijon lawyers] . . . are of the opinion that the right of eight *bichets* of oats demanded from the community in lieu of the right of watch and ward is not owing, that the sentence is untenable, and that the inhabitants will succeed in having it reversed.

The third matter concerns about three *journaux* of land which the community sold twelve years ago [and which it hopes to recover] . . .

The fourth matter has to do with several encroachments [on the commons] . . .

And the fifth matter has to do with rights of *corvée*, tithing and others which the [seigneur's] tax-farmers have introduced and want to exact from the inhabitants, while being unwilling to . . . show the title-deeds by virtue of which they want to levy the aforesaid rights, whereupon having appealed to the seigneur . . . asking him to make known his title-deeds and land-registers, this has been constantly refused.

The aforesaid Pierre Devevey advised the aforesaid assembled inhabitants to deliberate upon all these matters forthwith, so that nobody might impute to him the neglect of the interest of the aforesaid community during his time in office . . .

> Document from the Communal Archives of Combertault,
> Côte-d'Or, printed in Pierre de Saint-Jacob, op. cit., 47–9.

---

* An old measure, anything between 20 and 40 litres: eight bichets would be from $4\frac{1}{2}$ to 9 bushels. – Tr.

V · THE ELEMENTS OF RURAL SOCIETY

It is at once easy and pointless to trace the 'Orders' in the French countryside. There are one or two priests to each village, plus a distant tithe-owner, and some convent on the horizon. The members of the 'second order' either live in the countryside only temporarily or are fairly down-at-heel specimens. The bourgeois in the old sense of 'burgher' – wealthy town-dwellers who are neither noble nor clerical – rarely put in an appearance. But all the 'rude mechanicals' of the 'third estate' live here – more than four fifths of the king's subjects.

The vast traditional wealth of the realm is mainly produced here, and those who reap the greatest rewards are mainly elsewhere. The French countryside contains practically the whole category of the ruled.

1 THE EXPLANATORY FACTOR: FROM PRODUCTION TO RENT

Except for the remaining allodia, no part of the soil belongs wholly to the peasant. His 'property' is hedged with reservations. The right of the seigneur is always reserved. It is symbolized by the lightest, oldest and most significant tribute, the *cens*, as well as by the intervention of the seigneur whenever any plot of land changes hand, whether by inheritance, sale or exchange: the seigneur then collects a right which goes by a variety of names, and he can always take the place of the buyer by using the machinery of the *retrait*, which is 'feudal' on lands classified as noble, and *'censuel'* on the far larger category of commoner lands.

No crop may be gathered (except in gardens) until the tithe-owner's cart has come to call. And while the tithe is sometimes satisfied with three per cent of the gross harvest (as in Basse-Bretagne), it usually goes very much further, holding a level of between seven and eight per cent almost everywhere and from ten to twelve per cent in south-western France.

In two or three cases out of five, the peasant who has tilled the soil does not 'possess' it even in the limited sense of the word as used by the ancien régime. Whether as farmer, *métayer,* or in a more complex position, he has to pay the 'master' his rent, in kind, cash or work, and sometimes all three.

The technical conditions of the time force the peasant to keep back a high proportion of cereals in particular for next year's sowing. With the average yield on fairly good land running at about five for one (with tremendous variations in time and place), about a fifth of the harvest has to be stored for the next seed-time.

Naturally we cannot overlook the fiscal levies on the rural community – often slight, but not always – and the considerable growth of royal taxation after 1635 (to finance wars).

The historians have attempted to estimate this fourfold drain (not counting the indispensable seed) by provinces or years. The most reliable of their painstaking, conflicting and not always dispassionate analyses range between a fifth and a half of the crop.

This fifth or half (call it a third?) constitutes the ground rent – royal, seigneurial, tithe and proprietorial – which is the driving force of the realm and of its social system. Rent-payers are the ruled, receivers of rent and their agents the rulers. At least nine tenths of the population of the realm are bracketed by this elementary contrast, including the king himself up to a point.

But different types rule and are ruled in different ways and to varying degrees. In agricultural and rural society, the ruled are of at least three kinds and are divided by two fundamental partitions, those of residence and dependence.

2　BELOW THE 'RESIDENCE' THRESHOLD: THE WORLD OF THE VAGRANTS

The world of the vagrants see-saws between town and country; otherwise it would not be wholly vagrant. Its very mobility makes it elusive, but the records do enable us to glimpse the vagrants at times when their motion is arrested.

They pause when they ask for relief, and we can intercept them near charitable institutions: at the gate of a presbytery or convent, and oftener still within the urban organizations – the Hôtel-Dieu for the sick, the Hôpitaux Généraux and Bureaux des Pauvres for the rest, although they are often for citizens only.

The vagrants also come to a halt when they come up against the repressive organizations: the mounted constabulary (*maréchaussée*), which polices the main roads, the tipstaffs at the town gates ('rabble-drivers' – *chasse-coquins*), the militia, the watch or other 'sergeants' inside. Now we find them again hauled up in front of the seigneurial or royal tribunal, then in some jail or poor-house, since the *'Grand Siècle'* exerted its ingenuity to convert these houses of charity into houses of correction.

The vagrants sometimes stop of their own accord to try their hand at seasonal, intermittent or shady work. They people urban doss-houses, journeymen's hostels (for the most respectable) and the *cours des miracles,** and even encamp in the countryside, away from the villages, on the fringes of the *terroirs,* putting up flimsy huts, using natural caves, or allowed to live in some tumbledown building if they can be of service as labourers, ditchers, hedgers, mole-catchers, basket-makers, knife-grinders, clog-makers, charcoal-burners or rag-pickers. As squatters, or at least 'under cover', they now come under pressure from the fiscal organizations, which try to get them onto the tax-rolls, if only for a few *sous.*

We catch our last glimpse of the vagrant at the point when his motion is arrested for good. Whether he dies in a hospital, a barn, by the wayside or fording a stream, he is always entered in the re-

---

* Originally an area of medieval Paris notorious for its thieves, beggars and vagrants, then any such urban quarter. – Tr.

gister of his last parish, and the *curé* performs his usual function of providing a lengthy description of the foreign corpse and giving it Christian burial if any 'sign' of Christianity has been found upon it – a cross, a medallion or a rosary. There is not a parish in France which has not interred some beggar, poor maid or foundling at some time or another, and occasionally in considerable numbers in crisis years.

A careful approximate count of all the vagrants located by means of these laborious methods indicates that they must have been numerous enough to merit release from the novelettish straitjacket which has often confined them.

There are professional beggars and wayfarers. The Gypsies, a people apart, whose supposedly magical powers make them both respected and feared, hawk small items of handicraft and provide entertainment and dangerous services. Troupes with freak-shows and performing bears and others mounting static tableaux differ to only a small degree from the troupes of strolling players in which Molière made his second start. The world of the prostitute, urban by residence but recruited in the countryside among unmarried mothers and disgraced servant-girls, with its own code, hierarchy, districts and language, remains little known. Nearby is the different world of the *cours des miracles* and of organized, structured mendicancy, fuelled by a whole trade in children. Nobody is safe on the highways and in the forests because of their widespread infestation by powerful robber bands, of which Mandrin was one of the last popular heroes.[*] With smugglers and dealers in contraband salt (*faux-saulniers*) they were the raw material of the royalist uprisings of later years. All these professionals are not isolated adventurers but structured social groups whose combined strength could amount to several tens of thousands.

Certain groups of workers were long-distance travellers following precise itineraries by traditional stages, alternating between family dwelling and working area, or else embarking on their 'tour de France'. Among them were many highlanders who worked during the winter or in their younger years before returning – or not – to their

---

[*] Louis Mandrin was a notorious brigand of Dauphiné, broken on the wheel at Valence in 1755. – Tr.

native region: masons from Limousin, school-masters from Briançon, commercial travellers and chimney-sweeps from Savoy, and reapers and grape-pickers moving 'up' in disciplined bands from the forward Midi to cooler regions. The journeymen (*compagnons*) too have set destinations, travelling in some secrecy, with staff, water-bottle and bundle. More important, although less well known, the pedlars travelled on mule-back, sometimes with a handcart, to supply country backwaters with the hundred and one attractions of the town – needles, lace, trinkets, ointments and nostrums – but most of all they brought and sold for a few *sous* the essential agent of popular culture, the cheap book, small devotional compilations, almanacs, blue-bound booklets from Troyes* or elsewhere, even satirical and prohibited works. Their frequent comings and goings suggest that they must have existed in thousands, like all the above-mentioned types. Other and more sinister professionals paid periodic calls: these were the baby-farmers (*meneurs*), with their wagonloads of new-born babies bound for the provincial nurse or to be abandoned in Paris, in conditions which lightened the load at every halting place. The dead children were soon replaced.

This was not all. In addition to the professionals, there were all kinds of outcasts. Cripples or half-wits fit for nothing but to stretch out a hand; runaway apprentices, often sick of ill treatment and menial tasks; pregnant serving-girls and unmarried mothers turned away wherever they went, condemned without appeal by the whole of society; idlers, adventurers, eccentrics perhaps; much more frequently, army deserters wrongly impressed or suffering from the homesickness common among young peasants, or unable to stomach regimental or fighting discipline, in an era when the army was plagued by desertion, which usually accounted for as much as a fifth of its strength; lastly, 'demobilized' soldiers who had the utmost difficulty in readjusting to civilian life after long campaigns and licensed pillage. And we may as well add the regular army itself, which was seldom housed in proper barracks (barring the élite re-

---

* The reference is to the Bibliothèque bleue de Troyes, inaugurated by a bookseller called Oudot in the mid-seventeenth century, collections of medieval romances and legends, folklore etc., still being published well after the Revolution. – Tr.

giments), marching from station to station, still billeted on civilians, taking up its winter quarters here or there with a perpetual train of camp-followers, crooked merchants, women and more or less legitimate children.

Some years saw a steep increase in the vagrant masses: children at first, disowned by being sent begging or thieving, then whole families when dearth or famine struck a province, invasion threatened, or when the royal soldiery made camp. Panic fears drove entire villages onto the roads, and bands of paupers fled from pestilence, famine or their own fear. All these victims of circumstance took to the road with their sufferings, parasites and germs, spreading terror in their turn, often transmitting the epidemic they were evading, sometimes rioting at the sight of boats or carts loaded with what they took to be grain, and capable of screaming, plundering, smashing and occasionally killing.

An attempt to estimate the numbers of these vagrants, professional or occasional, taking into account the urban beggars (at least twenty thousand in Paris alone), deserters and even non-deserters, produces a figure upwards (possibly a long way upwards) of two hundred thousand – as many as the nobility, as many as the clergy. These elusive bands were very troublesome, especially at moments when they expanded abnormally: the last time was the period prior to 1789, when the crises in fodder (drought and epizootic diseases), viticulture (slump in prices) and cereals (dearth of 1788–9) interacted with the crisis in textiles (new machines, English competition) and spread unemployment and hardship among a population which had almost forgotten them and had probably been producing more children than before. When the avenues closed before these children, revolt, then war, became their outlet.

Certainly the Church, the State, town councils and provinces had been campaigning since the mid-seventeenth century for the 'great confinement' (*le grand renfermement*) of the poor, the mad, the beggars and the idlers – an indication of social fear rather than organization – but the 'hospitals general' were too few, and had neither room nor resources to confine men whose one ambition was to escape their filthy dormitories and sweatshops, forced-labour factories fitter to kill a man than feed him. The *maréchaussée* was undermanned (a few thousand constables and 'sergents', the gendarmerie of the future), not equal to the task of ferreting out and interning them, and seldom enjoyed the cooperation it expected or demanded from those with a roof over their heads. For the vagrants were occasionally useful, more often tolerated or feared; the deserter was systematically protected, and the *maréchaussée* was fairly unpopular.

A minority of these tens – or hundreds – of thousands of people might possess an occasional or seasonal home: there were even 'domiciled beggars'. But the majority slipped through the net of the police, the fiscal system and the census. Their numbers, character and above all their function do not merit the decent obscurity which has been their traditional fate. They are a guide to understanding some deep and mysterious aspects of the ancien régime mentality: beliefs, panics and revolts.

3 THE DEPENDENT PEASANTS

Throughout France, this group is certainly the most numerous. Its juridical membership of the 'third estate' (that which is neither noble nor clerical) is utterly academic: other men 'represent' and decide for them without consultation. These are the *'viles créatures'* who perform the *'viles besognes'* – the 'dregs of the people' as they are readily described in the conversation and writings of those men of culture who embody the indissoluble trinity of title, money and power. The clearest way to define this class (is there a better term?) is to say that it is divided into two groups, a lower and a more solidly established upper one.

The lower threshold concerns residence, which divides them off sharply from the vagrants, although some of the small peasants are liable to fall below this threshold in bad years, since social mobility tends in a downward rather than an upward direction, particularly in difficult periods like the seventeenth century. They are all ensconced in a *manse*, or at worst in part of a *manse*, clinging to their house or hovel, yard, a few outbuildings for their meagre livestock and a few ares of land cropped as often as local custom allows (there is seldom any appeal against the rules of the fallow system). The tenure may be either rented or owned, sometimes in partnership with a relative, and not excluding the rights of the seigneur. As residents, they enjoy the

benefits (and obligations) that derive from membership of a group
or complex of groups. Attachment to the *terroir* confers the right of
vaine pâture, where it exists, and of common and forest rights, where
they exist, so that a few sheep or a cow can graze off the common land
and timber can be collected for heating and minor building work.
Richer men will employ them at times when more manpower has to
be taken on – haymaking, harvesting, grape-gathering. As parishioners,
they enter a spiritual community which gives them the minimum en-
surance of a place at mass then in the cemetery, and provides solace
and the promise of happiness in the hereafter. The seigneurial court
judges their petty offences and will take custody of their orphaned
children when it has inventoried their furniture, implements, livestock and most of all their debts. Having become automatically liable
to the *taille,* the salt-tax and every conceivable levy, they are put down
on the tax-rolls, often for a few *sous* but never for nothing, otherwise
they would be classed among the 'poor', the 'destitute' or the 'beggars', still resident but threatened by imminent vagrancy, possibly
through eviction from their cottage and land. These small peasants
teeming just above the threshold of destitution and vagrancy are low
on the social scale but broad in the range of their activities as market
gardeners, small stock-breeders, day labourers, mixed farmers, part-
time craftsmen and ever-active handymen.

The upper threshold is naturally that of independence, principally
economic independence, although this brings all the other kinds in its
wake. The truly independent peasant is a man who, come what may,
can be confident of meeting every need of his family (and servants,
where necessary) by means of the land he rents or holds. He can
rely on paying his various dues without a struggle, and often on making
profitable sales enabling him to increase his herd or lands, line his
cash box and make provision for his children by elevating them beyond their initial station. The independent peasants (see section 4)
were very much a minority in every province.

Between these two thresholds lie the two or three million heads
of family who make up the majority of the population: small proprietors or non-proprietors, small farmers or *métayers,* stock-breeders
without real herds, craftsmen with a handful of tools. Their dwellings were thatch, their crockery wood or earthen, and their clothing

and furniture worth not more than a few *livres*. Their aim was quite simply to see the year out. They practically never participated in the parish assemblies (except as silent witnesses, if that); they were never churchwardens, never members of the 'body politic', nor of course syndics or consuls (two rough equivalents of the present-day rural 'mayor'). Except in a few northern and particularly in eastern provinces, they never learned to read or write, and received their spiritual food from the Sunday sermon, the cult of local saints and relics, and folk tales retold around the evening hearth. They preserved all the fears, panics, brutality and submission in a kind of obscure mental recess. And they gave their wives as many children as it pleased Heaven to bestow – children half of whom never reached adulthood, while those who did survive had no practical prospects of rising in the world. Their economic, social, political and cultural dependence was total, and as a rule they could hope for no improvement.

In the absence of physical, sometimes of mental resources, and no matter how brave they might be, these dependent peasants were continually threatened. Threatened by epidemics and their own low resistance to infection; by epizootic diseases which bring instant ruin (they cannot afford to buy more livestock); and by acute variations in harvests and above all in employment, since they rely on the work they do for other people to buy the bread which they themselves cannot produce. In cases of economic/demographic crisis, which was endemic until 1710 or 1750, they lapse into beggary, vagrancy or death. In this class, it is more usual to sink than to rise.

There is a growing number of monographs on the various types of dependent peasant, and it would be easy to linger over the variety of situations and provinces. We shall confine ourselves to four examples.

The weaver/day-labourer of Picardy often owns his mud cottage but 'holds' next to nothing apart from his garden and one or two tiny strips of ground which he crops as often as he can. His livestock never includes a horse; hardly ever a cow or a pig; it adds up to a few hens and a few sheep in the care of the communal shepherd. They graze on the stubble-fields and fallow, or munch straw in a fetid stall. He repays the big farmer for the loan of his horses and plough by working 'days' at harvest-time, which also provide a little grain for the winter, but not enough, and so he also spins wool, or weaves, or more simply prepares the warp to which the weft will be added by more specialist workers. As grain-grower and day-labourer he is dependent upon the '*bon laboureur*',* as a first-stage textile worker, he often has neither the raw material nor the loom, which is provided by some merchant-entrepreneur who lives in a large *bourg* or in Amiens. These lesser peasants consequently work in double jeopardy since the crises of their two activities arise at the same time and reinforce one another. They are the obvious victims of every kind of crisis, and constitute the vast majority of Picardy villagers throughout the duration of the ancien régime.

Another type of dependent peasant, in a very different setting, are the *métayers* of the West, tied to a 'master' who is often the seigneur, by contracts settled both by custom and by notarized deeds. These contracts are extremely various, and do not tally with our simplistic and anachronistic classifications, being neither for true *métayage* nor true farming-out, but a little of both, plus some even more ancient and 'feudal' conditions. Brittany in particular usually enforces a combination of ritual offerings, *corvées,* very arduous cartage rights (unpaid), *champarts,* prestations levied in cash or, more often, kind (grain, butter, flax, young beasts), tree-planting and more or less equal shares of some crops. With some exceptions, effective holdings are tiny, consisting of a few 'furrows' (work units which have become units of measurement), and if they are more than about twenty-five acres the peasants often have to combine into family *consorties* in order to pool their labour force and equipment. In practice subsistence, and occasionally success, is bound up with the considerable numbers of cattle made possible by variegated, extensive pasturage. A second favourable factor derives from the simultaneous cultivation of two kinds of grain, the high-grade for export (wheat), and the low-grade, cultivable at a different time of year (rye, buckwheat), for consumption. The contrasts and nuances in the various forms of hardship, bare sufficiency and semi-prosperity are governed by the structure of

---

* In this context, the word *laboureur* (worker, ploughman) has come to mean a man rich enough to own his own plough and team, consequently a fairly prosperous peasant who may even be able to afford to pay someone else to do the ploughing. See Doc. 23. – Tr.

holdings, variations in the yield of the livestock and in the severity of the seigneurial and feudal contracts and levies, and lastly by the luck of the weather. But one disturbing index does exist: in the Gâtine Poitevine,* a very well-researched region, half the *métayers* did not serve out their contracts: they lapsed into debt, absconded, abandoned their meagre belongings, or were just evicted. On the other hand, mainly because of their natural advantages, some exceptionally prosperous areas managed to support an unusually high quota of affluent peasants who almost always exported a substantial amount of their produce. These were the great low-lying meadows of Normandy and the Breton littorals, with their mild winters and soils greatly improved by marine fertilizers and incessant, intelligent activity.

The peasantries of the Midi have been less studied until recently, but they seem at once more varied and more fortunate. Certainly no area is devoid of its altogether wretched landless labourers, totally dependent upon their employers, but they are quite scarce and seem to be far outnumbered by smallholders who were hardly ever affected by dearth. In material terms, they possess only the *manse,* a few patches of land, some wooden implements, a donkey and a few sheep, but they enjoy the blessings of the soil and climate. Barring a few appalling marshlands, they inhabit the sunniest, healthiest regions in France. The structure of the *terroirs* preserves broad tracts of heath and scrub where sizeable flocks of sheep graze almost cost-free, and which can be cleared and planted if necessary. A good adaptation to the climate, with Mediterranean cereal crops in biennial rotation; skill in gardening and arboriculture – all too rare in France – with the benefit of the new plants introduced from Spain and the Orient; exceptional thrift, yet probably the most balanced diet in the realm; crops yielding saleable surpluses (olives, vines, dried fruits for Lent) when river or sea are never far away; the presence ever since the early seventeenth century of a plant with a near-miraculous yield, introduced by way of Navarre (American corn, which commonly returned 100 for 1, twenty times more than any other grain),

---

* Also known as the Gâtine de Parthenay, now in the department of Deux-Sèvres. – Tr.

invaluable as fodder also, and useful as an intermediate or catch-crop. All these factors made for fairly prosperous conditions among the small peasants of the Midi. We have already mentioned the prevailing climate of liberty – the persistence of the allodia, the necessity for both nobles and seigneurs to prove their claims to be accepted as such, the low level of the seigneurial rake-off (but the extremely high level of tithes), and the comparative strength of the municipalities or 'consulates'. No 'famine' worthy of the name has been identified among the southern population after 1660 at the latest, a precious, almost unbelievable dispensation. It is easy to understand why the wretched of every neighbouring region converge upon these favoured provinces, and especially the uncouth highlanders who littered all the Bas-Languedoc with beggars.

The image of these relatively fortunate southerners is counterpointed elsewhere by those types of peasant known locally by the graphic nickname of '*haricotiers*'. These peasants 'hold' a modest but respectable acreage of land; they own tools and a little livestock; they are diligent mixed farmers, making clever use of their time and resources– a little stock-farming, some market-gardening and arboriculture, which requires both care and expertise, a little grain, cottage industry and part-time work for others. This well-orchestrated activity (it was often typically French – that is, characteristic of the Paris region) frequently enables them to meet the demands of subsistence and taxation, and yet their diversified economy remains fragile: an epizootic outbreak, two bad years running, or even the illness of the head of the family can nudge them into debt, the usual prelude to relapsing into the massive category of the perpetually ruled, whose life and survival are always problematic.

The ownership and careful cultivation of a few *arpents** of vines is enough to guarantee a comparable, sometimes superior standard of living, provided that the grapes ripen and the wine sells well: in fact, it takes manpower and skill to work a vineyard, rather than expensive equipment. But, as with the *haricotiers,* many vine-growers

---

* The area of the *arpent* may vary from 20 to over 50 *ares*, between .5 and 1.25 acres. Like the English acre, the *arpent* was supposed to represent the amount of land which could be ploughed by a yoke of oxen in one day. – Tr.

hover on the brink of insecurity and can be dislodged quite quickly, especially when there is a glut on the market, in a social context in which failure is always more frequent than success.

All sorts of additional provincial and social nuances might be mentioned, but they would only add a few touches to the outline of the most widespread type of peasant, who lives a life of uncertainty and dependence. Uncertainty as to the coming winter and the more distant future alike, a function both of the frequent paucity of land, equipment and livestock and of the depletion of gross production by the host of dues exacted by successive or simultaneous rentiers. Uncertainty which also hinges upon weather conditions, fiscal variations, and the everyday ups and downs of family health, and is aggravated by a kind of chronic sense of desolation. Dependence all the way along the economic, social, juridical, political and cultural scale, whether upon the urban or rural employer, the 'master' of the farm or *métairie,* the seigneur, the body politic, or the Church in its twin roles of tithe-owner and sermonizer. Uncertainty and dependence do not necessarily involve rebellion or continual misery; adaptability, habit, and a kind of stupefaction caused by a non-existent, even positively damaging cultural life, more often result in the listless acceptance of dull, fitful mediocrity.

4   THE INDEPENDENT PEASANTS

No part of the countryside is without its share of truly independent peasants, but in varying proportions, and never in the majority. Barring disasters, their families and holdings are always secure. They work a sizeable '*corps de ferme*', usually upwards of ten hectares, sometimes more than twenty, although the land does not always belong to them. Many of the 'independents' are not 'proprietors' even in the old sense of the word: they tend to be well-entrenched 'farmers' on behalf of some wealthy family or thriving religious institution, and are hardly ever *métayers*. In every case, their considerable resources in terms of livestock and equipment are their own rightful property, and will include several teams of horses or oxen, at least ten cows or fifty sheep, big wheeled ploughs, harrows, rollers, scythes and carts with iron axles (the ownership of iron in any quantity is almost a badge of affluence). The utilization, often possession of well-made equipment for ploughing, cultivation and transportation determines and symbolizes their independence: these are agricultural entrepreneurs with their own capital stock.

They generally employ paid labour, either permanent (farmhands, serving-girls) or seasonal (day-labourers), and this brings them prestige, position, and the power of the employer over those lesser peasants who cannot do without their patronage. This subjection may go a very long way: in exchange for the plough, horses and often the supplies, seed or loans he usually needs, the small peasant signs IOUs which he often pays off in labour. The probate of estates records the index of dependence: the rich man's numerous papers contain entries for a mass of small debts owing; conversely, the little bundles of papers in lowlier homes show liabilities.

It is worth emphasizing that the independent peasant is often literate; in 'advanced' provinces – from Normandy to Alsace – he may even own a few books. The independent peasant is certain to be a member of the 'body politic' of the assembly of inhabitants, where he often plays an influential part as churchwarden, syndic or consul. And eventually it is most unusual for him not to acquire some kind of customary title in more or less official documents (parishional, notorial, fiscal, judicial), enshrining and proclaiming his '*dignité*' and reflecting his wealth and power. In the Paris basin, he is the '*laboureur*' (elsewhere a commonplace or non-existent title); throughout the Midi, he is the '*ménager*', more rarely '*maître de mas*', occasionally even '*bourgeois*'.

All the gradations between sufficiency and real affluence can of course be picked out. A great rift divides the '*bon ménager*' with two horses, twenty hectares and half a dozen cows from the big *fermier* who has a hundred hectares, the seigneury and even tithe-rights. But the division between them and the dependent peasant is greater still: in the most contrasted and developed provinces it amounts to a 'class' conflict which comes alive from time to time, and will do so increasingly in the future.

The topmost strata of these big *laboureurs* are the springboard for the more or less slow ascent from the peasantry into what are seen as more reputable (urban) circumstances or enterprises. A proportion, admittedly a small one, of the lower secular clergy is recruited from among this prosperous rural milieu, for it takes money – an income of between fifty and two hundred *livres,* according to date and diocese – to become a priest. Some urban shopkeepers and even minor officials also spring from this background, but the movement seems to become rarer after 1650. Usually the wealthiest and most prudent remain in the country, enlarge their lands, farms, livestock and staff, and deal in hides, timber or grain. These are the men who manage to garner some of the clergy's property after 1789, and become the local or provincial notables of the nineteenth century.

At the summit of the rural world, one or two men in every village occupy outstanding positions. They control the local agriculture, and have become dues collectors and occasionally stewards for the big landowners, seigneurs and even tithe-owners, in whose stead they collect the more or less 'feudal' rights which bring pride, profit, and access to a world previously beyond their reach. By this means they are instrumental in syphoning off ground rent, naturally retaining a percentage for themselves, and have a foot in two camps, being producers and production-managers as well as partial rentiers. Furthermore, their happy position enables them to go so far as to imitate their masters and seigneurs (subject to their consent) by giving orders, hunting, showing off, rearing pigeons, and even fixing a weathervane, the badge of the seigneur, atop their residence. These key figures have often been portrayed, but have never been systematically studied. In them the hierarchy of the peasant producers, the fundamental wealth of the ancien régime economy, reaches its peak and merges into the world of the rentiers, far above the heads of labourer and *haricotier.*

DOCUMENTS
20 A VAGRANT IN LANGUEDOC

... On 22 December 1684 in a secluded village in the Cévennes, it is freezing hard. Gabriel Georges, a vagrant, is breathing his last in the poor-house. He dies, and his body is buried in the special cemetery for poor outsiders. Where had he come from? By his own account, he was forty-six years old, born in La Familière, in Poitou. His fate was typical: working through the death-registers and poor-house records, one continually comes across these vagrants heading southward towards the sun and the Mediterranean, their entire baggage consisting of a small pot for boiling

soup and collecting coins . . . Tramps turned rag-pickers, they collect old
clothes and germ-laden rags, vectors of all kinds of diseases, and sell them
to paper mills . . . With the onset of winter they go to earth in barns and
métairies, to be turfed out by the farmhands in the early morning, stiff
with cold, sometimes frozen to death. Others are locked up in the poorhouses and are racked with hunger when fed upon a kind of greyish un-
leavened bread, as in Montpellier . . . But until about 1700 their way of
life was characterized much more by tramping than confinement: the
watch, gate-keepers, *chasse-coquins* and magistrates . . . try in vain to put
them behind bars. All those who share the old persuasion, and still believe,
as in medieval times, that beggars are a chosen race – small fry, lackeys,
the livery, children, nuns, inn-keepers or prostitutes – protect them, rescue
them from the clutches of the *chasse-gueux,* harbour them and set them free
again: thus in Montpellier in 1685, a woman named Gasconne, a man
named Barbe and a nun named Carabosse are fined for harbouring beggars
. . . A parish of any importance will see scores or hundreds of vagrants passing through every year; the Montpellier poor-house alone handed out over
forty thousand '*passades*' in sixty-five years. They haunt the churches in
jostling throngs but people claim that they will not pray; they offend the
faithful with their stink and noise and even venture to the foot of the altar,
at the elevation of the Host . . . They take up residence on threshing-floors
and farmyards, in barns and tile-works, woods and huts. They walk into
people's houses, fornicating with or without 'trollops'; murder and steal;
call themselves soldiers but produce no discharge; feign mutilation; form
begging bands of four or more, not including children; carry muskets, pis-
tols, bayonets and iron-shod staves; dog the path of great worthies, the
king and the Estates, so that they leave a long malodorous wake of squalid
poverty and beggary . . . It does no good to alternate kicks with ha'pence,
shave and flog them in tandem, sometimes shoot them down . . . burn their
flea-ridden bedrolls or drive them twenty miles away on carts or mule-back
'amid popular acclamation'. Nor to send them on their way in more humane
fashion with a bowlful of soup or a spoonful of beans and a piece of black
bread, shared with a few lepers. They always return.

Emmanuel LE ROY-LADURIE, *Les Paysans de Languedoc*
(S.E.V.P.E.N., 1966, 2 vols, 1035 pp.), 93–5.

21 THE DAY-LABOURERS, AS SEEN BY VAUBAN

. . . It only remains to take stock of two million men all of whom I suppose
to be day-labourers or simple artisans scattered throughout the towns,
bourgs and villages of the realm.

What I have to say about all these workers ... deserves serious attention, for although this sector may consist of what are unfairly called the dregs of the people, they are nonetheless worthy of high consideration in view of the services which they render to the State. For it is they who undertake all the great tasks in town and country without which neither themselves nor others could live. It is they who provide all the soldiers and sailors and all the servants and serving women; in a word, without them the State could not survive. It is for this reason that they ought to be spared in the matter of taxes, in order not to burden them beyond their strength.

Let us begin with the town-dwellers.

. . .

Among the smaller fry, particularly in the countryside, there are any number of people who, while they lay no claim to any special craft, are continually plying several which are most necessary and indispensable. Of such a kind are those whom we call *manoeuvriers,* who, owning for the most part nothing but their strong arms or very little more, do day- or piece-work for whoever wants to employ them. It is they who do all the major jobs such as mowing, harvesting, threshing, woodcutting, working the soil and the vineyards, clearing land, ditching, carrying soil to vineyards or elsewhere, labouring for builders and several other tasks which are all hard and laborious. These men may well find this kind of employment for part of the year, and it is true that they can usually earn a fair day's wage at haymaking, harvesting and grape-picking time, but the rest of the year is a different story ...

It will not be inappropriate [to give] some particulars about what the country day-labourer can earn.

I shall assume that of the three hundred and sixty-five days in the year, he may be gainfully employed for one hundred and eighty, and earn nine *sols* a day [*the date of writing is about 1700*]. This is a high figure, and it is certain that except at harvest- and grape-picking time most earn not more than eight *sols* a day on average, but supposing we allow the nine *sols,* that would amount to eighty-five *livres* and ten *sols,* call it ninety *livres,* from which we have to deduct his liabilities (taxes plus salt for a family of four say 14*l.* 16*s*) ... leaving seventy-five *livres* four *sols.*

Since I am assuming that this family ... consists of four people, it requires not less than ten *septiers* of grain, Paris measure [about 15½ hectolitres or 43 bushels], to feed them. This grain, half wheat, half rye ... commonly selling at six *livres* per *septier* ... will come to sixty *livres,* which leaves fifteen *livres* four *sols** out of the seventy-five *livres* four *sols*, out of which the labourer has to find the price of rent and upkeep for his house, a few chattels, if only some earthenware bowls, clothing and linen, and the needs of his entire family for one year.

But these fifteen *livres* four *sols* will not take him very far unless his industry [*handicraft, such as weaving*] or some particular business supervenes and his wife contributes to their income by means of her distaff, sewing, knitting hose or making small quantities of lace . . . also by keeping a small garden or rearing poultry and perhaps a calf, a pig or a goat for the better-off . . . ; by which means he might buy a piece of larding bacon and a little butter or oil for making soup. And if he does not additionally cultivate some small allotment, he will be hard pressed to subsist, or at least he will be reduced, together with his family, to the most wretched fare. And if instead of two children he has four, that will be worse still until they are old enough to earn their own living. Thus however we come at the matter, it is certain that he will always have the greatest difficulty in seeing the year out . . .

VAUBAN, *Projet d'une Dixme Royale,* 1707 (ed. Coornaert, Alcan, 1933, 296 pp.), 73, 77–81.

22 THE POOR PEASANTS OF NIVERNAIS, AS SEEN BY VAUBAN, JANUARY 1696

. . . all the so-called *bas peuple* live on nothing but bread of mixed barley and oats, from which they do not even remove the bran, which means that bread can sometimes be lifted by the straw sticking out of it. They also eat poor fruits, mainly wild, and a few vegetables from their gardens, boiled up with a little rape- or nut-oil sometimes, but more often not, or with a pinch of salt. Only the most prosperous eat bread made of rye mixed with barley and wheat.

. . . The general run of people seldom drink [wine], eat meat not three times a year, and use little salt . . . So it is no cause for surprise if people who are so ill-nourished have so little energy. Add to this what they suffer from exposure: winter and summer, three fourths of them are dressed in nothing but half-rotting tattered linen, and are shod throughout the year with *sabots,* and no other covering for the foot. If one of them does have shoes he only wears them on saints' days and Sundays: the extreme poverty to which they are reduced, owning as they do not one inch of land, rebounds against the more prosperous town and country bourgeois, and against the nobility and the clergy. They lease their lands out to *métayage,*

* Another of Vauban's calculations produced a figure of 23*l.* 17*s.* (there are several slightly different manuscript versions of the *Dixme Royale*).

and the owner who wants a new *métayer* must begin by settling his obligations, paying his debts, stocking the holding with beasts and feeding him
and his family for the coming year at his own expense . . .

The poor people are ground down in another manner by the loans of
grain and money they take from the wealthy in emergencies, by means of
which a high rate of usury is enforced, under the guise of presents which
must be made after the debts fall due, so as to avoid imprisonment. After
the term has been extended by only three or four months, either another
present must be produced when the time is up, or they face the *sergent*
[*debtors' bailiff*] who is sure to strip the house bare. Many others of these
poor people's afflictions remain at my quill's tip, so as not to offend anybody.

Since hardship can hardly go much further, its normal effects are a
matter of course: firstly, it makes people weak and unhealthy, especially
the children, many of whom die for want of good food; secondly, the men
become idle and apathetic, being persuaded that only the least and worst
part of the fruit of their labours will turn to their own profit; thirdly, there
are liars, robbers, men of bad faith, always willing to perjure themselves
provided that it pays, and to get drunk as soon as they lay hands on the
wherewithal . . .

> VAUBAN, *Description géographique de l'Élection de
> Vezelay . . .*, in Coornaert, op. cit., 279–81.

NB: the region is a particularly poor one, and the age particularly grim,
but Vauban had made an intensive study, and he lived in the region.

23 *LABOUREURS* OF THE ESSONNES VALLEY

The low-income masses contrast with the tight group of *laboureurs* who make
up less than eight per cent of the total population [*of the Essonnes valley*] . . .

What distinguishes and defines the *laboureur*, at least at the outset and to a
large extent in the seventeenth century also, is the exploitation of arable
lands with the help of his own equipment. . . . These are . . . essentially
lands held on lease and worked by the *laboureur*, who is consequently mainly in evidence as the lessee of those large farms . . . of two or three hundred
arpents. . . . It is not unusual for him to accumulate several farms. . . .
[*in 1691*] François Moreau holds the farm of Chêne-Coupé, 120 *arpents* of
arable land, as well as the farm of La Mézière, 35 *arpents* . . . . In 1700,
Gilles Labourer, who already holds the farm of La Verville, the biggest in
the duchy [*of Villeroy*], takes a nine-year lease on another of the duchy's
farms, Les Boulineaux (at Saint-Fargeau), consisting of 234 *arpents* of land
and 14 of meadow; his holdings therefore amount to 635 *arpents* of
land and 55 of meadow, about 740 acres all told. The latter example shows

that a *laboureur* may be anything but a simple husbandman. In fact it is barely imaginable that the holder of such an estate would have borne out his title of 'ploughman' by actually pushing the plough himself. We are dealing with a fully fledged agricultural entrepreneur.

In any case, it quickly becomes obvious that this entrepreneur has many more strings to his bow, so to speak, than the 'labour' of lands held in farm. He very often farms the seigneurial rights . . . . In this manner, Antoine Bige, *laboureur* of Fontenay-le-Vicomte, leases from the nuns of Port-Royal de Paris the estate of Mondeville, which comprises 'the seigneurial residence' (a tiled mansion 'with the chamber where the court is held' plus thatched outhouses) and 160 *arpents* of land, three of vines and four of heath, together with 'the entire seigneury of Mondeville, comprising seigneurial dues, cash, fowls or capons and grain, the whole payable to Saint Remy; item, the right of sub-letting to millers and of pursuit over the length and breadth of the aforesaid seigneurie in case of [*illicit*] removal and milling of grain'. At Ballancourt . . . First Jean Barbier then his son Robert hold the farm of Le Petit-Saussay (about 250 *arpents*) as well as managing the finances of the commandery of Saussay. This comprehensive system of leasing benefits the seigneur by simplifying the administration of his property, and is favourably regarded by the farmers. It takes large amounts of capital to manage a 350, to 500-acre holding [two or three thousand *livres* on equipment alone], and this could be partly provided by the farm of the seigneurial rights. Furthermore, on top of the prestige attached to the title of '*receveur d'une terre et seigneurie*', it enabled . . . pressure to be exerted on the mass of the rural population, increasing the farmer's supremacy over the world of the small earner.

The *laboureurs* sometimes obtain their capital from a third type of activity – trade. Many of them sell their marketable produce themselves, in order to avoid the middle-men, corn-chandlers and big grain-merchants . . .

Through his various activities, the *laboureur* therefore emerges as a sort of quasi-capitalist entrepreneur, a blend of businessman and agriculturist. This at any rate is the description, not of the majority of those who styled themselves '*laboureurs*', but of the type which they all aspired to resemble.

Michel FONTENAY, *Paysans et marchands ruraux de la vallée de l'Essonnes dans la seconde moitié du* XVIIe *siècle*, in *Paris et Ile-de France, Mémoires publiés par la fédération des sociétés historiques et archéologiques de Paris et de l'Ile-de-France* (1958), vol. IX, 245–9.

NB. The type described here occurs in the Ile-de-France and the rich cereal plains of the Paris basin; it is not at all prevalent in the realm as a whole.

24 THE FISCAL PATTERN OF A RURAL COMMUNITY: THE TAX-ROLL OF LA BELLIÈRE, 1698 (ANALYSES AND EXCERPTS)

This small Norman community is assessed at 904 *livres*; barring a single exemption, the *curé*, it comprises 41 domiciled tax-payers, 4 'old inhabitants' and 4 'entrants and new inhabitants' (farmers who have moved house).

Breakdown of assessments

Over 100 *livres* (150*l.* and 110*l.*)	2 ⎫	Note that these 5 tax-payers account
About 50 *livres* (53, 49, 48*l.*)	3 ⎭	for more than half the total.
24–32 *livres*	6	
16–21 *livres*	6	
9–12 *livres*	6	
3–7 *livres*	9	
2 *livres*	4	
10 *sols*	5	

Examples of assessments

150*l.*: Jean Horcholle, farmer for the marquis de La Bellière, at 1200*l.*; one plough, 15 cows, 30 wool beasts.

110*l.*: François de Gournay, farmer for the sieur de Saint-Arnoult and the widow Pierre Tabur, at 320*l.*; owns about 140*l.* of income, 2 horses, 6 cows.

53*l.*: Adrien Tabur, assistant clerk of the rolls [*a minor office*], farmer for the sieur de Mortemer at 400*l.*, 2 horses, 8 cows . . .

49*l.*: Pierre Horcholle and his son Estienne, farmer for the sieur Delestre d'Aumalle at 400*l.*, 2 horses, 6 cows.

27*l.*: René le Sage, miller for the sieur de Pommereux at 150*l.*, 1 horse, 1 cow.

16*l.*: Robert Mallard, weaver, farmer for Pierre le Clerc at 60*l.*, 2 cows.

8*l.*: Antoine Pinot, mason, owner of a small house.

6*l.*: François Fourgon, day-labourer and warden of a meadow.

4*l.*: Antoine Belleferme, day-labourer, tenant.

3*l.*: François Gambu, dominie, resident at the school.

2*l.*: Widow Nicolas Bailly, dowager.

10*s.*: 4 'absentees' [*probably absconders, beggars, or soldiers*].

> Excerpt from the archives of the département of Seine-Maritime, C 2099; like the other localities mentioned in the text, La Bellière is near Forges-les-Eaux.

VI · LANDED INCOME AND GROUND RENTIERS

Quesnay's mid-eighteenth-century *Tableau économique* distinguishes between producers and rentiers and portrays 'that class of proprietors . . . seated on a raised form at the centre of circulation . . and including the sovereign, land-owners and tithe owners'. In fact, gross peasant production is buried beneath a welter of levies which end up in the pockets of the 'proprietor class', or the class of non-peasant rentiers, to be more precise. In a predominantly agricultural society, it is hardly an exaggeration to say that whatever its form, juridical definition or psychological context, rent was the crucial factor.

1 THE PRINCIPAL CATEGORIES OF LANDED INCOME

THE ECCLESIASTICAL TITHE

Some eighteenth-century canonists were still prepared to argue that the tithe was of divine inspiration: they had only to mangle a few biblical passages which refer to 'consecrating to the Lord' the fruits of the earth. Expert jurists like Durand de Maillane were nevertheless aware that the Fathers of the Church had either held their peace or simply recommended that the faithful should give alms or part of their crops to the priests. The swing from suggestion to compulsion came between the sixth and ninth centuries, when Church councils threatened those of the faithful who did not pay their tithes with excommunication. A series of Carolingian capitularies, between 779 and 805 (the best-known issued in 801), fixed the terms and objectives of an age-old institution which was one of the strongest, most widespread, complex and controversial of any under the ancien régime.

The principle, if not the application, is straightforward: all men who enjoy the 'fruits' of the earth – fruits in the broad Latin sense of yield or crop – must give a proportion, theoretically of one tenth, to the Church, which will put it to three uses – provision for priests, upkeep of places of worship, and poor-relief. A sublimely simple concept, altered sometimes out of all recognition in the course of a millennium.

The universality of the payment is what changed least. It is true that privilege, in other words the constant priority of particular over general law, a fundamental principle of medieval and ancien régime law, has made some inroads into tithe law. A few ancient religious foundations (Cluny, Citeaux, Prémontrés, Chartreux) have succeeded, not without a struggle, in obtaining exemption and in having their privilege upheld by the Lateran Council of 1215. The outcome of a royal ordinance of 1475 attempting to give exemption to officials of the Parlement is not clear. *Curés* were naturally exempt on any property they possessed inside their own parishes – generally very little. Apart from these, everybody pays the tithe, even the poor man if he has land and livestock, even noblemen (but at a lower rate) and churchmen, while Protestants are forced to accept Article 25 of the Edict of Nantes, by which they had to subsidize a hostile religion.

But it should be pointed out that the payment is made in kind, takes precedence over all others, and is levied immediately after the harvest, on the gross yield, while it is the man who occupies and tills the land who also pays the tithe, and not the eminent proprietor. It is always the working peasant who pays.

The substance of the tithe – the 'fruit' – has been worked out little by little in pursuance of complicated, variable processes with numerous individual exceptions and local customs, amid a tangle of discussions and disputes. The *'gros fruits'*, or major products, are always subject to the tithe: these are primarily cereals and wine, not forgetting the 'increase of livestock', yearling animals. The tithe hardly ever applies to woods, except for some coppices; mines and quarries; hunting and often fishing; natural meadows (but not man-made ones, a detail which has far-reaching consequences); the produce of fruit-bearing trees when they are planted on titheable lands (hence the success of pear- and apple-trees, walnuts, chestnuts and olives in cornfields and vineyards) – by virtue of the old adage 'no tithe on both high and low', although this principle is violated in part of the Midi; also exempt are draught animals (hence the advantage of putting cows to the plough), crops gathered before they are ripe, if used for animal-fodder, and above all enclosures, parks and gardens, except those bearing titheable fruits such as grain or vines, or exceeding a (variable) area, and also excepting those located in the suburbs of certain towns, such as Paris. The freedom from the tithe enjoyed by enclosures, which accounts for so many features of the rural landscape, naturally constitutes a per-petual bone of contention. Need we add that no fruits are tithed in any one place other than those which it is customary to tithe (other-wise the tithe is 'unwonted' – *insolite*), that any new crop is tithed automatically, as well as any newly-planted land (the *'novales'*), that this is a serious impediment to agricultural progress, and that any change or switch of crops on the same piece of land gives rise to endless disputations? This simplified check-list is not beside the point: it goes to the heart of the institutions, customs, attitudes, dis-putes and complications which are so characteristic of the ancien régime, and so dear to its heart.

The rate of the tithe has changed even more than its content. Tithes of one tenth are not unheard of, but they are rare; rates higher than one tenth are rarer still; particularly low rates (one thirtieth, one thirty-sixth – under three per cent) exist likewise, and make the levies made by the popular *'recteurs'* of Basse-Bre-tagne, for example, easily bearable. The normal rates seem to come to between one eleventh and one thirteenth, about eight per cent, but in this field exception is the only rule – again a very typical feature of the ancien régime, as shown in the table at the end of this chapter, although it applies only to a scrap of Provence.

The biggest change has occurred in the character of the tithe-owners, the identity of the beneficiaries. Canonically and juridically, this tithe-owner is supposed to be the *curé* – 'his belfry suffices' to prove his claim, as the saying went – but others have contrary and over-riding claims. In nine cases out of ten the *curé* is not the exclusive recipient: he is fobbed off with odds and ends, *novales,* tithes on fleeces, flax and meat, which are meagre, unreliable and difficult to collect (what exactly is the tithe on the lambs and fleeces of a peasant with only two sheep?). This robbery of the *curé* is given official sanction by all kinds of legal documents, and is the work of the bishops, chapters of canons, convents and sometimes even laymen (the so-called 'subinfeudated' tithes, theoretically forbidden). It is true that all these *'gros décimateurs'* (big basically because they took the *'gros fruits',* but also because of their wealth) had duties towards the parish which produced their tithe. These they performed irregularly and reluctantly: poor relief hardly ever, despite all claims to the contrary; the upkeep of buildings, partially, and under pressure; the *curé's* living, grudgingly – they paid him an annual sum, the *'gros'* (part of the 'big' tithes), barely greater than the minimum which the kings tried to fix, often unsuccessfully (two or three hundred *livres,* then five hundred in 1768 and seven hundred in 1786). The bulk of the tithe did not revert to the parish, but was invested, or submerged in the fortunes of bishops, canons, regular clergy or seigneurs.

The effectiveness of the tithe system tempted the taxation theorists, including Vauban in his *Dixme royale* of 1707. It is generally held that the tithe could produce a return of between 100 and 150 million *livres* in the eighteenth century, almost as much as all the direct taxes together. The revenue from tithes made a considerable contribution to the income of the high and middle clergy. In Languedoc, the great cathedral chapters were essentially fed by the tithes; in Brittany, where the demands of the Church were moderate, tithes made up forty per cent of the revenue of the cathedral chapter of Rennes and fifty-five per cent of that of the modest bishopric of Dol.

In the wake of Protestant progress, sixteenth-century France was shaken by a real revolt against the tithe: even the most Catholic regions witnessed refusals to pay, and these were of no little account in the onset of the Reformation. The rebels were silenced by the containment and subsequent persecution of the Huguenots, together with the missionary efficiency of the Counter-Reformation and the monarchy of the seventeenth century. Resentment went underground for two hundred years, only to erupt violently in 1789, as so many of the *cahiers de doléances* testify.

The tithe was at once a type of landed income, a continual source of discontent by reason of the variations in its basis and collection, and a powerful revolutionary driving-force.

SEIGNEURIAL RENT

We have already referred to its extraordinary complexity (Chapter 4): moderate and almost universal *cens*, huge but localized *champarts*, remainders, erratic and often considerable *lods et ventes*, variegated, sometimes abundant *banalités*, a sprinkling of *surcens*, cash dues, *corvées*, tallages, cartage, honorific offerings, road- and bridge-tolls, the list goes on and on. Some rights are in fixed sums of money, subject to devaluation, and therefore the lightest (at least usually), but others, the heaviest, are in kind; some are immutable, others 'mutable'; some are regular and annual, others '*casuel*' (occasional); some are accepted without a murmur, others violently contested.

Passions have occasionally run high among historians clashing over the essential problem of the real burden of seigneurial rent. Only the impracticable study of tens of thousands of seigneuries, based on a whole new cartography, could produce reliable answers. It would bring out the unquestionably heavy toll of the *champarts* in most parts of France (*tierce* in Burgundy, *tasque* in Provence), unpopular levies in kind, milling rights throughout the West, a general scatter of transference rights, and conversely the unimportance of many others. Add to these contradictions a number of almost insoluble difficulties, such as how to differentiate between purely seigneurial receipts and those which represent land-leases in the old accounts ledgers. Finally, the seigneurs neglected or intensified the collection of their rights according to the times and the individuals involved: in the late eighteenth century in particular there were 'seigneurial reactions', which we shall encounter again later.

Provincial differences seem once again to testify to the disparities in seigneurial rent. In the Midi, and south of Paris, where the tithes were heavy (often eight per cent or more), the seigneurial toll was slight – three or four hundredths of gross production, sometimes no more than one hundredth. In Brittany, where the tithe remained slight, seigneurial revenue based on well-established usage seems to be substantial. Burgundy has been the subject of several fine studies, and must surely have broken all the records (possibly together with the whole of eastern France): the *taille,* the *tierce, corvées* and the widespread *mainmorte* blend into a grim picture. In places where the seigneur was also the tithe-owner – the great ecclesiastical seigneuries – this array of dues was not borne lightly. A good geographical survey of the distribution of specifically anti-feudal peasant uprisings, particularly during the 1788 – 90 period, would constitute quite a reliable index of those provinces where seigneurial revenue, with or without the concomitant feudal trappings, was considered both excessive and unbearable, since in this matter sentiment and self interest ran parallel.

Whatever the disparities in the seigneurial rake-off, one fact had become increasingly obvious: the seigneurial system no longer had much practical utility, any more than did the nobility, with whom the peasants often confused it. It was no longer a safeguard against invasion, or the sole guarantor of immediate justice. The various local monopolies it had retained (milling, baking, wine-pressing) had grown useless and expensive. Its law-enforcing function in the *terroir* had been taken over by the peasant magistracies, with the supervision and occasional assistance of the intendants and their subordinates. And in any case the seigneur was usually an absentee from the countryside, mainly after the Fronde, or only looked in to hunt and collect his rents; at the very most, if he was 'in' at court or with the intendancy he could protect his tenants and 'vassals' – the word was still in use – by having their contribution to the royal exchequer reduced, which meant shifting the burden of difference onto the backs of neighbouring communities. This was common procedure among the intriguing nobility, and it was continued later by those who came to power through elections.

In the sixteenth and seventeenth centuries, there were sporadic, hazy (or uncharted) peasant uprisings against the seigneurs, especially when they made changes, or appeared to be doing so; they

burned down châteaux and muniment rooms, looted, and occasionally withheld their payments, particularly of *champarts,* and mainly
during the aftermath of troubled periods such as the wars of religion
and the Frondes, when taxes had slackened off or could not be
collected. In the late eighteenth century the reaction was sharper
and more widespread. But its target was the existence of the nobility
as well as of the seigneurial system, both of these being shrewdly
lumped together under the name of 'feudal barbarism', which therefore safeguarded another and undisputed category of rent: 'proprietary rent' was becoming sacrosanct and has remained so for the
most part. It is a feature common to many old and 'new' régimes,
particularly in France.

PROPRIETARY RENT

Hundreds of scholarly investigations, based mainly on late eighteenth-century archives, have attempted to gauge what 'share' of
the French soil the various (and perfunctorily defined) 'classes'
may have 'possessed' under the ancien régime – possessed in the
feudal, not the Roman sense of the word, subject to the rights of
the seigneur and the tithe-owner. Predictably, these monographs
have emphasized to the point of caricature the long-standing, fundamental disparity in local conditions: here the great nobleman owns
almost everything; next door, next to nothing; in the North, the
Church owns as much as a quarter of the land; in the Midi, less
than one twentieth; around the big towns, peasants hold next to
nothing 'in their own right'; in the heart of Auvergne, almost everything. Amid these innumerable contrasts, it is hard to discern an
overall pattern, but it can be said that the peasants probably 'possessed' (again in the old sense) less than half of the land on which
they did all the work.

It follows from this simplified account that a good half of the
land belonged to people who did not farm it or live on it, but who
returned from time to time to collect their revenues. The contracts
concluded between these landlords and the occupants of the land
are bewilderingly various, and do not correspond to our summary
and anachronistic classifications of *fermage* and *métayage.* The
study of these contracts in the French setting alone would necessi-

tate a fat volume; we shall attempt to make the basic generalizations.

The 'landlord' takes from his 'tenant' (variously known as *fermier, miège, métayer, bordier, closier,* etc.) an income which is supposed to pay him back for the use of his landed capital, in the form of a share of the yearly revenue. This share is sometimes on a fixed, sometimes a sliding scale; it may or may not be in proportion to the yield; it is paid here in kind, there in cash, elsewhere in labour, often in any combination of the three; sometimes it consists of a single product (grain), sometimes of many. The contract is usually written and covers a varying number of years or harvests, mainly between one and nine, but possibly longer – twenty-seven, fifty-four, ninety-nine years, one or several 'lifetimes' (during difficult times) – not to mention the many *'baux à rentes'* which are sales in disguise, subject to payment of a fixed annual sum. The contracts gradually evolved towards greater simplicity and efficiency, especially noticeable in the more 'advanced' provinces (such as the Paris basin): a nine-year lease and simplified, perhaps single payments, preferably in cash, and in ever-increasing sums in the second half of the eighteenth century.

The outlying provinces retained more archaic types of contract for a long time, and their combined idiosyncrasies put them in an overall majority. The south-west almost revelled in contracts of *métayage* in which the most trivial shares were specified, down to the amount of grass which the livestock were permitted to graze, or the amount of goose-fat which would or would not suffice when the traditional *confits* (meats cooked and cured in their own fat) were shared out. Western France long continued to enforce a tangled mass of clauses of an altogether feudal kind (*corvées,* ritual gifts, homages) together with specifically seigneurial (*champarts,* milling rights) and more general clauses (grain, butter, cash, some variable, some defined). The list is inexhaustible.

The next logical step is to evaluate the share of the crop which a tenant might 'pay' his landlord. In the regions of *métayage* proper, it is obviously half, when the master provides half of the advance; despite endless bargaining and mutual trickery, and no matter how capable the *métayer* may be, this is a tremendous amount, and in fact the

métayers were generally a fairly wretched crew, as contemporary observers and historians both point out. Nevertheless they did scrape a
livelihood, and not always a wretched one. The question of *métayage*
warrants a fundamental re-examination. In regions where the landlord mostly leases out his land, it is difficult to obtain a clear view
even in the eighteenth century. Near Paris, the cost of the lease is always higher than that of the tithe, even when this stands at eight or
nine per cent, as it often does. In southern Picardy in the seventeenth
century, the landlord tries to make at least a bushel of grain on every
bushel sown on the land he leases; in northern Beauvais, this works
out at a rate of $1\frac{1}{2}$ hectolitres (about four bushels) on every hectare
under cultivation (two out of three courses), and over two hectolitres
per hectare overall (fallow included). In other words, the landlord
claims distinctly more than the farmer must set aside for next year's
sowing. It is impossible to estimate these exactions at less than one
fifth of the actual harvest. Even allowing for the farmer's additional
profits (garden, livestock, timber, hire of equipment, etc.) and the entire gamut of special circumstances, it is undeniable that proprietorial
rent swallowed up the greater part of the 'gross yield' (harvest minus
seed, the cost of reaping and threshing, and the consumption of the
farmer and his labourers). This is no small return, even when the
farmer could feed his family or store sufficient seed-corn on top of
finding his (always obligatory) 'rent'. Even the best-equipped holdings had their difficult, sometimes tragic years.

As was normal at that time (at least until 1750 or thereabouts),
yearly variations take on greater significance than rough averages,
foreign as these often are to the spirit of the times. We know that
the crop yield could vary by a factor of two. In a good year, and on
a good farm, the rent is easily settled, especially if it is in kind; but if
it is in cash a great many bushels will have to be sold, since prices are
low. In a bad year, rent fixed in kind puts a strain on the farmer and
benefits the landlord, who will be able to sell much more dear (at
least double); if the rent is in cash, the farmer may be forced to sell
what he should have stored away as seed-corn or food: only the
very big farmer will manage. In other provinces, where there is a
system of proprietorial rent in proportion to the harvest, the landlord will receive less produce in a bad year, but will sell it more

profitably: his *métayer* has to make out as best he can! It is
important to realize that 'bad years' usually benefit the landlord
(if he can collect his dues) and usually harm the peasant, except
on really big holdings. 'Conjuncture' is hard on the small and
medium farmer, but almost always smiles on the landlord. A succession of three or four bad years is all it takes to produce debt, bankruptcy, foreclosure and flight among many *métayers* and farmers.
Similarly, their plight may constitute a windfall for the clever and
almost inevitable creditor, who can now make a clean sweep of land,
goods and even entire holdings. This dichotomy is not unique to
ancien régime France, but it is very much a basic characteristic. It
also enables us to grasp a little-known and seldom explored type of
landed income which we shall make no bones about calling 'usurious
rent'.

'USURIOUS' RENT

The word 'usurer', even in its surviving sense of a man who makes
short-term loans at extortionate interest, often against pledges, may
also be applied to the type of mainly urban but occasionally rural
figure symbolized by Molière's Harpagon. But when the theologians
and moralists referred to usury they meant not just any illicit form of
interest but interest itself; in the mid-eighteenth century, there were
still Jansenists who followed in the footsteps of Pascal and Bourdaloue by holding that a loan of money might only be an act of charity,
and consequently unconditional. Nevertheless, usage and even legislation had been evading these purely scholastic prohibitions for some
time. The simplest method consisted of disguising a loan as a simulated sale, and this was done under the most diverse and subtle
legalistic forms.

All these procedures start with the creditor-debtor duo. The
former 'advanced' seed-corn, food, wool, livestock, materials and
sometimes cash (rarely mentioned in the contract) to the latter. To
square his debt, the debtor offers the simulated sale of a piece of land,
or more often the annual payment of a 'rent' on his future harvests;
this rent is stipulated in kind, but may be converted into cash according to a yearly valuation reached either privately or by court
decision (the '*apprécis*' of grain, wine, livestock, faggots, etc.). Con-

sequently it often happened that real estate, land and even houses were saddled with non-seigneurial 'rents' sometimes originating in the distant past and payable to rich creditors or their descendants. A key clause is that non-payment entailed, by a well-established legal process, the seizure of the property on which the loan was based.

French archives are crammed with records of 'constituted rents' or '*constituts*' of a similar kind. These were loans at interest camouflaged as bills of sale. The investor would 'buy' for a lump sum an 'annual rent in perpetuity until repayment' which represented the lawful 'interest' rate on his capital (this rate gradually decreased between the early sixteenth and early eighteenth centuries from twelve to five per cent, disregarding brief reversals or regional variations). The rent constituted in this manner was secured against the entire property of the borrower, and namely against certain specified lands. The mechanism was universal, but the payment, which fell due at a fixed annual date, put a considerable strain on the property of the borrower. The creditor's profit was also increased by various kinds of swindle, for example when he had not always really paid the full amount listed by the notary. In the event of payment lapsing for a few years, seizure was a legal right.

The usual beneficiaries of this type of rent, which masqueraded under a number of different titles, were often members of the legal profession, officials and all sorts of 'bourgeois'. The notaries of central France and the Midi made huge gains from these practices, usurious both in the contemporary sense and in our own. Even churchmen and venerable abbeys did not scruple to add this type of income to their other sources of profit. No matter what their status, the nobles were likely to appear among the borrowers, therefore the victims, for a while at least; but the usual and countless victims were that majority of the peasantry who had some small amount of landed property.

STATE INCOME

In spite of some stubborn misconceptions, it was a long time since any French king had lived off his estate '*en bon ménager*', any more than his great provincial forerunners had done. Taxation was nominally 'extraordinary' but actually permanent, and had gradually entrenched itself in the realm, although not without sporadic armed resistance and regional and local accommodations.

The general distribution and uniformity of royal taxation was at odds with the institutions and customs of each province, 'country' (*pays*) and town absorbed by the realm, as well as with the astonishing tangle of personal and collective 'privileges' which were much more than the prerogative of the two ancient 'orders' of priests and warriors. Volume two of this textbook will go into privilege and taxation at length, but at this point we must underline a factor so glaring and so commonplace that it has often been overlooked.

Whatever its form – and it took several dozen, if not several hundred – royal taxation could be raised on nothing else but the income of the realm, whether at source or in circulation. And it has already been established that more than three quarters of this income was of agricultural, peasant, rural origin. Since it is also established that practically the entire rentier class was either privileged or exempt, in whole or in part, it was therefore the peasant producer on whom taxation was essentially levied, and levied in cash. Outside his 'domain' (reconstituted by Colbert), the king was actually the biggest rentier in the realm.

Historians are in disagreement as to the rate of the royal levy, which varied from year to year and still more from province to province. It is certain that it made a sudden spurt in the time of Richelieu, who doubled the direct taxation (and increased the rest) in order to wage war against the Habsburgs, and that subsequent reductions were only episodic. Two examples may help to throw light on the situation.

In the heyday of Louis XIV, an 'average' peasant of the Paris basin – the small *laboureur* or sound *haricotier* – paid the tax-collector about twenty *livres* a year. Twenty *livres* was the price of a calf, six or seven sheep, or five hectolitres of grain in a good year (less in a bad year); five hectolitres was the yield of half a hectare of ordinary land; if the peasant in question was harvesting four hectares to the course (twelve hectares in three-course rotation), the fiscal rate is one eighth or 12.5 per cent of the gross yield of the first course. Assuming that the produce of the second course, livestock, garden and part-time work double this gross income, royal taxation would work out at six per cent of income. The outlying provinces and the *pays d'État** were certainly taxed at a lower rate.

The day-labourer occupying a cottage and a plot of land might pay about five *livres* during the same period, the equivalent of ten days' work. Allowing for Sundays, saints' days and seasonal unemployment, he could work for a maximum of two hundred days a year, which means that the *taille* removes about five per cent of his wage-earnings, which are less than his total income – say three per cent overall?

We should also take into account the salt-tax – heavy, light or non-existent, depending on the region – plus a host of lesser taxes. The royal levy on gross production can rarely have fallen short of five per cent, and sometimes rose to ten per cent; this is as far as we can reasonably go in the guessing-game. The levy is not a crushing one in itself, but it is compulsory and imprescriptible, gradually rises from the time of Richelieu onward, takes practically no account of 'bad' years (dearths, unemployment, sickness), and above all comes on top of all the rest – those of the seigneur, the tithe-owner, probably the landlord and usurer, who are powerfully guarded in law and jurisprudence at a time when almost every judge is also a rentier.

The inroads made into gross peasant production by this spate of rents, very unevenly distributed, can never be assessed at less than one fifth and must often have reached twice and in local instances three times that amount (some historians have suggested even higher rates, but these are rarely admissible, in the long term at any rate).

A tightly-knit rentier class – a few hundredths of the population of the realm – lives, more or less comfortably, off this array of levies. Now is the convenient moment for introducing that class.

* Provinces still possessing their own Estates, such as Artois, Béarn, Brittany, Burgundy, Dauphiné, Languedoc, Provence and various others, although there seems to be no general agreement on the numbers or identity of the *pays d'État*. In fiscal law, they contrast with the *pays d'élection* (roughly speaking, *généralités* whose taxes are settled by the central administration rather than by consultation with the Estates), and are easily outnumbered by them. – Tr.

2   THE COMMON FEATURES OF THE RENTIER CLASS

RANGE

Practically every important, brilliant or commanding figure in the realm lives in whole or in part off the various categories of landed income. The only exceptions are some few great merchants, ship-owners, financiers, businessmen and the occasional entrepreneur, and these warrant separate consideration. The entire clergy, barring dependent wage-earners such as curates, non-beneficed priests and the few real mendicant monks; the entire nobility, save the odd fallen gentleman; everybody of any note in the administration, the law, officialdom and what we shall for the time being call the urban bourgeoisie; and lastly the thin upper crust of the peasant world – all these derived all or most of their income from the land.

DISPARITY BETWEEN TYPES OF RENT AND OF RENTIER

But there is no congruity between the types of rent and the types of rentier. One and the same person or institution will commonly be the recipient of two, three, or four types of rent. The king is the principal recipient of taxation, but he also gets a little seigneurial and proprietorial rent; he can even collect tithe income, since he was entitled to the revenues of vacant bishoprics (the '*régale temporelle*'). Like every influential church institution, the abbey or the chapter of canons collects seigneurial and proprietorial rent as well as tithes, and is not always above stooping to what we have called usurious rent. The nobleman of the West, '*chef de nom et d'armes*' as he dubs himself in Brittany, collects what is still a feudal rent, a rough blend of seigneurial and proprietorial rent. The prosperous bourgeois is the big specialist in usurious rent and also assumes the function of state tax-collector – retaining a share for himself. He is nearly always the landlord of one or more estates or seigneuries, which bring him other types of rent, as well as honour. Even the well-to-do peasant, farmer of lands, mills, *champarts* and tithes, can be the recipient of two or three types of rent while remaining a producer or production overseer.

THE RENTIER, A TOWNSMAN

Under the ancien régime, therefore, the rentier is commonly identified by the receipt of a mixture of rents. Another general characteristic is that his principal dwelling-place is not or is no longer at the centre of his landed wealth. The rentier is becoming more and more removed from his source of income. More and more, he is becoming a stranger to the fields, those 'deserts' despised ever since the age of Molière; he belongs to the town, even the capital, whether provincial, national or royal. True, the abbeys still stand in the heart of their ancient estates, but the abbot parades at court, and is present only in the person of his business managers. True, a few seigneurs of the West and central France still live on their manors: they are usually the most hard up. True, *métayage* is unthinkable without the frequent presence of the landlord, but nowadays he often enlists some steward to supervise the minutiae of sharing out. The mainstays of the rentier group, and the biggest landowners in particular, have long been absent, enticed to the towns, especially the big towns, by office, business, prestige, ambition and worldliness.

Their rents have taken the same path, and this flight from the land and non-reinvestment of most landed income probably constitutes one of the greatest failings of the ancien régime economy. The way it worked was relatively simple.

It will be established in volume two of this work that half of all state taxation was consumed by war and the debts incurred by war, the rest by the operation of the system and prestige spending; a trivial amount went into national investment, especially prior to the 1730s. It was practically compulsory for the greatest nobles, lay or clerical, ancient or recent, to adopt a way of life which forced them to spend for the sake of appearance, and keep on spending to the point of debt and even bankruptcy, unless the king made a timely intervention, as he usually did. *Cens, champarts,* tithes and leases paid for coach and pair, fine clothes, cooks and chambermaids, diamonds and gaming, opera girls and rare books, antiquities and medallions. Yet all this conspicuous expenditure, so necessary for 'living up to one's station' gave employment to decorators, builders and artists. The few great nobles with enough sense to make practical investments arrived late in the day and were active in the plantations of the Caribbean, business and the new industries rather than in the countryside.

The bourgeois tended to be more prudent and far-sighted, at least so far as the earlier generations were concerned. They saved and lent, and invested some of their cash in building but a great deal more in official posts which the king allowed to be sold and resold piecemeal. The more affluent were almost alone in being able to buy and build up estates, although they hardly ever made improvements. Essentially, their motives for acquiring landed income were not so much financial as social; they thirsted for the propertied seigneurial status and semblance and half-illusion of nobility that went with the addition of the name of a farm to their family name. The progression from Arnolphe to M. de la Souche was a long-lived and fundamental process, and Molière is not alone in describing it.*

The rarity of rural reinvestment expressed a lack of confidence in the land which remained a brake on the economic fate of the country for a long time. After 1750 – again this key date – the physiocrats bent their efforts towards denouncing and remedying this mistake, but their efforts came late and their efficiency is unproven – was it enough to publish pamphlets? was the 'back to the land' craze among the enlightened nobility deep-rooted, widespread and lasting? We know that the experiments of the marquis de Turbilly in Anjou existed only in his imagination.

The peasants occasionally realized how little they mattered to those who might have helped them or given them a lead. Many of the *cahiers de doléances* attacked this drainage of the countryside's best resources into the towns; true, their accusations were mainly levelled at the higher clergy and the unpopular regular clergy who misappropriated the tithes, took straw away only to sell it again, and did not even provide poor relief for the tithed parishes.

BEYOND RENTS AND RENTIERS

The interests and residence of rentier and rent-payer put them all too clearly on opposite sides, and this *de facto* opposition often

---

* In *L'École de femmes,* Arnolphe also styles himself M. de la Souche. – Tr.

became a very conscious one in the long run. Yet it does not account for every aspect of the ancien régime, for at least three reasons.

Firstly, it ignores a host of middle-men who are the link between the places where the goods are produced and collected, as well as the various intendants, farmers general, sub-farmers, excise-men and tax-collectors. These are essential spheres in which social mobility is surprisingly rapid.

Secondly, an increasing (but very minor) number of merchants, manufacturers, businessmen and financiers are gradually coming to the forefront and occupying the growth sectors of the national economy, and the cornerstone of their activities and power is certainly not land revenue. They live in the big towns, and whether they are bourgeois or noble, native or foreign, their adaptation to the ancient system of landed revenue and rentiers is negative, indirect or secondary. They are the men of the future, and some of them are aware of it.

Even in what might be called the 'classic' ancien régime – prior to 1750 – it is not enough to identify, isolate and characterize the types of rent and the rentier class in order to get a full and detailed picture of the social machinery and the upper strata of society. In a world which is hypersensitive to tradition, appearances and rank, the juridical and outward structures often conceal those deeper structures to which we have drawn attention. They are concealed, but they are there. Instead of hemming ourselves in with the age-old categories of *oratores, bellatores, laboratores,* we shall therefore have to make the attempt to understand at least what the nobility and bourgeoisie, or nobilities and bourgeoisies, really were.

DOCUMENTS
25 SOCIETY AND STATE ACCORDING TO QUESNAY

I

The nation comprises but three classes of citizen: the productive class, the proprietor class, and the sterile class.

The productive class is that which recreates the annual wealth of the nation by working the land, which advances the costs of agricultural labours, and pays the annual revenues of the landowners . . .

The proprietor class comprises the sovereigns, the landowners and the tithe-owners. This class is kept by the revenue or net yield of agriculture, paid yearly by the productive class after that class has deducted from its annually recreated produce the wealth necessary in order to reimburse itself for its annual advances and to maintain its working capital.

The sterile class is made up of all the citizens employed upon services and works other than agriculture, and whose costs are paid by the productive class.

> François Quesnay, *Analyse de la formule arithmétique du tableau économique*, June 1766, printed in *François Quesnay et la physiocratie* (Institut National d'Études Démographiques, 1958), vol. II, 793–4.

II

... SECURITY OF PROPERTY IS THE ESSENTIAL FOUNDATION OF THE ECONOMIC ORDER OF SOCIETY [in capitals in the text].

... The sovereign authority should be one and indivisible, and above every individual in society and all the unjust undertakings of private interests.... The idea of checks and balances in government is a pernicious one.... The division of societies into different orders of citizens some of whom exercise authority over others destroys the general interest of the nation and introduces a clash of private interests among the various classes of citizens: this division would overthrow the governmental order of an agricultural realm, which ought to bend every interest towards one main objective, the prosperity of agriculture, which is the source of all the wealth of the State and of all the citizens.

> Quesnay, *Maximes générales du gouvernement économique d'un royaume agricole, 1767,* ibid., 949–50.

26 TITHE-RATES IN BASSE-PROVENCE, *c.* 1730
(in 179 rural communities)

Rate	No. of communities	Rate	No. of communities
1/8	1	1/13	14
1/10	5	1/14	19
1/11	8	1/15	25
1/12	12	1/16	36

Rate	No. of communities	Rate	No. of communities
1/17	7	1/21	5
1/18	8	1/24–1/50	8
1/19	1	Varying	17
1/20	13		

Table based on René Baehrel, *Une Croissance, la Basse-Provence rurale (fin du* XVIe *siècle-1789)* (S.E.V.P.E.N., 1961), 752.

27 TITHE-RATES IN THE DIOCESE OF COMMINGES

Tibiran (seneschalcy of Auch)

4 in 31 for grains, 1 in 10 for wine, flax and small livestock.

Barbazan (seneschalcy of Pamiers)

The chapter of Saint-Bertrand customarily receives the entire tithe. Wheat, maslin, oats, barley and other fruits which are known in the area, maize, flax, hemp, etc. 4 in 31 for grains; 1 in 10 for wine and for small livestock.

Nizan (seneschalcy of Toulouse)

Tithes on: wheat, rye, barley, beans, marrowfats and green peas, maize, flax and wine. Rate: the tithe is paid at one in ten. . . . The chapter of Saint-Bertrand takes $\frac{5}{8}$ of the fruits, the archdeacon of Riviere $\frac{1}{8}$, the curé . . . $\frac{1}{4}$.

Oô (seneschalcy of Auch)

Tithes on: wheat, maslin, barley, black and white millet, peas, lentils, beans, hemp and flax . . . The wheat, maslin and hemp pay one in eight. The barley, millet, peas, lentils and beans, one in nine. Tithe-owners: the chapter of Saint-Bertrand for three quarters of the grains and small livestock; the prior of Sarrancolin receives the remaining quarter.

Encausse (seneschalcy of Pamiers)

Tithes on every kind of fruit, but hay by composition, wine by the bottle. Rate: one in 10.

Tithe-owners: the bishop, archdeacon and commander of Monsaunes.

From Dr Armand Sarramon, *Les Paroisses du diocèse de Comminges en 1786, Collection de Documents inédits sur l'histoire économique de la Révolution française* (Bibliothèque Nationale, 1968), 45, 46, 201, 329, 426.

NB: These tithe-rates, almost always of one tenth or more, are found in nearly all the parishes examined; they appear to be usual throughout the South-West.

28 INVENTORY OF THE ESTATE AND MARQUISATE OF MAULE (YVELINES) IN 1736

... Which estate includes the *bourg* of Maule, consisting of two parishes ... in which place there is high, middle and low justice ...

To which marquisate ... is joined the fief of Bataille-Poucin, which includes part of the parish of Aunay, adjoining the aforesaid Maule ... [where] there is the right of high, middle and low justice ...

Item, the right of *grurie* [on woodland produce] over the aforesaid estate ...

Item, the right of exchange, consisting of one twelfth of the price of any parcel of land changing hands within the bounds of the aforesaid estate of Maule.

Item, rights of *censives, lods et ventes, saisines* and fining over all houses and lands situated within the length and breadth of the aforesaid marquisate.

Item, the right of *rouage* [on cart-wheels], which is 4 *deniers parisis* per wine-waggon ... two per cart [Paris coinage, a relic of earlier times, is worth one fourth more than Tours coinage].

Item, *banalités* of baking, milling and wine-pressing over all the subjects of the aforesaid marquisate.

Item, right of market each week ... and two yearly fairs ...

Item, right of measuring wine and grains, and stallage ... both on fair- and market-days and other days ...

Item, transit right on all beasts, harness and merchandise ... entering the aforesaid marquisate by land or water.

Item, right of wine-shipment ... measurement and weighing ... prohibition on the sale of wine [except by the seigneur] for one month each year ... right of fishing in the River Mauldre ... game right ...

All which rights are well established by the ancient vows of the said estate, and recently confirmed by decision of the Châtelet and decree of the Parlement ...

The following farms belong to the aforesaid marquisate.

1. The barony of Palmort, consisting of one large farm ... 60 *arpents* (1 *arpent* = 51 ares) of pasture ... 230 of arable ... five of meadow, leased for the annual sum of	2,266 *livres*
2. The farm of Bois Henry ... 234 *arpents*, leased at	2,661 *l.*
3. The farm of La Baste, leased at	762 *l.*

4.　The farm of the Radet mill (mill, house, lands), leased at 1,251 *l.* 10 *sols*

5.　The farm of Les Granges 1,798 *l.*

6.　The farm of the La Chaussée mill 839 *l.*

7.　The farm of the town mill 939 *l.*

8.　Also the 3 millers . . . deliver an annual 24 *septiers* of corn to the château, of which 23 go to the prior of Maule; remainder, 1 *septier* 25 *l.*

9.　The farm of grain measurement 535 *l.*

10.　The farm of stallage . . . under the market-hall . . . and in the square 560 *l.*

11.　The farm of the cloven hoof [livestock] 200 *l.*

12.　The Aunay wine-press 50 *l.*

13.　For the office of clerk of the court, and scrivening 120 *l.*

14.　The great meadows 1,500 *l.*

15.　The underwoods of Maule 3,463 *l.* 12 *s.*

16.　The château wine-press 100 *l.*

17.　The château pigeon-house 300 *l.*

18.　*Censives* in cash, grain and poultry 415 *l.*

19.　*Lods et ventes* at 1/12 690 *l.*

(plus eleven other minor sources of revenue)

Total annual revenue of the marquisate 19,069 *livres* 8 *sols*

Document printed in Marcel LACHIVER, *Histoire de Meulan et de sa région par les textes* (Meulan, 1965), 428 pp., 159–62.

29 EXAMPLE OF *MÉTAYGE* NEAR PARTHENAY (DEUX-SÈVRES) 1649

. . . in the Parthenay court of contracts for Marshal de la Meilleraie, the following were in attendance . . .

Noble homme [indicating a commoner] Pierre Buignon, sieur des Belles-Foyes, resident in this town of Parthenay, in the name and under the authority of Matthieu Vidard, chevalier [therefore noble], sieur de Saint-Clair, King's counsellor [standard title for an office-holder], treasurer of France [a financial office] in the Généralité of Poitou at Poitiers, and resident there, for the first part;

and Toussaint and Mathurin Vernin, father and son, ox-drivers in joint association . . . for the second part;

the which sr. des Belles-Foyes . . . has this day leased and farmed out . . . [to] Vernin father and son, for seven years . . . commencing . . . next Michaelmas . . . the place and *métairie* of Besançay in the parish of Tallud . . . consisting of houses, barns, stables, pigsties, yards, vegetable gardens, threshing-floors, gardens, orchards, meadows, pastures, arable and non-arable lands, woods etc.

And this farm is made on one half of every kind of grain, wheat, maslin, oats and others . . . together with the fruit-trees of the aforesaid places, whether these be apple-, pear-, chestnut- or cherry-trees or any other kind. The which arable lands the aforesaid Vernins, father and son, shall be bound and have promised to plough, cultivate, manure and sow at the proper time and season each year in the amount customary in the fashion of the country, the aforesaid lessor to provide one half and the aforesaid Vernins, the lessees, the other half of the necessary seed. The lessees shall reap and gather in the grain at their own expense . . . and thresh, winnow, clean and prepare it to be shared out; likewise they shall be bound to pick and gather the fruits of the trees . . . And as soon as the aforesaid grain shall be threshed . . . and the aforesaid tree fruits gathered, the aforesaid lessees shall be bound to inform the aforesaid lessor so that . . . the half-share may be made . . . and the aforesaid lessees shall be bound to take and transport this half to the aforesaid town of Parthenay to the house of the aforesaid lessor . . .

The aforesaid lessor reserves one garden for himself . . . and as regards the other gardens, the lessees shall be in duty bound to lease them and to pay the aforesaid sieur des Belles-Foyes the annual sum of two kids, six pullets, six goslings, two capons, one two-year-old pig, four pounds of flax, four pounds of hemp, one bushel of green peas, twelve cheeses in season, six cream cheeses, four cartloads of faggots at fifty-two faggots per cartload . . . one cartload of rye-straw, one hare and six pounds of butter [some on All Saints' Day, the rest at Easter, Pentecost, Midsummer and Michaelmas], all deliverable to the house of the aforesaid sieur des Belles-Foyes in Parthenay, free of transport charges.

The aforesaid Vernins shall also be in duty bound to make twenty spans of ditches on the lands of the aforesaid *métairie*, at their own expense . . . and to plant live plants and also a dozen seedlings, apple- or pear-trees, for grafting . . . The aforesaid parties shall pay [the seigneurial rights owed by the *métairie* – half of those in cash, the whole of those in kind].

It is agreed between the parties that the aforesaid sieur des Belles-Foyes shall provide half of the cattle, rams and ewes necessary to stock the aforesaid *métairie*, and the aforesaid Vernins the rest of the aforesaid animals . . . their increase and profit to be equally divided.

. . . The aforesaid lessees shall keep the houses, stables and outbuildings in repair by their own labours, whereas the aforesaid lessor shall provide the requisite materials, which the aforesaid lessees shall collect and transport . . . without claiming any wage . . . They shall not fell any trees . . . They shall enjoy the aforesaid *métairie* as good heads of family . . . and keep the hedges . . . thick and close . . . [etc.].

. . . Made and concluded in the aforesaid Parthenay in the office of Bourceau, notary, on the afternoon of this fourteenth day of April sixteen hundred and forty-nine, the lessees having declared themselves unable to sign.

Signed: P. Buignon, Gaultier and Bourceau, notaries.

Minute from the Bourceau archives, printed in Dr Louis
MERLE, *La Métairie et l'évolution agraire de la Gâtine
poitevine de la fin du Moyen Age à la Révolution* (S.E.V.P.E.N.,
1958), 252 pp., 218 – 20.

30 EXAMPLE OF A 'CONSTITUTED RENT', 1647

[Contrary to normal practice, this document is given in textbook form so as to clarify the basic process.]

'On Tuesday April 16th sixteen hundred and forty-seven, in the forenoon'

1. The 'rent-vendors' or '*débirentiers*' – actually the borrowers

'In the presence of the high and mighty seigneur Messire Adrian Pierre de Tiercelin, marquis de Brosses, residing at the château of Sercus (Sarcus, Oise), both in his private capacity and in the name of and as attorney to . . . Messire Françoys de Tiercelin, counsellor-chaplain to the King, commendatory abbot of the Abbey of Saint Germer de Fly [a wealthy Benedictine foundation], to the high and mighty Lady Henriette de Joleuse, wife of the aforesaid Marquis, ànd to *noble homme* Pierre Adrian, advocate at Parlement resident in Beauvais [the Tiercelins' business adviser], who each and severally, once and for all . . . acknowledge having sold, created, settled, fixed and assigned, and hereby sell, create . . . promising to guarantee . . . against all trouble and hindrance . . .'

2. The rent-buyer, or *crédirentier* – actually the lender

   'to the profit of Jean Boicervoise, merchant burgher of Beauvais . . .'

3. The rent (*au denier* 18,* which is legal, as emerges in section 5)

   'the sum of three hundred and thirty-three *livres* six *sols* eight *deniers tournois* of annual rent in perpetuity . . . on the 17th day of April each year . . .'

4. The 'assignment', or blanket mortgage

   '. . . on each and every good, land and seigneury of the said contracting gentlemen and lady, now and in the future, wherever they may be . . . [this is the blanket mortgage] . . . and in particular on the lands and seigneuries, goods and gifts brought to the marriage contract of the aforesaid marquis and lady, drawn up before Motelet and Drouin, notaries royal, at the Châtelet of Paris, on 26th March 1646 . . . the which goods, both general and particular, the aforesaid marquises, and their sieur Adrian in their names, have to this purpose assigned and hypothecated in payment and continuance of the said rent . . . and the aforesaid marquis has [in the name of his brother the abbot] consented and agreed that the amount of the aforesaid rent shall be received from the widow Nicolas Lefevre, burgher of Beauvais, part-receiver of the aforesaid Abbey, each year . . . and the sieur Marquis . . . has transferred the farms of his lands and seigneuries to the amount of the aforesaid rent'

5. the 'rent-price' – that is, the sum lent

   '. . . this sale being made subject to the payment of the sum of six thousand *livres tournois*, counted out and paid at this present by the said buyer in *louis d'or*, and Spanish pistoles, quarter-crowns and royals, all legal tender, which the aforesaid marquis has received and removed . . .'†

6. Further legal guarantee of payment of the rent

   '. . . and in so doing, the aforesaid contracting gentlemen are disseised and divested of their goods, lands and seigneuries to the profit of the aforesaid buyer to the amount of the aforesaid rent . . .'

7. Redemption clause

   '. . . and whereas the aforesaid rent be called perpetual, nevertheless it is stipulated that the aforesaid contracting gentlemen shall have the option of redeeming it outright . . . upon paying the aforesaid buyer a like sum of

---

* This is the current method of expressing interest-rates. *Au denier* 18 means a rate of $\frac{1}{18}$, about 5.5 per cent; *au denier* 2 would be 50 per cent. – Tr.

† The notary's minute which succeeds this one on the afternoon of the same day reveals that part of the 6000 *livres* was actually lent, through Boicervoise, by the Tiercelins' own business adviser, Adrian (who appears in the bill of sale as a borrower!).

six thousand *livres* . . .' [The rent was in fact redeemed by the marquis's son, as shown by a marginal note added to the minute on 29/7/1682.]

Signed: Adrian Pierre de Tiercelin

Adrian Boicervoise

Leclerc (notary) de Nully (notary)

Excerpt from the minutes of Maître Jouan deposited in the archives of the département of Oise, series E, Étude de Nully, 1647.

31   A FARMER-USURER IN GAILLAC:
GUILLAUME MASENX (BASED ON HIS DAY-BOOK)

Guillaume Masenx is born in Castelnau-de-Montmirail, western Langue-doc, around 1495, of a family of proprietors, merchants, priests and simple *métayers*. His uncle Antoine, a priest of Castelnau, gives him a tiny smattering of education. Guillaume is never to know either Latin or French. He speaks the *langue d'oc* . . . and his spelling is atrocious . . . To make up for his lack of instruction, Guillaume has a nose for business: in 1516, he marries the daughter of a farmer who works one of the properties of the commandery of Saint-Pierre de Gaillac. Guillaume moves in with his father-in-law; by 1518, he has taken charge, has become the titular lessee and is laying down the law to father-, mother- and brother-in-law, who supervise the farmhands, sell wine and corn and collect rents and *cens* on his behalf. In 1530 Guillaume, whose acumen has impressed the com-mandery, takes over the farm of another of its estates, Senouilhac, and sets up his mother-in-law there. In 1535 he is given the farm of a third estate, and also becomes the farmer general and factotum of the com-mandery. . . .

Everything is grist to his mill. At first he lends, grain or cash, at short terms and high interest: for a month (*dins un mes*), a week (*deo paga d'aysi* VIII *jorns*), or else, in his own grim formula, 'at will, from day to day'. He lends his *bordiers* (who do not even receive seed) the wherewithal to marry off their daughters or sisters: cash, cloth . . . old wine, grain; the sheep for the wedding-feast – on credit. The loans are made against pledges of land: later on, Masenx will expand his own estates with the fields of his debt-ridden borrowers.

Furthermore Masenx, the farmer-usurer, sometimes refers to interest, or *paga*, in spite of the Church: his accounts mention the loan of grain to the younger Mandret, of Vors, at fourteen per cent in ten days, which comes to four hundred per cent a year. On other occasions, the interest is disguised by cooking the books. . . . Sometimes a deliberate mistake lets usury into the deal: *deniers* become *sous, livres tournois* turn into *écus,* three quintals of hay lent in 1538 have mysteriously transformed themselves into five quintals by the time they are paid back. Masenx's account-book is crammed with swindles.... Our man is also a grain-banker.... Masenx's secret lies in lending barley, rye, oats or vetch and having himself repaid, bushel for bushel, in wheat. Or else he plays on price-variations, often of his own devising: in 1545, he prices the corn he lends at 4*l.* 10*s.* per *setier*; the following year he is repaid (in kind) at 2*l.* per *setier*, and the borrower is forced to pay back twice the amount he received ... meanwhile, Masenx is selling his wheat on the Gaillac market at 5*l.* 6*s.* per *setier.* ... He is also a labour-creditor if need be; Paul Bru, of the Bru *mas*, buys a quintal of hay from Masenx in 1535, and has neither the cash nor the grain to pay it back – never mind, he signs on for a day's ploughing. Likewise with Pierre Toulouse: in 1535–6, he borrows grain, rye, vetch and old wine. Insolvent, he squares his debt by labouring for our man. Other needy debtors reap, ditch, cart or repair Master Guillaume's roof. Masenx gives nothing away.

.... Indebtedness ... leads to transfers of land: one of Masenx's neighbours, Ramon Fabre, buys cloth from him on credit; in April 1531, an expensive spring, he borrows grain. Seven years go by, and Masenx leaves the debt dormant. In 1539, Fabre borrows grain again, giving as security various lands which pay Masenx an 'annual pension' from now on. Finally he liquidates his grain debt by selling his land at Resals to Master Guillaume (1545). In 1546, a year of dearth, the scene repeats itself. On 8 April, the Fabre family has run out of grain. Once again, Raymond comes knocking at Masenx's door ... and he provides the starving man with seven *demi-cartières* of grain (about 3.3 bushels) to feed a whole family until the next harvest. Raymond Fabre has the knife at his throat; the debt is repayable 'from day to day' at the lender's pleasure. To pay if off, he has to sell his remaining piece of land: *paga cant vendet la terra*, Masenx notes drily in his journal. In 1546, the land pays for the bread, and from now on the Fabres are *bordiers* delivering to Masenx half the yield of the very same land which their ancestors once owned.

Masenx is nothing if not consistent ...

Le Roy-Ladurie, Les Paysans de Languedoc, op. cit.,
303–6.

FURTHER READING
FOR CHAPTERS 4, 5 AND 6
(THE RURAL WORLD)

1

The basic works have already been cited (chapter 3, p. 75).

There is a more detailed outline by the author of this book in vol. 2 of the *Histoire économique et sociale de la France moderne, 1660–1789* in the section entitled 'Le poids du monde rural' (P.U.F., in preparation).

2 WRITTEN UNDER THE ANCIEN RÉGIME

ESTIENNE, Charles, and LIEBAULT, Jean, *L'Agriculture et maison rustique . . .*, 1st ed., 1561, numerous reprints.

SERRES, Olivier de, *Théâtre d'agriculture et ménage des champs . . .*, 1st ed., 1600, numerous reprints; the best is the François de Neufchâteau edition (1803), under the Consulate.

Boisguilbert, Pierre de, ou la naissance de l'Économie politique (Institut National d'Études Démographiques, 1966), 2 vols, 1,031 pp. (particularly vol. II, which contains the author's own texts).

VAUBAN, *Project d'une dixme royale*, 1707 (ed. Coornaert, Alcan, 1933), 296 pp.

Quesnay, François, et la physiocratie (published by the Institut National d'Études Démographiques, 1958), 2 vols, 1,005 pp. (particularly vol. II, which contains the texts).

3 GENERAL BACKGROUND WORKS

BLOCH, Marc, *Les Caractères originaux de l'histoire rurale française* (A. Colin, 1952 and 1956), 2 vols., 2nd vol. completed by R. DAUVERGNE.
(This is the great pioneer work, first printed in 1931 – in Oslo!)

BRAUDEL, Fernand, *Civilisation matérielle et capitalisme* (A. Colin, 1967), 463 pp.

DEVÈZE, Michel, *La Vie de la forêt française au XVIᵉ siècle* (S.E.V.P.E.N., 1961), 2 vols, 473 + 325 pp.

DION, Roger, *Essai sur la formation du paysage rural français* (Tours, Arrault, 1934).

Ibid, *Histoire de la vigne et du vin en France des origines au XIXᵉ siècle* (Paris, 1959), 768 pp. (probably the finest history book of the last few decades).

DUBY, Georges, *L'Économie rurale et la vie des campagnes dans l'Occident médiéval* (Aubier, 1962), 2 vols (in this area, the Middle Ages are already the ancien régime).

MEYNIER, André, *Les Paysages agraires* (A. Colin, 1958) (sober and indispensable contribution from a geographer).

SLICHER VAN BATH, B.H., *The Agrarian History of Western Europe, 500–1850* (London, Arnold, 1963), 364 pp. (the standard work).

L'Agriculture en Europe aux XVIIe *et* XVIIIe *siècles*, reports by Meuvret, Hoskins and Slicher van Bath in Xe *Congresso Internazionale di Scienzi storiche, Roma, 1965, Relazioni*, vol. IV (Florence, Sansoni), 137 – 226. (Point of departure for European comparative studies.)

Étude comparée du grand domaine depuis la fin du Moyen Age (by several hands) in *Première conférence internationale d'histoire économique, Stockholm 1960* (Paris and the Hague, Mouton et Cie), 309–432. (Useful and uneven, as usual in this type of compilation.)

Villages désertés et histoire économique, XIe–XVIIIe *siècle* (several hands), S.E.V.P.E.N., 1965, 619 pp. (exceptionally fine English and German contributions; the rest uneven).

4 REGIONAL STUDIES
(In the last analysis, these are the works which are extending our knowledge; here the historians have followed in the footsteps of the geographers.)

A. Northern France and the Paris basin
Add to the works by LEFEBVRE, GOUBERT and DEYON, already mentioned:

BRUNET, Pierre, *Structure agraire et économie rurale des plateaux tertiaires entre la Seine et l'Oise* (Caen, Caron et Cie, 1960), 552 pp., illustrated. (Social geography thesis based on detailed research in archives.)

DEMANGEON, Albert, *La Picardie et les régions voisines* (or *La Plaine picarde*) (Hachette, 1905). This geography thesis has not been superseded for historians, in spite of its date.

DEYON, Pierre, *Contribution à l'étude des revenus fonciers en Picardie, les fermages de l'Hôtel-Dieu d'Amiens et leurs variations de 1515 à 1789* (Lille, R. Giard, n.d. (1967)), 129 pp.

DION, Roger, *Le Val de Loire* (Tours, Arrault, 1933), unusually penetrating, and particularly important for historians.

FONTENAY, Michel, *Paysans et marchands ruraux de la vallée de l'Essonne dans la seconde moitié du XVIIᵉ siècle,* in *Paris et Ile-de-France, mémoires publiés par la fédération des sociétés historiques et archéologiques de Paris et de l'Ile-de-France,* vol. IX, 1958, 157–282 (one of the best studies in depth, a lot more useful than cursory syntheses, and very much more vivid).

MIREAUX, Émile, *Une Province française au temps du grand roi: la Brie* (Hachette, 1958), 352 pp. (valuable only for the archival documents utilized: this eminent polymath is no expert on the seventeenth century).

VENARD, Marc, *Bourgeois et paysans au XVIIᵉ siècle. Recherches sur le rôle des bourgeois parisiens dans la vie agricole au Sud de Paris au XVIIᵉ siècle* (S.E.V.P.E.N., 1957), 126 pp. (same comments as for the Fontenay, above).

B. Western France

BOIS, Paul, *Paysans de l'Ouest* (Le Mans, 1960) (late ancien régime and nineteenth century).

GOUBERT, Pierre, *Recherches d'histoire rurale brettone, XVIIᵉ – XVIIIᵉ siècles* in Bulletin de la Société d'Histoire Moderne, series XIII, No 2, 1965 (summary of work carried out by a number of good students).

MERLE, Dr Louis, *La Métairie et l'évolution agraire de la Gâtine poitevine de la fin du Moyen Age à la Révolution* (S.E.V.P.E.N., 1958), 252 pp. (altogether first-class: scholarly base, brilliant format).

MEYER, Jean, *La Noblesse bretonne au XVIIIᵉ siècle* (S.E.V. P.E.N., 1966), 2 vols 1,292 pp.; this thesis from Rennes naturally concentrates on the Breton rural world, dominated by the nobility.

MUSSET, René, *Le Bas-Maine* (Paris, 1917). (Geography thesis, still not superseded.)

PLAISSE, André, *La Baronnie du Neubourg* (P.U.F., 1961), 760 pp. (precise, excellent monograph).

SÉE, Henri, *Les Classes rurales en Bretagne, du* XVIᵉ *siècle à la Révolution* (Alcan, 1906). (Never superseded, in spite of occasional superficiality.)

SION, Jules, *Les Paysans de la Normandie Orientale* (Paris, 1909). (The best of all the theses on regional geography.)

C. Eastern France

Thanks to Roupnel, Saint-Jacob and a few others, Burgundy has been and remains particularly favoured by the best kind of rural history.

ROUPNEL, Gaston, *La Ville et la campagne au* XVIIᵉ *siècle, étude sur les populations du pays dijonnais* (2nd ed., Colin, 1955), 357 pp. (Paris thesis which went almost unnoticed in 1922, but in fact the first great book on rural history, acute, eminently readable, sometimes rather hasty – the author was also a novelist and poet.)

SAINT-JACOB, Pierre de, *Les Paysans de la Bourgogne du Nord . . .* (1960). See Further Reading, chapter 3.

Ibid., *Documents relatifs à la communauté villageoise en Bourgogne du milieu du* XVIIᵉ *siècle à la Révolution* (Dijon, Bernigaud et Privat, 1962), 157 pp.

Ibid., *Etudes sur l'ancienne communauté rurale en Bourgogne,* in *Annales de Bourgogne,* years 1941, 1943, 1946, 1953 passim.

The other regions are, for the moment, under-represented. These may be consulted:

JUILLARD, Étienne, *La Vie rurale dans la plaine de Basse-Alsace* (Strasbourg, 1953, geography thesis).

Paysans d'Alsace (Strasbourg, F.-X. Le Roux et Cie, 1959), 638 pp. (By several hands, and uneven.)

D. Southern France

For the moment there are three top-class works: BAEHREL (Basse-Provence), the outstanding LE ROY-LADURIE (Bas-Languedoc) and POITRINEAU (Basse-Auvergne), already cited. A number of fresh studies are in preparation.

These may still be consulted:

DEFFONTAINES, Pierre, *Les Hommes et leurs travaux dans les pays de la Moyenne-Garonne* (Lille, 1932, geography thesis).

Various works by the excellent rural geographer Daniel FAUCHER, such as: *La Vie rurale vue par un géographe* (Toulouse, 1962).

LÉON, Pierre (et al.), *Structures économiques et problèmes sociaux du monde rural dans la France du Sud-Est* (Lyon & Paris, 1966). Good detailed monographs.

VII · THE NOBILITY:
IN SEARCH OF A DEFINITION

The position occupied by this chapter will come as no surprise. It has seemed logical first of all to locate the foundations of ancien régime society, and these we have found in the countryside. More, perhaps, than any other 'order', 'estate', 'body' or 'class', the nobility is inconceivable outside the rural context, would not exist without it, and derives almost all its sustenance from it.

As regards the first traditional 'order' – which might have been expected to claim precedence – its spiritual unity (sacred 'unction') and remarkable organization (mainly material, and monopolized by the prelates) have not prevented it from separating socially into two classes that were clearly antagonistic – not too strong a word. We shall find them here and elsewhere (particularly in volume 2) and first, quite naturally, among the nobility.

Except in England and Sweden, where its boundaries are quite well known, it is seldom an easy task to define the nobility. In France the reality, already fluid and hard to grasp, has been so blurred by futility, incompetence, pride and passions that it is necessary to dwell at some length upon what the nobility is not, or is no longer.

1   THE NEGATIVE ELEMENTS
COMMON FALLACIES
The common fallacies arise out of generalizing from particular identifications which were not necessarily false at a given time or place. The most popular errors have to do with the particle, titles and coats of arms.

The particle, the little *de* joining the true 'name', given at baptism, to the 'surname' which has become the patronymic, usually indicates a family's place of origin. It is frequently found among commoners, and especially among peasants: thus Pierre de Frocourt and Jacques de Lihus, seventeenth-century burghers of Beauvais, were descended from peasants born in the two neighbouring parishes whose name they bore. Among the many Frenchmen of Flemish descent, the *de* is simply the definite article: De Ridder is the same as Le Chevalier. Many genuine noblemen – the Gouffiers of the sixteenth century, for example – did not take the particle, and the really great would not bother to include it in their signatures, which were often reduced to a Christian name, or that of a principal estate: 'Louis' or 'Noailles'. Not that this debarred the particle from hinting at greater things, even under the ancien régime – any number of stout burghers played on the illusion by tacking onto their father's name the name of their *métairie,* and often brought off the deception. But the particle proves nothing in itself.

It must also be emphasised that true titles (from baron to duke) belong to estates, not men, and that only one man in every generation may assume them. It is true that 'courtesy' titles – mainly that of marquis – were sold or countenanced, especially during and after the reign of Louis XIV, who cashed in on everything and pursued a deliberately anti-noble policy. And yet the majority of noblemen were not 'titled'. All the same, there is one short word, placed immediately before or after their name, by which they can often be quite reliably identified in nearly every province in France. This is the word '*escuyer*', or on a higher plane, '*chevalier*'. Except in Normandy, apparently, the commoner is distinguished by the title '*noble homme*'. Throughout the Midi, south of the Gironde-Geneva line which is one of the great 'frontiers' of the realm, the standard mark of nobility is the epithet 'noble' placed before the name. '*Noble homme* Jean Dupont' is sure to be a commoner (with the possible Norman exception); 'Jean Dupont, *escuyer*' is a genuine nobleman (or a clever fraud) and so is 'noble Jean Dupont' in the *langue d'oc* lands; writing his name 'Du Pont' makes no difference anywhere.

As for coats of arms, they are no longer of interest under the ancien régime except as puzzles. Anybody could award himself a coat of arms, and even have it registered, for hard cash, by a royal dispensary which did a roaring-trade from 1696 onward. After that date, and even a little previously, heraldry stopped registering anything except vanity. Even the old noble privilege of 'crested' escutcheons (surmounted by a helmet, a crown, or both) is in decline; soon we find Voltaire adopting a marquis' coronet, and not in jest.

THE EXPLICABLE CONFUSIONS
SEIGNEURS AND NOBILITY

In everyday parlance, a *'grand seigneur'* was definitely an indisputable, wealthy, powerful nobleman of ancient family. But possession of a seigneury was no longer a legal indication of nobility (cf. chapter 4, p. 82), since seigneuries were bought and sold like any other piece of property. But there still existed vivid memories linking nobility with the possession of great estates and the exercise of important rights such as justice, so much so that the acquisition of a seigneury by some *bon bourgeois* still represented one more step up his personal ladder towards nobility, or the semblance of nobility.

FIEF AND NOBILITY

The word 'fief', whose meaning seems so clear in the works of the medievalists, became an extraordinarily vexed question under the ancien régime, and a pitfall for the wariest jurist: Guyot, the last and most subtle of them, fought shy of defining it. In Burgundy, 'fief' was just everyday parlance for seigneury, but tends to refer to the 'central' part of the seigneury, the *'réserve'* or *'domaine'*. In the most common usage, 'fief' indicates a noble estate (and sometimes various special rights, which we shall not go into). In many provinces these noble estates, as opposed to commoner estates (the *censives*), have a special status: they are not handed down and divided like the rest (passing to the eldest son, where primogeniture obtains), do not pay the same dues and are not subject to the same taxation. In the Midi, they are subject to none at all. But the great innovation of the ancien régime is the separation of the condition of men from the condition of estates which was gradually written into the various customs (except in Béarn) in the late sixteenth century, as ratified by article 258 of the Decree of Orléans in 1579. This produced two consequences:

a) Any commoner who 'holds' a fief, and therefore a noble estate, and cannot, by virtue of his condition, discharge the duties of a fief-holder – basically military service – owes instead (barring local privilege!) the right of *'franc-fief'*, which has been appropriated by the king's treasury. This right is an expensive one: usually a year of the fief's revenue in every twenty, plus an additional year's revenue at each change of ownership. It was extremely unpopular, being both humiliating (proof of common birth), costly, and likely to lower the value of the estate concerned.

b) In the northern half of the country, noble estates do not diminish the incumbent commoner's liability to the *taille*; conversely, an *'exempt de taille'* (nobles always are) pays nothing, even on his commoner estates. The exact opposite holds true in the southern half, where noble estates never pay the *taille*, whatever the station of their holder may be, but the most blue-blooded noblemen pay the *taille* on their commoner estates. From the point of view of the relationship between nobility and the principal tax, North and Midi are worlds apart.

Notwithstanding these complications, which seem so distant today, the upshot is that under the ancien régime the noble status of an estate is never transmitted to an individual, except in Béarn (but it takes a hundred years there!). Similarly, individual status does not ennoble an estate, although it may be that exceptions will emerge in provinces formerly belonging to the Habsburg Empire.

2　THE SURVIVAL OF THE OLD DEFINITIONS
A MILITARY CLASS?

Aristotle, and after him Christendom, St Thomas, and most ancien régime theoreticians divided society into *oratores, bellatores, laboratores* according to the model provided by ancient Indo-European sources. The juridical and rhetorical tradition was an extremely stubborn one, in spite of the fact that it no longer bore a relationship to the reality. From the sixteenth century onward, the 'military class' tends more and more to include a considerable majority of commoners, although command generally devolves upon the nobility.

Yet at this point we do approach the elements of a definition, albeit an old one: at the height of the Middle Ages, the nobleman was usually the man who fought on horseback, hence the survival of the terms *chevalier* and *écuyer* as common designations for true nobles. Hence too the military ideal which held good among most of the French nobility, even – and perhaps particularly – among the poorer of them. The same ideal also took root among the recently ennobled: to wear and wield a sword, preferably at the head of a bought armed company, reinforced the dignity of a new-born, often despised nobility. Similarly, it is clear that in the far-reaching 'sectarian' reaction which set in during the eighteenth century the nobility laid the main emphasis on its military vocation and tried to squeeze the utmost advantage out of it, including a quasi monopoly of the higher ranks of the army, increasingly realized towards the end of the century.

But it is more obvious still that whereas the nobility is (partly) descended from the old warrior class, tends to serve by means of the sword and has concocted a warlike image of itself, it is not certain that the majority of noblemen were soldiers, still less their ancestry. What we have here is the survival and resurrection of an ancient ideal.

A FEUDAL CLASS?

Like the word 'fief', 'feudalism' under the ancien régime denotes a tangle of confusion and controversies. Nevertheless it still contains a nucleus of antiquity, whether it is now seen as something sacred and worthy of respect or as outworn and ludicrous. It may be argued that at this point the word had two sets of connotations:

1. The chain of vassalage which had bound man to man, from the lowest vassal to the highest suzerain – a position which the king had managed to occupy from a very early date. Complementary symbols: the inferior pledges 'fealty and homage' to the superior, and receives from him the 'gift' of a 'fief'. This ceremony is supposed to occur between noblemen (which is no longer the case under the ancien régime), and has not completely disappeared, but it has branched out and profoundly changed.

It has been extended to commoners, in the first place because they held fiefs, as we have seen, in the second place because those whom their noble seigneurs sometimes called 'vassals' sometimes continued to believe that they were protected by the seigneur from the depredations of the royal '*gabeleurs*'* until the mid-seventeenth century. Again, in the more backward provinces (the West, the Centre and the duchy and county of Burgundy), some peasants clung to various forms of ancestral homage to their seigneur: kneeling at the château gates, kissing the latch, presenting newly-weds, ritual offerings etc. At the end of the eighteenth century, the 'vassals' usually rejected such practices.

At and even below the level of the gentry, one custom survived for some time – until 1660 at least: that of the poorer 'commending' or 'giving' themselves to the more powerful. The latter would feed, house and equip the former, whose person, sword and goods were at their disposal. Most of the noble, and even a few peasant uprisings took their strength from this kind of subordination, clientship and fealty, for a while at any rate. Not that these commitments of one man to another are exclusive either to the 'feudal' era or the ancien régime: they are prevalent both in ancient civilizations and in our own, and may be observed in the retinues of the French kings and their principal ministers, notably around Richelieu, with his '*créatures*', and even Colbert, who was surrounded by a kind of 'lobby' which remains to be investigated. We need not look very far to find phenomena of the same order in the twentieth century.

It is certain that these original ties, which typify particular eras rather than groups, were now especially prevalent in the world of the nobility, where they constituted a kind of substitute for old-time vassalage. Yet they do not in themselves suffice to define the nobility, since they existed outside it.

2. The usual association with feudalism is the image of a strong castle girded with stout walls and surrounded by rich estates, law-giver to a whole region or province; in the remote but not forgotten days of royal instability, this law could maintain a modicum or order, organization and security in the area concerned. The great feudal magnates had taken over some of the royal prerogatives, including those of justice, recruitment, levying taxes and striking coinage. The early decades of the ancien régime would baffle com-

---

* Originally salt-tax collectors, *gabeleurs* in common parlance were any collectors of unpopular taxation. – Tr.

prehension without the reminder of this recent past, or 'past present'. The former power of the dukes of Normandy, the counts of Toulouse and Provence and the dukes of Anjou and particularly of Burgundy was still a living memory. The religious wars and the regencies had given a new lease of life to the '*grands*' who had been granted appanages or provincial governorships as a result of royal weakness. The power of Mayenne and of the Condé family, to take only two examples, resided in the lands, fortresses and governorships they held, where they thought of themselves as owners and near-kings, and whose financial and human resources they tapped. Even after the Fronde, which closes a great 'feudal' period, a number of troublesome fiefs still belonged to foreign monarchs (Charolais) and others retained the altogether medieval right of striking coinage at the height of the 'great king's' reign (Orange, Dombes, Sedan, Cugnan and the duchy of Henrichemont).

It is certain that all the provincial power slowly eroded by successive monarchs had some sort of relation to the nobility – the higher nobility at any rate – and might be seen as representing it.

A PROPRIETARY AND LANDED CLASS?
The link between the nobility and the land which provided its various kinds of revenue constitutes one of the basic elements of its make-up, but decreasingly so, since noblemen are drifting away from the land, as we have seen, and the land is drifting away from them, taken over by 'masters', even seigneurs, who came straight from the wealthy commonalty. There should be no illusions about this ancient and still living link between the nobility and the land: it is not proven that the nobles had been the seigneurs of the majority of French estates, and it is certain that they held less than a third of them. The landed class *par excellence* – whose combined smallholdings outnumber all the noble estates – was still the peasantry.

The definitions we have suggested are therefore either inaccurate, inadequate, or outdated. Then what does constitute nobility?

3   ELEMENTS OF A DEFINITION:
THE NOBILITY, A RACE?
It is practically meaningless to reproduce the jurists' definition of the nobility as the second of the 'three orders' of the realm. The first

order merges into the other two, and the third constitutes either a sort of dustbin (which is neither clerical nor noble) or a sham – the wealthier bourgeoisie and officials make up and claim to 'represent' the Third Estate to the exclusion of a vast majority which is not worth even mentioning. To add that the nobility is 'one of the two privileged orders' hardly gets us much further, since it is one of the characteristics of the ancien régime that just about everybody has privileges, except for the peasants of the Capetian *vieux domaine*. It cannot be often enough reiterated that the ancien régime was a world of 'private laws' (*leges privatae*, privileges) which held out to the end against 'general' law.

The nobility is defined by its antonym, the commonalty. In the contemporary view, the commoner, non-noble or ignoble – rather like the old serf or villein whose lowliness he has in a sense inherited – bears a stain, blot, or leavening of impurity: it was often argued under the ancien régime that a candidate for nobility ought first to undergo a lengthy waiting period, a kind of purgation during which he would be 'decontaminated' of his common clay. These elemental, quasi magical concepts are basic and vital, and it will not be long before the nobility is echoing the tradition articulated by Boulainvilliers (in works appearing in 1727 and 1732) and claiming descent from a special race of conquerors, the Franks, who enslaved the Gallic peasants and whose 'blue blood' attested to their racial individuality. Without necessarily going to these extremes, the ancien régime nobility certainly does see itself as belonging to a race apart, whose ancient virtues of honour and military courage run undiminished in its blood. This race has been passing on its superiority since time immemorial solely by virtue of birth, or so it believes, and any number of non-nobles are attracted to the concept. It is not too gross an anachronism to qualify this position as racism.

But the French concept of a hereditary noble race is at once narrow and broad. Narrow because it is confined to legitimate offspring – only royal bastards are recognized as noble. At once broad and narrow, because only the man communicates nobility and the woman is immaterial, a mere 'vessel' communicating her husband's status, not her own. As Valéry once put it, 'nobility is seminal fluid'. Contrary to the practice of the Austrian Empire (and this is why some former imperial provinces, such as part of Franche-Comté, allow nobility to be communicated 'by the belly'), the woman may just as well be a commoner: her husband will do the ennobling. This cardinal rule has a very convenient application in the matter of what Mme de Sévigné calls 'manuring the land' – the marriage of penurious noblemen to well-endowed commoners. It also explains why nobility in France is usually counted by degrees (in the male line) and not by quarterings (in both lines), and why it is that young noblewomen and their families paid so little heed to possible common suitors: these were the true *mésalliances*.

Ancient lineage therefore lies at the heart of the matter, both for the nobles themselves and for all legislation, first customary, then royal. But how is it to be proved? It is quite obvious that no family can trace its 'proofs' back to the Franks, often not even to the Crusades. Three ways to 'prove' are usually distinguished:

a) A small number of great and powerful families never have to prove their nobility, which is established 'since time immemorial'. To ask for proof from a Rochechouart, a Rohan, a Harcourt or a Montmorency would be just as insulting as to ask it of a Capetian.

b) Various less illustrious or less powerful families may have to 'prove'. These proofs are sometimes required by the king (campaigns against fake noblemen were frequent under Louis XIV), sometimes because they are requesting an official post reserved for noblemen only, either at court, in the army, or among the Knights of Malta. Now it is only possible to 'prove' by means of authentic written documents deriving from recognized authorities such as court decisions, notarized deeds, royal decrees or, at a pinch, parish deeds, which must usually extend over three generations or one century. These documents must prove that the family has lived nobly, without derogating from its rank, serving the king and always bearing the prevailing noble designation in the province (usually '*escuyer*'), whereupon the 'race' is assured of a century's legitimate continuity.

It is immediately obvious that the law or 'custom' of the province plays the key part in this as in so many other matters; and customs vary. It is also obvious that the 'source' of nobility is not specified; it is assumed, quite optimistically perhaps, to be 'chivalric'.

c) The third instance is the simplest, and became the most usual:

the 'race' is young because the family has been ennobled at a known date by order of the sovereign, the sole creator of new noblemen. The resulting nobility was called 'modern' by the jurists, in contrast with the nobility which harks back to a remote but unknown past, the 'old' nobility.

Naturally the old self-styled nobility 'of race', 'of extraction' or 'of the sword' looks down upon this new nobility, especially that which owes its existence to venal offices, and equates it, like Saint-Simon, with the *'vile bourgeoisie'*. Notwithstanding these clashes of vanity and petulance, the fact remains that the entire nobility was juridically equal, enjoyed much the same privileges and was communicated in the same manner, by way of the 'seminal fluid' of lawful fathers. Putting it simply, and in the absence of proven descent from the companions of Clovis, the 'race' had been born an indeterminate number of centuries or generations before. Internal squabbles among the nobility are squabbles of seniority, combining duplicity, fake genealogies and diseased egos.

The nobility is singled out by its status and by its recognized privileges. What are these privileges?

4   PRIVILEGES AND DUTIES OF THE NOBILITY

It is harder than is commonly believed to give an account of the privileges of the nobility because they varied so much in time, place and interpretation. We can make a fairly academic division into three categories, and discard a fourth.

HONORIFIC PRIVILEGES

Wearing the sword remains fundamental. Unless he is very powerful in his own locality, severe action is taken against any unauthorized wearer, with the exception of soldiers, whom Vauban classified together with the gentlemen among the *'gens d'épée'*.

For a long time, it was essential to bear a crested coat of arms; Louis XII and his son felt the need to confirm this privilege in 1634 and 1665. After 1696, as we have seen, the excesses of the *'Grande Maîtrise d'Armes'* in selling cut-price coats of arms devalued this ancient privilege, and prosperous social-climbing commoners transgressed it with impunity.

The third honorific privilege is plain enough: the nobleman is judged in civil courts by the chief magistrate, and in criminal courts by the Parlement: the penalties he incurs differ from those incurred by commoners, and everybody knows that he is never hanged, but beheaded.

The privilege of hunting has usually been their exclusive preserve (but not always in Brittany). However, wealthy non-noble seigneurs have encroached upon this right, and it should be added that large-scale poaching made its own inroad.

Although we are dealing here with attitudes of mind rather than privileges, there was clearly a specifically noble life-style – lavish entertaining, horsemanship, being a good shot, fighting no duels with commoners, and above all never working with one's hands at profitable, base and 'mechanical' occupations (to do so is to 'derogate').

PRIVILEGES OF SERVICE
The nobility have access to what we may anachronistically term 'reserved occupations', in particular in the army, at court and in the Church.

ARMY
Further to the general obligation to 'serve' and to provide one's own equipment (the old vassals' duty of *auxilium*), in élite regiments such as the Gardes du Corps, and in almost all the others, there were posts open only to noblemen. In most regiments, an ordinary lieutenancy cannot usually be granted to anybody who is unable to prove four degrees of nobility. Here the rules and customs varied. In the later eighteenth century the 'noble reaction' was particularly fierce: it got much harder for commoners to become officers, or they would be confined to the lower ranks or to 'technical' corps like the Sappers, where race could not deputize for competence. This is undoubtedly one of the many causes of the Revolution.

As for the Navy, all the ranks of the fleet were restricted to noblemen only. Commoners could only become administrative officers (who were utterly despised), otherwise they confined themselves to commerce and privateering.

COURT
As a nobleman among noblemen, it is standard practice for the king to award the important and even the minor posts and functions to

what the seventeenth century called, with unconscious irony, his
'*fidèle noblesse*'. The best 'offices of the King's Household' (venery
and falconry, for instance) and the posts of squire and page were
their exclusive province. Louis XIV increased the number of pages but
required candidates to prove two centuries of nobility, and the
difficulty of doing so gave rise to a number of 'derogations'. Only
noblemen of four degrees could enter many of the bodies and
institutions close to the king's person. At least four degrees for the
Order of the Holy Ghost; four degrees for the Collège des Quatre-
Nations founded by Mazarin (the present-day Institut); 140 years
for the young ladies admitted to Madame de Maintenon's beloved
Saint-Cyr; four degrees again for the various military schools founded
in the eighteenth century, even the schools of artillery (1772) and
engineering (1776), where aptitude might have seemed essential.

CHURCH

Since the Concordat of 1516 (cf. vol. 2) the king has retained the
right of 'presenting', which in practice means making the nominations
to all the 'major' benefices, in particular to almost all bishoprics and
most abbeys. He nearly always decides in favour of the nobility, and
in the eighteenth century in favour of the 'old' nobility, so much so
that a number of noble families naturally reached the point of thinking
that certain ecclesiastical benefices were somehow a part of their
lawful patrimony. In Beauvais, for example, five of the eight successive bishops between Henry IV and Louis XVI belonged to that
great family of Parisian *parlementaires,* the Potiers, who were
ennobled under François I, while the rest were descended from a
still older nobility, since their names were Forbin, Beauvillier and
La Rochefoucauld. All the former and nearly all the others collected
revenue from more or less distant abbeys held *in commendam* and
where they hardly ever set foot. Through the king, the finest ecclesiastical benefices are available to the nobility – a convenient and
inexpensive kind of subsidy.

Lastly, only noblemen can become Knights of Malta, and are
required to furnish exacting proof, in spite of occasional compromises.

FISCAL PRIVILEGES

Because in principle they serve the king by bearing arms (or giving counsel), the nobility are exempt from paying taxes – the badge of the commoner – and especially from direct taxation, the *taille* and its various successive supplements and adjuncts. That is the principle, or rather the fiction. It was open to at least three types of exception.

a) First we must repeat that this principle is altogether inapplicable to the Midi, where it is the land on which the *taille* is paid. A nobleman was just as liable as a commoner on his common lands, which always constituted the greater part of his landed property (ninety to ninety-five per cent in Haut-Languedoc), while he still had to prove the 'nobility' of the rest.

b) After the institution of the *capitation* in 1695 – a crucial date, to which we shall have to return – the king tried to make the nobles pay. In general he can be said to have succeeded, but they were soon granted a special, lower rate.

c) The nobility (like the clergy) were by no means the only group exempt from most of the direct taxes. A host of wealthy commoners, several towns and whole provinces (such as Brittany) were exempt.

The same also applies to the entire complex financial system of the ancien régime (which will be outlined in vol. 2): noblemen are partly or totally exempt but are not at all unique in this respect (wealthy commoners, towns and provinces, as for the *taille*), and the royal administration keeps trying to compensate for these exemptions by inventing new and would-be 'general' taxes.

On the whole, the nobility was only slightly affected by taxation.

SEIGNEURIAL AS DISTINCT FROM NOBLE PRIVILEGES

It has already been pointed out that the seigneurial rights which the ancien régime called 'feudal' (*cens, champart, banalités,* etc.) are no longer the sole preserve of the nobility, since they belonged to anybody who possessed a seigneury.

Apparently the same holds true of various long-standing honorific rights – the weathercock over the seigneurial mansion, sometimes the banner and coat of arms; the nearby pigeon-house; the pew on the gospel-side, tombs in the chancel, the mourning-bands or '*litres*' painted or hung on the church walls, etc.

DUTIES OF THE NOBILITY: SERVICE, NON-DEROGATION

In return for these advantages the nobility has its duties, which can be summed up in two words: serve, uphold.

Serving the king: The main residue of the medieval '*auxilium et consilium*' is the military duty, most fitting for a nobleman; but there is also the less dangerous function of assisting the king in government and administration: Councils, justice and finance if need be. When the king gathers commoners or upstart nobles about his person the old nobility always feels slighted.

To uphold its rank means first of all not to derogate, secondly to communicate nobility by means of procreation within lawful wedlock and if possible to enhance it by earning distinctions, orders and titles from the king. Where necessary, the family should be able to provide clear proof, although not all of them preserve the relevant archives. It must also uphold the above-mentioned 'noble life-style'.

The most important and delicate of all these honorary duties determines all the others, and at the same time throws new light on the deeper nature of the nobility: this duty is non-derogation.

Derogation, the loss of one's nobility, means engaging in common, ignoble activities. What are these activities?

Any 'mechanical' manual activity, with the exception of glassmaking, ironfounding and eventually mining, which counts as 'extending' the estate;

Any commercial activity, both retail and, in certain fastidious provinces and periods, wholesale;

Farming evades derogation within certain limits, provided it is practised in the enclosed '*parc*' or over an area of one or two 'ploughlands' (*charrues*) – not more than twenty hectares – or within a 'capon's flight' radius of the manor, although taking land in farm always means derogation;

A crime involving loss of civil rights deprives the criminal of nobility, but not usually his family.

Contrary to English (and the similar Breton) practice, the legislation of many French provinces comes down hard on derogation, and the collectors of the *taille* keep a sharp eye out for it. The majority of noblemen not only accepted but cordially approved of this severity, and tended for the most part to refrain even from the 'honourable trade' of shipping, in spite of several royal decisions exempting it from the stigma of derogation. Thus the creation of a 'trading nobility' was ultimately prevented, notwithstanding the good arguments in its favour. There is no doubt that this die-hard attitude was highly detrimental to the nobility and to the entire realm; the standard comparison with England in this respect is still a valid one.

THE NUMBERS OF THE NOBILITY

'Ancient' or 'modern', rich or poor, court or provincial, sword or desk, legal or naval: what is the sum total of all these noblemen?

Nobody knows. Contemporary estimates range between eighty thousand (for the 'old' nobility) and four hundred thousand (for the combined total). Historians generally arrive at the cautious number of three hundred thousand, roughly 1 to 1.5 per cent of the population. Reliable recent researches mention a figure of at least forty thousand for Brittany alone around 1670, or about two per cent of all Bretons, but Brittany was particularly rich in noblemen, which indicates that this proportion is hardly likely to apply to the entire realm. Greater precision is not possible.

There is no point in trying to detail the twenty or so types of noble which make up the sum total. Barring the unifying factors of race, blood and rent, the major distinctions lie in the setting, mode and style of life, and the greatest contrast is between the 'ancient' and the 'modern' nobility. Why not accept the standard version? It does at least correspond to the reality experienced by the many.

In the following chapter we shall attempt to introduce a few of the better-known types of noble.*

---

* Documents and further reading for this and the following chapter will be found on p. 193 et seq.

VIII · TYPES OF NOBLEMEN

1 TYPES OF 'ANCIENT' NOBLEMEN
THE 'GRANDS'

Ancien régime writers were much preoccupied with the *Grands*, whether from scorn or admiration. The following criteria will help to provide a summary identification:

a) A very ancient nobility: they are never required to 'prove' and it would be an affront not to acknowledge their nobility as 'immemorial'. Their titles derive from their estates, which will be baronies at least, and usually counties. All the *ducs et pairs* (about a hundred 'peerages' had been created prior to 1715, half of which were vacant at that date), all the 'princes of the blood' (the king's relations), and most of the great prelates (archbishops and the upper crust of the bishops and abbots), by reason of their office and often of their birth, belong to this group of a few hundred people.

b) Tremendous wealth, but dispersed and unstable

All the Great (prelates included) own several large châteaux, surrounded by parks and game-preserves, in the heart of the provinces. They also have an *hôtel* in Paris, but this will tend to be rented rather than owned, at least under Louis XIII.

The estates, fiefs, *mouvances,* seigneuries and seigneurial rights of the Great extend altogether over hundreds, sometimes thousands of hectares – much less than the great estates of the 'magnates' of Central Europe – but they are hardly ever concentrated on a single region, or even a single province. Princes of the blood such as the Contis of the mid-seventeenth century had lands and seigneuries scattered from Soissons to Languedoc and from Brittany to Dauphiné. Less famous figures like the marquis de Vasse, owner of the renowned château of Azay-le-Rideau, had estates from Normandy to Poitou. This kind of dispersion did not make management any easier, and it had to be entrusted to '*intendants*', '*amodiateurs*' and '*fermiers généraux*' who were more often competent than honest.

The annual revenue of the Great usually ranged between 50,000 and 250,000 *livres* in the seventeenth century (the first estimate applies to the Vasses, the second to the Contis); twice that amount in the eighteenth – the duc de Beuvron, a Harcourt, had an income of 260,000 *livres* in 1786. At a time when a labourer could earn one or two hundred *livres* year in, year out, these incomes may sound enormous, but in fact they are deceptive. For the most part, the outlay of the Great exceeded their income, and by large amounts – not that this irked them much, since they could avoid prosecution, compulsory selling up and foreclosure by appealing to the king, who usually bailed them out by granting either additional church benefices or posts at court and in the provinces, or simply by paying their debts. The practice never lapsed, and the extravagant gifts made to her dear friends the princesse de Lamballe and the princesse de Polignac by Queen Marie Antoinette are all too familiar instances of a custom which had become an institution after being a means of subjection under Louis XIV and earlier still a sign of royal weakness, especially during the regencies, as well as a reason for rebellion.

It was the way of life of the owners as well as the dispersion of the property which caused the fortunes of the Great to be so unstable.

c) *Political pretensions*

Except when coerced or pensioned, most of the Great never accepted either the 'absolute' power of the king or the overlordship of ministers and their underlings. They had memories, traditions, vague ideas and illusions which led them to believe that the king could not govern without themselves, their assistance and their counsel, particularly in the event of royal minority and a regency, during which the royal 'family' and the 'great vassals' combined were supposed to close ranks around the young monarch. Theirs was a fairly vague political ideal, but it kept cropping up from time to time especially in periods of royal weakness. It boils down to the following points.

1. The Great of the realm, namely the princes of the blood and even the *ducs et pairs,* ought to enter the King's Council. In fact they did clutter it up for a long time. It took the repeated efforts of Henri IV, Richelieu and Mazarin, then the iron hand of Louis XIV and even the good sense of the duc d'Orléans in 1718 to get rid of them. But they always yearned to reassert themselves as 'natural counsellors', and the special pretensions of the *ducs et pairs* became linked with those of the parlements, grafting themselves, with the help of Saint-Simon, onto the traditional wishful thinking (we shall come back to this subject in vol. 2).

2. The Great should hold important commands in the provinces, generally as governors, and ought to be supreme even over the Intendants, who moved in during the seventeenth century nevertheless. In fact the monarchy was threatened for a long time by the powers, clients and ambitions of the Great provincial governors, up to and including the time of the Fronde. The reign of Louis XIV broke these habits, and they never set in again.

3. Those of the Great who had purchased or been given regiments, admiralships or the grandmastership of the artillery claimed to be their own masters in these posts. Richelieu and Louis XIV exploded their claims, put a stop to quarrelling among the generals, and initiated the practice of 'civilian' supervision of the army by the *Intendants d'armée,* but the military commands on land and sea were nearly always the preserve of the Great. The occasional lesser nobleman, like Vauban, or recent nobleman, like Catinat (less than a century's nobility), got there all the same, through merit. But these promotions grew rarer in the eighteenth century, during the strong reaction among the older nobility.

4. The Great usually took a very critical line against royal fiscal policy, refusing all taxation on themselves, more out of pride than self-interest. A strange blend of generosity and personal interest, in varying proportions, found them readily supporting the '*bon peuple*' and their 'vassals' against the continual inroads of royal taxation, which was dangerous competition for their own. This was the complex motivation underlying their ready participation in the numerous

tax-rebellions which jolted seventeenth-century France in particular.

The political behaviour of the Great was always a significant element in the evolution of the realm. Indiscipline and revolt endemic until 1652; then gilded submission; then the reawakening of an assertive, 'reactionary' aristocratic ideal around Fénelon, Boulainvilliers and Saint-Simon soon after 1700; the short-lived triumphs of 1715-18, and the far more serious aristocratic revival late in the century: these, briefly, are the principal phases.

d) General mediocrity of mind and conduct

We are always being reminded of those great noblemen who left their mark on literature and thought – La Rochefoucauld, Saint-Simon. It is doubtful if the churchmen – even Bossuet, Fénelon and Gondi, Cardinal de Retz (grandson of Italian financiers) – truly belonged to their milieu. What is much more striking about the Great is their frivolity. Prior to 1700, they had formed no coherent body of aristocratic doctrine. Can we take their intrigues, plotting and swashbuckling seriously? Many of them smack of the romantic (Turenne going over to the Fronde for the sake of Mme de Longueville) or the ridiculous (the cabal of the *Importants* in 1643). So often they act on impulse or have no idea what they really want, like Condé at the time of the Fronde. Some are the embodiment of weakness and cowardice, like Louis XIII's brother Gaston. Patently venal figures are legion: for men such as the older Condé, the duc de Longueville and many others, rebellion is basically a matter of money.

Although some of the Great seem to be highly cultured men – and we turn once more to the Grand Condé – others are uneducated and proud of it, and put on a deliberate show of vulgarity, like Beaufort, the 'king of Les Halles'. Their devoutness is often the kind of sham which was castigated by La Bruyère. Many of them have been and still are scandalous libertines who hardly bother to conceal their inclinations, except momentarily under Louis XIV. Even at court, they are inveterate gamblers, and their uncouth and scabrous demeanour is common knowledge, except in the case of various morbid and subtle spirits such as Louis XIV's bejewelled and perfumed brother. Many were compromised in the so-called Poisons Affair, and Louis XIV was reduced to burning the dossiers with his own hands. Many believed (like the common people) in magic, witchcraft, astrology and heavenly 'portents'. The practising *dévots* were sometimes utterly ludicrous, like duc Mazarin, the cardinal's heir, epicene precursor of Molière's Arsinoé, or repellent (the systematic delations of the pious Company of the Blessed Sacrament, founded by the duc de Lévis-Ventadour, Molière's obvious target in the person of Tartuffe), or else were eleventh-hour penitents like the beautiful sinners who prayed at leisure in the shadow of Port-Royal. Apart from genealogical and heraldic treatises and the occasional school-book, the libraries of the Great usually contained the complete Nostradamus, astrological treatises and any number of chivalrous romances, including *Don Quixote*, which was probably misinterpreted.

With a few exceptions, and discounting the late eighteenth-century evolution of the 'enlightenment' and of the aristocratic reaction, it seems certain that the culture and religion of the Great were inferior to those of the so-called '*noblesse de robe*'.

THE PARLEMENTARY NOBILITY: BRITTANY

According to a persistent myth upheld and fostered by the court nobility, the fanatical self-styled 'immemorial race' of noblemen and the snobbish society of the capital, the magistrates of the twelve (later thirteen) parlements of the realm belonged to the 'bourgeoisie' and constituted the '*bourgeoisie parlementaire*'. Even if it is to be understood as meaning that the parlementary nobility was relatively recent by contrast with various other types, the interpretation is radically in error. Only one concession can be granted to contemporary opinion: the parlementary nobility was 'newer' in Paris than elsewhere. The majority of seats in the provincial parlements are held by the Great and the old nobility.

The Breton nobility played a very early part in parlementary activity. The distinction between 'robe' and 'sword' is meaningless in Brittany, as it is in the provinces in general. The Parlement of Brittany represents that section of the nobility which wields the judicial power and which is also the most exalted section. From 1660 onward, no true commoner was admitted to the Parlement: in the space of 130 years, at most five candidates of recent or dubious nobility dared to knock at its door.

This parlementary nobility is exceptionally old: a study of 216 families shows that in 1670 there were 136 whose nobility dated indisputably from the pre-1500 period. The entire two thousand or so families of the Breton nobility give a rather lower percentage (twenty-eight per cent prior to 1500), although some way above the French mean, and well above that of the Paris Parlement.

This group of nobles contracts very few misalliances. Out of 412 known marriages, 119 came from within the parlementary milieu and nearly two hundred others from among the rest of the old nobility. Only about sixty *parlementaires* married burghers' daughters, and in any case these were often well on the way to ennoblement, as well (of course) as being richly endowed. They hardly ever stooped to marrying into trading or financial circles (4 cases out of the 412).

The fortunes of the members of the '*auguste Sénat*' varied fairly widely. No poor or struggling members at all; a few 'moderate' incomes of less than ten thousand *livres* – but these belong to cadet branches, hard done by under Breton law, which always gives two thirds or more to the eldest son; in the eighteenth century, the majority can reckon on an income of twenty thousand *livres*, which comes to half a million of capital. The biggest are millionaires twice or thrice over. This old nobility is very wealthy, certainly wealthier than in Toulouse, and perhaps than other provinces.

Until (and even after) the fall of the ancien régime, this wealth is feudal, seigneurial and landed. The eldest son of the dynasty always sets great store by his status as '*chef de nom et d'armes*', which means more in Brittany than some dubious marquisate. The 'Messieurs' of the Parlement own the lion's share of the two hundred greatest seigneuries in the province, leaving the residue to the new nobility (ten per cent), with the court nobility trailing raggedly behind. By any reckoning, rural assets make up at least two thirds of all annual incomes and of every individual fortune appraised or divided. In 1752, the comparatively modest estate of the father of the famous Breton *parlementaire* La Chalotais came to over half a million: more than four fifths of this sum was in landed property, while the parlementary office (with almost negligible revenues) made up less than six per cent. And this vast rural income is still feudal and seigneurial: the *censives* bring in more than the personal estate, and there is nothing

symbolic about the revenue provided by the *banalités du moulin* and
the *lods et ventes*.

It turns out that the administration of the parlementary nobility
was harsh, just as it was at Dijon. The least grasping and the most
humane were either the very wealthy or the most impoverished, while
the rest were tough, efficient managers, brooking no delays in payment or delivery, alert to the least of their rights, even those of an
honorific and symbolic nature, and making the most of established
usages by demanding submission from the 'vassal' and especially a
high rate of cartage dues, so that the peasant of the West retains
some resemblance to the villein liable to *corvées* 'at will'. With a
few exceptions, *Messieurs du Parlement* are detested in Rennes and
Dijon alike.*

These are proud, high-living, rapacious noblemen who build,
decorate, entertain, read and write a great deal. Some were well
known as book-collectors, although their libraries consisted mainly
of devotional and historical works and were almost immune to the
thinking of the philosophes and physiocrats. They preferred the
abbé Pluche and his *Spectacles de la Nature,* but pride of place went
to the great classics from Antiquity onward until the seventeenth
century – even Molière and Pascal. The intellectual and political
upheavals of the later eighteenth century are to overturn this sober,
traditionalist culture: meanwhile these *parlementaires* usually retain
their pious severity (many of them are Jansenists) and step up their
political aspirations (cf. vol. 2 of this work).

The Breton example is well-documented, but has the possible
drawback of being limited in its application. Rennes is not Paris, and
these Bretons cling stubbornly to their individuality in face of the
universally detested 'administration'. It seems, however, that '*Messieurs*' of Rennes bear a strong resemblance to their less familiar
noble colleagues in Dijon, Aix, Toulouse or Grenoble. In any case
their uniquely long pedigree alone makes these haughty *parlementaires* evidence of an important aspect of the second 'order', although they relapsed into utter apathy with the first breaths of the
Revolution.

---

* Provincial capitals of Brittany and Burgundy respectively. – Tr.

THE COUNTRY GENTLEMAN

Novels from *Capitaine Fracasse* to *Les Célibataires** have overpopu-
larized the stereotype of the poor gentleman with nothing left but
his nobility and his pride. These '*hoberaux*',† as they were at first
derisively nicknamed, are hard to investigate (they left few records)
but seem to answer to the following criteria:

1. They live in a more or less tumbledown manor at the heart of
what remains of the domain proper, fiefs and *censives*. Being hard up,
they are obliged to squeeze the last drop out of their rightful feudal
dues, and their peasants do not always fall over themselves to obey,
less impressed by poverty than by wealth. We even find cases of
gentlemen who are seigneurs of a quarter of a parish coming to blows
with their *censitaires* over a few *sous* or a stray cow. Their circumstances are supposed occasionally to have reduced them to tilling
their own land, and we have the well-worn image of the Breton
gentleman ploughing with his sword at his side. At the lowest level,
those who have lost fief and manor work in the cloth industry or
clerk in the offices of the *subdélégation* or the provincial tax-farmers,
thereby running the risk of derogation. This they could avoid, at
least in Brittany, by a particularly generous system of temporary
'dormition' of nobility, but impoverishment and the necessity of
making a living drove some of them into commoner status, and they
were entered on the tax-rolls.

2. This noble poverty is often put down to snowballing debts incurred by living above their means. A major factor was the rising cost
of equipping sons for the army and providing dowries for daughters
marrying or entering convents (although the latter is cheaper and
must have swelled the number of compulsory 'vocations'). It is also
worth bearing in mind the cunning of the moneylenders – usually
bourgeois, but sometimes clerics or even peasants – who were not
slow to take advantage of weak, careless or legally feckless gentry.
In some provinces a grinding primogeniture law (at least two thirds
to the eldest son and the remainder equally divided in Champagne,
Brittany, Normandy, Poitou and Guyenne) multiplied the number of

---

* By Gautier and Balzac. –Tr.
† Hobby – a *small* bird of prey. – Tr.

near-destitute younger sons, especially in populous unmilitary regions like Brittany.

3. This poor nobility is usually deeply devoted to the military profession, whether in the service of some great provincial family or of the king. The bereavements and disabilities caused by war are common visitants and put a further strain on family finances – they also testify to a great deal of courage and pride.

4. With some exceptions, the intellectual level is fairly low. Stray examples of private correspondence and the occasional day-book which comes to light here and there display a no more than passing acquaintance with the language, and the spelling is sometimes phonetic. 'Libraries' are rare, poor and steeped in the past: works of piety, feudal usage, blazonry and heraldry, the inevitable chivalrous romances and Nostradamus, always. Theirs is often a rough and ready faith, allowing for frequent clashes with the *curé* or tithe-owner, usually over wounded pride. Drunkenness is common, and so are bastards (not so shocking when they belong to gentlemen). Brutish morals are not unusual and brigandage is quite widespread in the sixteenth and even the seventeenth century (Fléchier's evidence on Auvergne is irrefutable and by no means exceptional*), but tails off considerably in the eighteenth century. Relationships with the peasantry are not always idyllic. Side by side with those '*bons seigneurs*' who are loved, respected or tolerated are others who are openly detested. Above all, their privileges, pride and swaggering appear less and less justified: the *cahiers de doléances* are clear on this point, when the small peasants manage to get a word in.

This colourful social category has nearly always been sympathetically described, but the historian has to ask himself whether the real position of the *hobereaux* warrants all the attention they have received. Their poverty is often very relative: the Breton capitation-rolls of 1710 enable us to pinpoint them, especially around Tréguier and Saint-Brieuc, and show that practically all of them had servants – a detail which scarcely tallies with genuine poverty. It is even

---

* The reference is to Fléchier's *Mémoires sur les Grands-Jours d'Auvergne*, written in 1665 but not published until 1844, an account of the extraordinary sessions held to investigate and stamp out brigandage in that region. – Tr.

questionable whether their numbers were at all significant. Out of all the hundred thousand inhabitants of the Beauvaisis, just twenty-three families of poor *écuyers* are recorded in 1690 – one hundred people, one thousandth of the total! Even so, they still declare incomes of three to five hundred *livres,* which cannot be called destitution (a *curé*'s stipend amounted to three hundred *livres* at that date). Their total number cannot be assessed at more than a few thousand families, mainly in the West and South-West, probably the victims of a variety of primogeniture which bore heavily on younger sons. But their customary hostility to all innovation, especially when it comes from the State, their deep-seated provincialism and strict, often heavy-handed exploitation of their 'rights' (they have to live, and keep up appearances) gives them something of the function of a social 'reagent', around which passions gather and crystallize. They play a greater part than their numbers suggest, as well-entrenched centres of resistance in the more traditionalist provinces against the accelerating evolution of society.

THE INTERMEDIATE PROVINCIAL NOBILITY: THE '*BONS MÉNAGERS*'

Did the *Grands,* the parlementary nobility and the more or less beggarly gentlemen between them make up the largest fraction of the 'old' nobility? Is it always the best-known, most 'type-cast' groups that represent the majority? Surely representativeness would be something more ordinary?

There did exist a kind of 'intermediate' nobility, the subject of a few isolated and revealing monographs. The Breton capitation-rolls of 1710 give us their number: over fifty *livres,* a high rate, 750 prosperous families; under ten *livres,* rather more than 1300 designated as 'poor'; between the two, forty per cent of the total. In provinces where the law of primogeniture was less strict, the proportion must have exceeded fifty per cent.

Ordinary is the word for this 'intermediate' type, which has been best described in the Midi. They own a house in the country and an '*hostel*' in town; the town house gradually takes over. They also have a few hundred *arpents,* some woodland, game preserves, a park and several thriving farms, the best always adjoining the manor and keeping it supplied with food. Two or three seigneuries where a few thousand peasants may live and pay dues, a few mills or wine presses, the patronage of a parish, a few bits and pieces of tithes and, unfailingly, a court in good working order, with its magistrate, *procureur fiscal,* clerk and often its notaries. These are steady sources of income if wisely managed, as Olivier de Serres advised his fellow '*bons ménagers*' in 1600.

It is always the same hardships and dangers that confront these landed rentiers: excessive expenditure for appearance' sake, and the readiness of bourgeois moneylenders to proffer their services – so easy to mortgage such a comfortable fortune. But this stratum of the old nobility put up a fairly staunch resistance to temptation. Some traded in wool or leather on the side; others kept a very tight rein on their farmers, *métayers* and '*laboureurs*' (a *laboureur* in Languedoc is a farmhand employed by the year); others transformed open country into closed fields, as in the Gâtine poitevine, and split it up into *métairies,* which produced a higher return; many of them delved into dusty muniment-rooms and came up with unauthenticated tomes by whose authority they demanded ancient and forgotten rights, when they did not simply invent new ones with the help of the *feudistes.* Of the few dozen known examples of one or the other technique, we are particularly well acquainted with that of the Sarret de Coussergues family, in Languedoc: in spite of prodigal sons and disputed successions down the centuries they succeeded in keeping together a fine estate of some thousand hectares of agricultural and pastoral land, which was bringing in the respectable sum of about thirty thousand *livres* annually towards 1750.

It took courage to hold out in face of the temptations of Paris and Versailles, the lure of the easy life and the by no means disinterested offers of the people with cash in hand. We have no statistics for gauging the number of those who lasted the pace, weakened or foundered. One thing is certain: a fair percentage did hold out. What is still more certain is that a 'new nobility' risen from the ranks of the bourgeoisie was hard on their heels, and sometimes dislodged them even from their most prosperous domains.

2 THE 'MODERN' NOBILITY

THE MACHINERY OF ENNOBLEMENT

It is a universally recognized principle that the king, and only the king, can create new noblemen – a prerogative that none of them failed to exercise. The rapid extinction-rate for ancient lineages (between a third and a quarter of the *ducs et pairs* each century) makes some kind of official replacement system inevitable in any case, given that the survival of the nobility is seen as a desirable end. True, the self-styled noblemen 'of ancient extraction', not to mention the commoners, made no secret of their contempt for those whom they persistently lumped together with the *'vile bourgeoisie'*, in Saint-Simon's phrase, retailing subtle distinctions such as the comtemporary dictum that: 'The king can make a noble, but not a gentleman'. None of these petty sneers prevented recent ennoblement from being as valid as any other type and more susceptible to cast-iron proof. The new nobility enjoyed all the privileges of their kind, including the crucial one of siring a permanently noble race, and in any case within two or three generations the 'new' had aged sufficiently not to be food for conversation, except in the mutterings of the lunatic fringe. The historian must draw attention to these quibbles over seniority as indications of mental attitudes before going on to probe more deeply.

The urge to be set apart from the common herd and to join both a legal order and a kind of racial group whose ultimate belief is that its rituals and way of life stem from a special physiological make-up is still a thought-provoking phenomenon. Monarchic or otherwise, states have always succeeded in utilizing it, even when not altogether believing it, as a rallying-point for subordinates, faithful followers and essential allies. And what we may term public opinion has practically accepted it: the bitter disagreements which the phenomenon arouses tend only to give it greater substance. The monarchy of the ancien régime succeeded in utilizing this physiological, mystical and mythic thirst for separateness. It also succeeded, sporadically at least, in believing in its own doctrine, and anybody who had amassed wealth and influence and wanted to turn it into power and prestige yearned to be merged into the mystic passion of the nobility.

Two means of entry were available: the letter of ennoblement, and the official post.

ENNOBLEMENT BY LETTER

The *lettre d'anoblissement* seems to have originated in the late thirteenth century, becoming a standard practice during and after the fourteenth and surviving until the time of the Revolution, to be resuscitated by some of the nineteenth-century French kings. As soon as this letter had been authenticated and registered by the principal financial and judicial institutions (first the Chambre des Comptes, then the Cour des Aides and the Parlement), its holder and all his legitimate descendants enjoyed the full plenitude of noble rank. The customary wording of the letters patent is most precise:

> . . . By Our special grace, plenary power and royal authority, given under Our own hand, We have ennobled and do hereby ennoble *sieur* X, and have conferred and do confer the title of noble and squire, being pleased and desirous that he be held and reputed noble . . . together with his children, posterity and descendants, male and female, born now or in future, in rightful wedlock; that as such they may in all documents and in all places assume the rank of squire, that they may have access to all the degrees of chivalry and other dignities, titles and qualities set apart for Our nobility, be inscribed upon the roll of noblemen, and enjoy all rights, privileges, prerogatives, preeminences, franchises, liberties, exemptions and immunities which the other nobles of Our realm enjoy and are accustomed to enjoy. . .

The kings of France did not abuse this method of ennoblement. According to the list recently compiled by Jean-Richard Bloch, François I authorized no more than 183 in a thirty-two-year reign. No more than a hundred such letters have been located in the whole of Brittany in the last century of the ancien régime, which suggests a total of not more than a thousand for the entire realm over the same period. Louis XIV appears to be the only king to have abused the procedure, as when he issued close on a thousand blank *lettres de noblesse* through his Intendants at the time of the League of Augsburg at six thousand *livres* apiece. No one dared publish the list of buyers. The historians have reached conflicting conclusions as to the extent of the vanity-market: Jean Meyer has unearthed only forty or so buyers in Brittany; he believes that there were no more than six hundred sold throughout the country, there being no takers for the rest. But most estimates are far less modest. The eighteenth century certainly showed more restraint, and the letters of ennoblement went to influential merchants (the great ship-owners), high-ranking soldiers, and the more loyal servants of the crown, in particular to the most distinguished of the Intendants' local assistants, the *sub-délégués*.

Examination of the numerous known examples shows that the king's choice was rarely arguable and often excellent. Some of the commoners selected really were outstanding individuals. We must emphasize, however, that this kind of ennoblement seldom came free.

Legally it could not, since the recipient had to fork out 'registration dues' as well as to 'compensate' for the loss of his former contribution to the *taille* (from which he was now exempt), in addition to making a donation to any charitable bodies in his parish. Moreover the king had not been slow to consider his own pocket. As early as François I's time, at least a hundred and fifty-three of the extant letters of ennoblement went hand in hand with the payment of a '*finance*' to the royal exchequer, which rose from a few hundred to over a thousand *livres* by the end of the reign. The wording of the letters makes no bones about this point: they are sold 'in order to subsidize, satisfy and provide for the great, costly and pressing affairs which we must bear and direct' (1522) or else to help with the 'excessive and extreme expenditure that we are constrained to make for the maintenance and governance of the great forces which we have mustered on land and sea... in order to resist the hostile enterprises of our enemies' (1544). It is no accident that merit or services rendered tend to coincide with wealth; the letters of ennoblement always go to wealthy commoners: impecunious merit does not make a nobleman. All the same, the monarchy was moderate in its use of letters patent, which is more than can be said of the wholesale ennoblements conferred by official posts or '*charges*'.

ENNOBLEMENT BY OFFICE

This was by far the most common type of ennoblement, but the legislation and usage that governed it display the usual tangled complexity of ancien régime institutions, with conditions varying from one post, province or period to the next. The one constant factor is the high prices for which posts are bought, bequeathed or sold. We can provide little more than an outline here, but not before making one important distinction:

Some posts conferred immediate, outright ennoblement provided that the incumbent held them for twenty years, or died 'in charge', and these were the most sought after and the most expensive. The rest conferred only 'gradual nobility' whereby at least two generations had to have held office for twenty years (or died in harness) in order for their descendants to claim noble rank. This common procedure eventually created a kind of temporary bastardy, neither flesh nor fowl (which was particularly hard luck on those who came to office after 1768, since the Revolution left them in suspense as to their noble status and their descendants had to arrive at their own interpretation, according to which way the winds of political change were blowing).

Four main types of office conferred potential nobility:

a) The office of 'commensal du roi'

The idea behind this kind of ennoblement, which is usually of the first degree, is that anybody who shares the king's life and theoretically his table (hence commensal) ought himself to be noble. Thus the great Crown offices of secretary of State, counsellor of State and *maître des requêtes** conferred first-degree nobility, although those whom the king accepted as purchasers of these prestigious and expensive posts were nearly always noblemen already. The exception was the much sought-after office of 'secrétaire du roi'.

In theory, the 'conseillers et secrétaires du roi' came under the aegis of the royal chancellery, dispatched and sealed the royal mail and were close to the king's person. They therefore acquired first-degree nobility together with additional privileges such as being allowed to engage in wholesale trade. Originally they probably number about sixty, rising to two or three hundred under Louis XIV and possibly nine hundred under Louis XVI, according to Necker,

---

* Lawyers employed by the king in several administrative capacities, as judges, recorders attached to various Councils and as royal representatives in the provinces: most of the Intendants came from among their ranks. – Tr.

who is an exaggerator. As well as the secretaries of the 'grand chancellery' (attached to the king), additional companies of secretaries
were created for the 'chancelleries' of the provincial parlements.
These were out-and-out sinecures. The price of office, and consequently of nobility, reached seventy thousand *livres* in Paris in 1700,
passed the hundred thousand mark towards 1750, bordered on
two hundred thousand after a reform in 1771, and hit three hundred
thousand *livres* towards the close of the ancien régime – the cost
of a well-appointed *hôtel* in a provincial capital! The price of the
corresponding posts in the small provincial chancelleries came to
about half these amounts. In spite of these disparities, 'serf-soap'
('*savonnette à vilains*'), as it was commonly called, reached an exorbitant price – we may venture to compare it with that of a dozen
racing cars in the later twentieth century. Usually it would be
bought by a grandfather; since he did not have long to live and
would necessarily die 'in charge' (no residential condition was required) he automatically ennobled all his offspring, who proceeded
to re-sell the miraculous soap, possibly without losing on the transaction, for the venality and (since 1604) inheritability of all these
offices ensured their continuation and circulation, as well as pro-
longing their ennobling properties. Naturally the 'soap' gave rise to
any amount of scoffing, but it nevertheless created a sizeable fraction
of the ancien régime's nobility; from the sixteenth century onward,
this included a number of families who were to become prominent
in the parlements, ranking among the very great, like the Le Fèvres,
who became the Lefèvre d'Ormesson family in 1568, or among
those who added lustre to the realm in an altogether different manner,
like Racine, Boileau, Jussieu, Mahé de La Bourdonnais, and even
Beaumarchais.

b) Judicial office

First-degree nobility was conferred by membership of two
courts of law which sat in close proximity to the king: the Grand
Conseil and the Requêtes de l'Hôtel (which contained the *maîtres
des requêtes*, offices that served as a nursery for the administrators
mentioned above). But their members were often noble before they
were admitted.

The parlements ennobled their counsellors, 'king's men' (members of the office of the public prosecutor), and sometimes their chief clerk, to the first or second degree, but most *parlementaires* already possessed ancient and sometimes 'immemorial' nobility, especially in the provinces, as we have seen. Even in eighteenth-century Paris, only a tenth of those influential and wealthy enough to purchase a parlementary post were commoners. The *parlementaires* tended to constitute an exclusive noble caste, although this had not always been the case prior to 1660: the Lamoignons, for example, had to buy office in the Parlement of Paris in order to join the nobility.

Lastly, the counsellors of the Châtelet de Paris were the sole judges at bailiwick level to be ennobled by their posts, either to the first or second degree, according to their importance.

c) Financial office

This was undoubtedly one of the principal sources of ennoblement (together with the office of *secrétaire du roi*), although it was slow – two generations to qualify – and slightly despised. With any number of local variations, the great financial courts of the realm (the *chambres des comptes, cours des aides* and the *cours des monnaies* in Paris and Lyons) and the financial departments of the *généralités*, gradually 'cleansed' their principal officers of their commoner clay.

d) Municipal office

By a long-established practice, the '*capitouls*' of Toulouse, like the *prevôt des marchands** and municipal magistrates of Paris, were automatically ennobled (but the king accepted only noblemen in these positions from the seventeenth century onward). There were about fifteen towns which conferred nobility on all or part of their municipal magistracy: former frontier towns which had held off sieges (La Rochelle, Angoulême, Poitiers, Niort, Saint-Jean d'Angély, Abbeville, Péronne) or had given financial support to Louis XI (Angers, Tours, Bourges), plus latecomers like Lyon and Nantes. Many of these towns lost their privileges in the course of the seventeenth century, or saw them become restricted to the mayor alone. This '*noblesse de cloche*' (the bell of the town hall) was something of a laughing-stock in any case, and those who had it often tried to

---

* Virtually the 'mayor' of Paris. – Tr.

obtain glossier titles (letters patent or secretaryships) so as to be taken a little more seriously.

We have seen that nobility is never conferred by ownership of a fief. Add to this the fact that the profession of arms does not ennoble the commoner, other than by special royal decision, and that it was not until after 1750 that thought was given to ennobling general officers and families which had worn the order of Saint-Louis (a military decoration) for three generations. Even so, Louis xv's rulings affected only a handful of great soldiers and were practically cancelled out by subsequent regulations which reserved almost all the commissioned ranks for the nobility. Apart from these, the army consists mainly of commoners.

Neither ennoblement by letters patent nor by office can operate unless the candidate is a man of substance. True, there was always an element of choice exercised at any given moment by the king, his representatives, or the official body concerned. The candidate's 'life' and 'morals' are investigated (a *curé's* affidavit will do), and conditions of age and ability are enforced in theory (but easily circumvented in practice through generous dispensations). The fact remains that the main gateway to nobility is wealth.

Wealth even confers the appearance of nobility, and the appearance eventually leads to the legal reality by a process which has been referred to as 'graduation'. This has often been described, but more as a series of haphazard incidents than a comprehensive social mechanism. It works as follows:

A wealthy commoner buys farms, a manor, a seigneury and the concomitant 'feudal' rights. With his court, notary, river, miller, farmers and pride of place in church and in the communal assembly, he is now the seigneur and more or less 'master' of the village. If he has a smattering of law he has also bought some kind of office in the bailiwick or *élection*, which does not carry nobility but does exempt him from the *taille* and brings prestige and power: now he is a regional magistrate and tax-official. Like their parents before them, his peasants – 'vassals' – probably call him 'master' or 'lord', and if he is seigneur of the village of Plessis they call him 'Monsieur du Plessis'. This is the moment he has been waiting for: from now on Du Plessis is his name. He will judge, command, strut, hunt and eventually buckle on a sword; some day a clerk, notary or priest will voluntarily promote him to '*écuyer*' in their records. One or two generations later, the custom will be time-honoured enough to convince the investigator of a 'nobility inquiry' – these men may be friends, or endowed with a healthy respect for money, or they may simply observe that the Du Plessis have borne the title of *écuyer* on their estates without let or hindrance, do not appear on the tax-rolls, and have 'lived nobly'. The family now duly graduates into the nobility.

How frequently did this type of ennoblement occur? There is no way of knowing: traces were well covered, and now the trail is cold. Some authorities have argued that this artful, gradual method was the most common of all, but this is hard to credit, first of all because in a number of traditionalist provinces and during certain periods (the eighteenth century) the old nobility kept a close watch on its own 'purity', and secondly because it was still advisable for a wealthy man to buy a sound ennobling office, if only to speed up the process.

Whatever method they used, the race for the supreme consecration among wealthy commoners demonstrates the prestige of nobility. It could almost be maintained that it was the most stubbornly cherished ideal of the bourgeoisie, their final metamorphosis, were it not that the true situation was more complex than we have shown, for nobility and bourgeoisie alike.

3   TWO PROBLEMS FOR THE NOBILITY

To account for the phenomenon of the French nobility in its entirety, it is not enough to attempt to see into its nature, stratification and methods of self-renewal. We would need to make a systematic study of all the mental images conjured up by the term, within and above all outside their own ranks. We would need to pursue them into the clergy and the army, where they are the ruling force, and we would need to observe their reaction to the eighteenth century 'enlightenment' at close quarters – it was more complex and more nuanced than is sometimes thought. Recent studies (some of them not yet complete) are beginning to throw light on at least two aspects, one political, the other economic.

NOBILITY AND MONARCHY

Roughly between 1560 and 1660, there were two important categories of the old nobility whose political attitude towards the monarchy
was questionable – the *Grands* and their adherents, the provincial
gentry. Whether as active rebels, supporters of lesser rebels, plotting
at will with foreign powers (usually Spain) or simply malcontents,
they were a constant thorn in the king's side not only in the sixteenth-
century religious wars but also during the two Regencies and even
under Richelieu. Add to this their aspirations to membership of the
Council, and their tendency to turn their provincial governorships
into quasi satrapies and maintain their own loyal private armies. The
kings of France took the first available opportunities to dispense with
their services: in order to rule, they needed reliable, competent men
whose first obligation was to the throne. 'Race' was a secondary consideration.

The essential selection came in a single century between Henri II
and Mazarin, and was carried out with the utmost efficiency by two
men, Henri IV and Richelieu. Henri III may have shown the way, but
we are not too familiar with that intelligent, cultured king. Thanks
to the work of Mousnier and his pupils we are beginning to build up
a working model of these great executives of the monarchy. They
are for the most part jurists and Parisians, usually training in the
sovereign courts and therefore noble, but very recently. Like so many
others, these Parisians come from the provinces (but seldom from the
Midi), where their parents were officials and landowners, their grandparents often merchants. Their remarkable political flair has enabled
them to pick the right (the winning) side at the ideal moment, early
in the day – the group of '*politiques*' at the time of the Catholic
League and Richelieu's supporters thirty years later. Their families
were well entrenched around them, and they had wide contacts,
'*créatures*', money, ability and dedication. Those who were not noble
had their status changed in due course, like the Colberts, who came to
the top after being supporters of the Le Tellier family. Louis XIV inherited these able, biddable men, this nobility backed or created by
his predecessors, and had the good sense to retain and reward them
and to heap them with honours and riches. Every one of the ministers of the 'great king' was inherited from the ranks of previous

royal followers and was absolutely noble, in spite of the waspish allegations of Saint-Simon. There is biographical interest in the fact that their nobility was not usually of long standing, but politically it is meaningless, and in any case this governmental aristocracy possessed an abundance of titles and had no difficulty in allying itself with the '*noblesse de race*'.

We find both of them closely allied in the eighteenth century, after the abortive reactionary interlude of the Polysynody (1715–18), based on a new group which rears its head now and then under Louis xv and is full grown by the time of Louis xvi, unluckily for him. This was the 'party of the court', which failed in its efforts to reform the monarchy.

Those groups of noblemen who governed or were close collaborators in government after 1660 do not usually belong to the 'immemorial' nobility, but they are not conspicuously recent either, and made little use of 'serf-soap'. Part of their prestige derived from their 150 or 200 years of noble ancestry, but its essence came from the king, the state and the practice of government. We might assign the name of political nobility to the families of Séguier, Le Tellier, Colbert, Phélypeaux and Le Voyer d'Argenson.

NOBILITY AND WEALTH

'In fact it is money which controls a family's social evolution. Wealth hastens this evolution, just as poverty hampers it.' This was the conclusion of Gaston Roupnel in 1922, in his study of the seventeenth-century parlementary society of Dijon. Forty years later François Bluche, writing about the nobility of the Paris *parlementaires,* bluntly declares that: 'The first qualification is to be rich and influential.' Lastly, we should recall that for a sum which ranged from sixty thousand to two hundred thousand *livres* in the eighteenth century the fast-acting and ennobling post of *secrétaire du roi* was open to any rich bidder.

Where did all this money come from? Was landed income sufficient? In the absence of a systematic study, which would probably be a difficult undertaking, a few examples may provide indications which are considerably at variance with the usual versions.

For the eighteenth century, the details are in agreement. Of the fifty-eight men who sat to elect the noble representative for the bailiwick of Beauvais in 1789 twenty-seven belonged to families ennobled in the course of the same century, nearly all of them by way of the office of *secrétaire du roi*; five went by the name of Regnonval, five Danse, and six Michel (with a few names of seigneuries tacked on); all of them were sons or grandsons of men who had dealt in serge and linen goods in the seventeenth century. Some of their wealth was of course invested in land, manors and seigneuries, but there can be no doubt that their rapid rise to fortune was attributable to the accumulation and concentration of raw materials for finishing and distribution, followed by large-scale mercantile activities in the Caribbean, China and the Pacific. The profits from commercial concentration and colonial trade were quite literally 'invested' in nobility. Of the three hundred or so noblemen created by one method or another in eighteenth-century Brittany, big businessmen make up the most sizeable group: every one of the great families of shipowners, financiers and slave-traders is accounted for on the list, where we find the names of Danycan, Magon and Trouin of Saint-Malo side by side with those of Michel, Grou, Piou, Montaudoin and the other great trading families of Nantes. Nobility put the finishing touch to the success of a commercial dynasty. The great shipping trade in slaves and materials reaped its ultimate reward – to be the founder of a superior race.

Perhaps these observations apply only to the eighteenth century? Yet as we cast further back in time we find comparable factors, though working in a different way. One of the most striking of these emerges from François Bluche's work on the origins and finances of the Parisian parlementary families of the eighteenth century.

The Parlement of Paris displays a number of distinctive features by contrast with the provincial parlements. These come under the headings of age, prestige and pretensions. In particular, its nobility is much more recent than in any other parlement – less than six per cent of 590 families could trace back their origins prior to the sixteenth century. It was a derisory number, and it scandalized provincial conservatism. These families are a boon to the historian, however, because they involuntarily bequeath him the history of their ennoblement.

The general outline is well known. Somewhere in the past there is nearly always a merchant ancestor (and before him, a blank), a grandfather holding legal office in the provinces, or a parlementary lawyer. Noble rank has often been attained before entry into the Parlement, frequently by way of a financial post (membership of a *chambre des comptes* or of the *trésoriers de France*) or the office of *secrétaire du roi*. In most of these social genealogies there comes a point at which the family seems to make a sudden jump in the scale both of honours and of prosperity. An element of increased wealth and social standing emerges as the essential step towards real success: in Paris it stems not from trade but from what we may call 'finance'.

Finance could mean managing the estate of some high personage: the Lamoignons paved the way for their ascent by administering the property of the dukes of Nevers in the fifteenth and sixteenth centuries, and the Doublets did likewise for the houses of Soissons and Longueville a century later. The same results came from handling the vast assets of the French clergy (the La Briffes, from Armagnac, became marquis de Ferrières in 1692) or receiving on behalf of the bishoprics of Poitou (the Dreux became marquis de Brézé in 1685). Nevertheless, the principal source of fame and fortune was still the royal exchequer. There is no counting the number of powerful noble families descended from big salt-tax collectors like the Feydeaus; suppliers to the army, like some of Mme de Sévigné's ancestors; tax-farmers to the provincial Estates of Languedoc or Brittany, like the Crozats or Pennautiers; and from all the necessary unscrupulous host of farmers, sub-farmers and even the ordinary *receveurs généraux de finances* of the *généralités*, who speculated against the future yield of the taxes they were commissioned to collect. Bluche's 'dictionary' teems with examples.

Reversing the process, Bluche has shown that if we focus on the wealthiest of the Paris *parlementaires* the biggest fortunes (several millions) turn out to have been accumulated or bequeathed by the financier father or godfather of the parlementary noble. The one exception discovered is that of the Aymeret de Gazeau family, and this lasts only until 1733, after which two female descendants of farmers general give a shot in the arm to the quiet family fortune.

The business affairs of the *Grands,* the clergy and the king therefore brought new blood to the French nobility, so that while the ancient feudal nobility tended for the most part to derive their income from landed sources, the total number of the nobility was increased and replenished by altogether different types of revenue. In sixteenth and eighteenth centuries alike, the most outstanding of the new nobility came from commercial backgrounds, and still more from 'finance', tax gathering, supplying to the army and a whole system of collections, loans, advances and deductions from the revenues of others. The ablest servants (or parasites) of the nobility and the state easily found their way into the one and the other. The fulminations of the *mazarinades* and of La Bruyère and Lesage against the *'partisans'** and 'financiers' have been charged with exaggeration: they may well have understated the reality.

But once they were noble, did these descendants of intendants, tax-farmers and army suppliers not settle down to living respectably and traditionally off their estates and their office? It is usually argued that in order not to 'derogate' they had to steer clear of trade and the business world, and some historians have made play with the 'economic sterility' of the nobility, pausing to congratulate the few enlightened gentlemen attracted by the doctrines of the physiocrats. It is beginning to seem as if these impressions do not often correspond to the reality.

Firstly it must be realized that the nobility conferred by the office of *secrétaire du roi,* and even by some letters of ennoblement, did not involve even a moral obligation to discontinue the *'grand Commerce'* of shipping, the Indies and the slave trade. There is no known example of any Nantes shipowner calling a halt to his activities as a result of ennoblement.

Secondly, the oldest noble families engage in maritime ventures – we find Chateaubriand's father becoming a shipowner, even a slave-trader, and he is not an isolated example. The great nobility is not above investing its capital in ships and the Indies: it simply works through dummies or nominees, like the Montaudoins of Nantes, who acted on behalf of the families of Bourmont and Maurepas. The

---

* Those who made a contract (*parti*) for the right to assess and collect the royal taxes. – Tr.

Charettes (ancestors of the Vendée leader) were lending money against ships sailing for Martinique as early as 1715. In Paris, none of the eighteenth-century farmers-general was prepared to remain a commoner in order to recoup in taxes what he advanced to the king: high finance would no longer stomach common status.

Industry in turn, and especially new industry, attracted many members of the old nobility. The so-called 'Brécilien' ironworks belonged to the two great Breton parlementary families of Andigné and Farcy, who retained control until the Revolution. Other great owners of ironworks in the distant provinces were the families of Condé, Rohan and Villeroy and the duc de Chaulnes. Yet another bought a pottery and founded a textile factory. These people, the Pinczon du Sel des Monts, had the financial backing of the States of Brittany, a bastion of the most ancient nobility.

While the vast majority of noblemen held aloof from any kind of manufacturing activity for a long time, there was a profound transformation in the eighteenth century – unless it is just that the documentation becomes more plentiful and explicit during that period. Under Louis XVI, the topmost strata of the nobility moved into industry (after moving into 'business' very much earlier). The duc de Penthièvre owned foundries in Champagne, the maréchal de Lorges in Burgundy, the big Dauphiné families in the Alps, and the newly ennobled Wendels where they remain to this day. The marquis de Coeuvres and the prince de Croy proved themselves first-rate businessmen at the Anzin coalmines near Valenciennes, like the Montmorencys and others at Saint-Gobain. The marquis de Waldner and the duc de Deux-Ponts created the first textile factories in Alsace during this period, and the duc d'Orléans took an interest in the newborn chemical industry, while when it comes to speculation in real estate and on the stock market the princes of the blood and the archbishops held their own with the gamblers of every nation. In other words, one section of the nobility was already ensconced in an economic 'new régime' while what would soon be known as the 'ancien régime' gasped its life away in political display and social myth.

DOCUMENTS

32 THE *GRANDS*: ASSETS OF THE CONDÉ AND CONTI FAMILIES

1 THE CONDÉS, 1701–10

Total revenue: 1,680,000 *livres* (according to surviving accounts)

Real estate revenue	783,000 *livres*
Personal estate revenue	897,000 *livres*

Breakdown of real estate revenue:

Ile-de-France, Enghien, Chantilly	138,920
Burgundy	60,374
Berry and Bourbonnais	193,863
Anjou and Brittany	102,450
Senonches and Guercheville (Beauce)	57,838
Clermontois (Argonne & environs)	150,500
Normandy	31,500
Other sources	77,625

Breakdown of personal income

Annual royal pensions (for four people)	443,000
Royal offices of 'M. le Prince' (son of the Grand Condé)	365,000
Dowries and inheritances payable in annual instalments	79,000
Various, including a share in the Compagnie des Indes	10,000

Estimate of total capital at the start of the eighteenth century, based on probate of wills

Total: 31 to 32 million *livres,* consisting of:

Personal estate of about 12 million ($5\frac{1}{2}$ million in pensions and royal offices);

Real estate of more than 19 million.

> Based on Daniel ROCHE, 'Aperçus sur la fortune et les revenus des princes de Condé à l'aube du xviiie siècle', in *Revue d'Histoire Moderne et Contemporaine*, July–September 1967,
> pp. 217–43.

2 THE CONTIS

Average annual revenue (based on family accounts)

1655–60	1,130,000 *livres*
1661–65	1,220,000 *livres*
1666–70	725,000 *livres* (the prince has lost royal offices and pensions)
. . . .	
1676–80	529,000 *livres*
. . . .	
1789	3,743,000 *livres*

Total assets (according to the partition settlement of 1752)

13,110,266 *livres* – including 7,235,363 *l.* in real estate (55%)
(In 1783, real estate alone, which was sold almost lock, stock and barrel, came to 17 million *livres*.)

Distribution of real estate

1 Estates grouped in the Oise valley (Isle-Adam and Vexin area).
2 Other lands in the Paris basin (Fère-en-Tardenois, Beauvaisis, Perche, Normandy).
3 Central France: Berry (Sancerre), Burgundy (Vosne, Nuits . . .) and Auvergne (duchy of Mercoeur).
4 Estates in Languedoc and Dauphiné (centered on the county of Pézenas).

Revenue from real estate

Examples of estates:	1671	1752
Barony of Fère	11,000 *livres*	40,000 *livres*
Barony of Isle-Adam	25,000 *livres*	50,000 *livres*
Beauvaisis (Mouy)	11,060 *livres*	15,000 *livres*
Pézenas, Bagnols, Pierrelatte	30,200 *livres*	40,500 *livres*
Total real estate revenue	138,515 *livres*	350,000 *livres*

Based on François MOUGEL, *Fortune des princes de Bourbon-Conti, revenus et gestion,* master's thesis in modern history, Nanterre, June 1968, 145 pp., unpublished ms., to be published in article form.

33 REVENUES OF NOBLEMEN OF THE BAILIWICK OF BEAUVAIS IN 1697

I The revenues of 109 noble families were estimated (probably generously) by the *lieutenant général* of this bailiwick. The following is a breakdown in summary:

A. Gentlemen resident outside the bailiwick: 39.

Total revenue of these 'outsiders': 188,000 *livres* (70% of the total; an average of 4,800 *livres* apiece).

Three largest incomes:

the marquis de Mannevillette (Hanyvel, an ennobled financier)	20,000 *livres*
the prince de Conti	14,000 *livres*
the maréchal de Noailles	12,000 *livres*

B. Resident country gentry: 70 families with a total revenue of 81,000 *livres* (an average of 1,160 *livres*); 23 of these families have incomes valued at 500 *livres* (the average income of a country *curé*).

II Excerpts from letters written by rural gentlemen asking for tax-remission or exemption from the '*arrière-ban*' (by which they had either to do military service for the king or pay him a tax theoretically of one fifth of their annual income):

Jean de Courvoisin, 1692:

'Are you not quite convinced that it [the tax] is beyond my means? Must you know more? I have sufficient pride and awareness of what is due to my birth to conceal the wretched condition in which I find myself over so mean a sum. If I could borrow, I would rather not mention it. But where to find it? and when to repay?'

Adrien de Villepoix, 1693 (he is in debt to the tune of 25,000 *livres*):

' . . . so that not only does he not have a *sou*, but he lacks more than half of what it will take to pay off his debts . . . his creditors have put his assets under distraint . . . and have agreed to put them up for private auction . . .'

Demoiselle de Pauville, wife of Antoine de Sulfour, 1695:

'If you will trouble to send someone to our house, you will see whether I am being honest with you and whether the whole house is not half in ruins and the coverings threadbare . . . We are in desperate straits, and will soon have to turn to charity . . .'

> Documents from the archives on the *arrière-ban* in the departmental archives of Oise, excerpted in Pierre GOUBERT, *Beauvais et le Beauvaisis . . . de 1600 à 1730* (S.E.V.P.E.N., 1960), 210–12.

34 THE NOBILITY OF POITOU AND
RURAL REORGANIZATION

A few examples:

In the late seventeenth century, La Lunardière is a noble *métairie* of over sixty hectares' area on the banks of the little River Saumore, a tributary of the Autize. Raoul de La Porte, great-grandfather of maréchal de la Meilleraie and of Cardinal Richelieu, began building it up in 1537 . . . His son François, the famous lawyer of the Paris Parlement, carried on the good work by concentrating on invoking the feudal right of the *retrait* at every opportunity. Through seven contracts spaced out between 1558 and 1580, he attached all the village peasants' holdings to his fief . . .: we witness the progressive eviction of the villagers as they abandon the place to the *métayer* working on behalf of the seigneur of La Lunardière.

Part of the leasehold property at La Follardière belongs to the fief of the La Portes, and here Raoul embarks on a similar process of acquisitions over the period of 1531–4, when eleven contracts show village tenant-farmers ceding parcels of land or meadow. After this burst of activity, there is a protracted lull until about 1560, which marks the onset of a new campaign initiated by François and continued by his son Charles. It goes on until 1609, when the *métairie* is completed.

. . . Georges Thibault de la Carte, seigneur of Vieux-Brusson, part of whose fief consists of the holdings [of La Berlandière and La Perrochère, straddling the parish boundaries of Allonne and Fenioux], comes into his inheritance . . . 1646 . . . He sets to work the following year, carries on without a break, and completes his task in less than twenty years (1647–64). A series of twenty-one contracts of acquisition or exchange replaces the jumble of smallholdings which used to surround these two villages by two *métairies* of about forty hectares each. The operation came later and proceeded faster than the above, took the same course, and arrived at the same end.

Conclusions:

The crisis which followed the Hundred Years War, like that occasioned in the sixteenth century by the fall in the purchasing-power of the *livre*, caused the nobility of the Gâtine to begin a lengthy process of land-reform, with the object of sustaining and even increasing its revenues.

The nucleus of this process was usually the fief, and it was furthered by manipulating the feudal *retrait*. The result was the fusion of the *censitaires'* smallholdings into a single new agricultural unit . . . the disappearance of a considerable number of inhabited places and the transformation of a great many hamlets into *métairies* harbouring a single family.

The fusion of the smallholdings into *métairies* had only a minor impact on agricultural methods ... at the end of the ancien régime, the Gâtine was still failing to produce sufficient grain to feed its inhabitants.

... The progressive impoverishment of the *métayers* in the course of these three centuries converted this social category into a true rural proletariat ... By increasing the revenues of the lesser and intermediate nobility, the creation of *métairies* seems to have kept the gentry of the Gâtine on their lands. They certainly remained plentiful there in 1789.

Dr Louis MERLE, *La Métairie et l'évolution agricole de la Gâtine poitevine* ... (S.E.V.P.E.N., 1958), 60–1 and 202–3.

35 GOING RATES OF 'SERF-SOAP' IN THE PROVINCES

Brittany (posts of *secrétaire du roi* at the Breton Chancellery)

1680-1700	(five examples)	23,000-27,800 *livres*
1723-36	(five examples)	37,000-43,000 *livres*
1751-5	(ten examples)	51,000-67,500 *livres*
1766-88	(seventeen examples)	70,000-95,000 *livres*

Jean MEYER, *La Noblesse bretonne au XVIIIe siècle* (S.E.V.P.E.N., 1966, 2 vols, 1292 pp.), vol. 1, 257–60.

Bordeaux

... This is 'serf-soap' *par excellence*. No qualifications are required of the candidates. In theory, the *secrétaires* at Bordeaux seal and dispatch judicial communications in the chancelleries attached to the Parlement or the Cour des Aides. In fact, they do nothing whatsoever ...

During the latter years of the reign of Louis XIV, secretaryships sold at quite a moderate price: ... 17,750 *livres*; in 1717, they can be had for as little as 10,000 *livres*. But a steep rise begins at this point. Between 1720 and 1730 as much as 52,000 ... Between 1730 and 1740, the price never fell below 25,000 *livres*, with a maximum of 61,000 ... Towards 1775, they were selling at over 70,000 *livres* ... They topped the 100,000 mark by 1780, and the highest price of the century, 125,000 *livres*, was paid in 1785. This was therefore the most expensive post in Bordeaux, costing even more than the presidency of the Parlement.

W. DOYLE, 'Le prix des charges anoblissantes à Bordeaux au XVIIIe siècle', in *Annales du Midi*, January-March 1968, p. 75.

36 NOBLE SHIPOWNERS AND SLAVE-TRADERS IN EIGHTEENTH-CENTURY NANTES

. . . 6,300 cases have been analysed . . . Our sample of families is therefore concerned with most of the commerce with the Indies, the slave trade, and also the shipments to the Bourbon [now the Mascarene Islands], Louisiana, Canada and the English colonies in America. These 6,300 shipments were undertaken by about two hundred shipowning families, an average of 31–32 ventures each. . . The traditional nobility . . . are fairly small in number – five family groups – but they commission 385 voyages, an average of seventy-five apiece . . . [of these] the de Luynes, offshoots of the Talleyrand-Perigords . . . commission at least 182.

A group of eight families ennobled early in the century and almost totally absorbed into the nobility produce the enormous sum of 748 ventures . . . The Montaudoins . . . commissioned at least 357 voyages . . .

Nine families ennobled in the second half of the century account for the high figure of 592 voyages, due largely to the activities of the Drouin and Bouteiller families (at least 112 and 171 respectively). On the eve of the Revolution these families are closely bound by commercial as well as familial ties.

The three above-mentioned categories represent therefore numerically very few – barely a score of families (out of 200) – but their commissions amount to twenty-seven per cent (at least 1,725) of the cases analysed.

Jean MEYER, *L'Armement nantais dans la deuxième moitié du XVIIIe siècle*, D. Litt. thesis, Rennes, 1966, pp. 44–5, typescript.

37 SOME VIEWS OF THE NOBILITY

1. MOLIÈRE AND THE PARTICLE (1662)

Chrysalde: Who the devil put it into your head, at forty-two years old, to unchristen yourself and make a seigneur's name out of a rotting old tree-trunk [pun on *souche* = tree-stump] on your farm?

Arnolphe: The house is known by that name, and besides, La Souche sounds better than Arnolphe to my ear.

Chrysalde: It's wrong for a man to get rid of the true name of his ancestors for the sake of a fabrication. Most people long to do it, and I know one peasant – no comparison intended – who used to be called Gros-Pierre, whose entire worldly goods were a single plot of land. So he digs a muddy ditch around it, and takes the splendid name of Monsieur de l'Isle.*

Ecole des Femmes, I, i

2. LA BRUYÈRE AND THE *GRANDS* (1692)

While great nobles are content to know nothing, not merely about matters of State and the interests of princes but about their own private affairs; while they remain ignorant of household administration and all that the head of a family should know, and pride themselves on this ignorance; while they let themselves be robbed and ruled by bailiffs, while they are satisfied with being gourmets or connoisseurs of wine, with frequenting *Thaïs* and *Phryne,* talking about the first and second pack or how many stages there are between Paris and Besançon or Philisbourg, certain bourgeois have been learning all about the internal and external affairs of the kingdom, have studied the art of government, have become shrewd politicians, acquainted with the strength and weakness of the whole State, have sought promotion, have risen high, grown powerful; and relieved the prince of part of his public responsibilities. Those nobles who once scorned them now revere them, and are happy to become their sons-in-law.

Caractères, IX, 24 (trans. Jean Stewart, Penguin Books, 1970)

Chrysalde: Qui diable vous a fait aussi vous aviser,/A quarante de deux ans, de vous débaptiser,/Et d'un vieux tronc pourri de votre métairie/Vous faire dans le monde un nom de seigneurie?

Arnolphe: Outre que la maison par ce nom se connaît,/La Souche plus qu'Arnolphe à mes oreilles plait.

Chrysalde: Quel abus de quitter le vrai nom de ses pères/Pour en vouloir prendre un bâti sur des chimères!/De la plupart des gens c'est la démangeaison;/Et, sans vous embrasser dans la comparaison,/Je sais un paysan qu'on appelait Gros-Pierre/Qui, n'ayant pour tout bien qu'un seul quartier de terre,/Y fit tout à l'entour fair un fossé bourbeux,/Et de Monsieur de l'Isle en prit le nom pompeux.

3. A FORGOTTEN POET: ÉTIENNE PAVILLON,
*Le Gentilhomme de l'arrière-ban** (1689)

With a few happy country neighbours,
Fonder of amorous than warlike labours,
Without a want or care, I lived at ease
'Mid mansion, shepherdess, springs, fountains, trees

Our talk was all of love, and never war.
Though I bewailed the king of England's plight,†
It never crossed my mind to go and fight.
. . . My pride in noble status solely lay
In being exempt from what the commoners pay.
Today I mourn my birth's nobility:
This glorious rank will be the death of me
By forcing me, in this ill-omened year,
Among the *arrière-ban* to appear.
O great-grandsire, of tranquil memory
(Pen and ink were your only armoury,
Bourgeois in caution and timidity),
Behold in me your true posterity.
Yours was the cash your son and grandson spent
To bring me to this dire predicament,
This noble duty, which I must fulfil,
To be a warrior against my will.‡

Étienne PAVILLON, printed in Maurice ALLEM, *Anthologie poétique*
française, XVIIᵉ *siècle* (Garnier-Flammarion, 1966), vol. 2,
p. 301.

---

* Published after Pavillon's death in 1705. The *arrière-ban* was an old feudal custom revived on several occasions in the seventeenth century, by which the gentry were supposed to render military service; in fact, they mostly bought themselves out.

† The reference is to James II, exiled by the Glorious Revolution of 1688-9.

‡ With apologies to Pavillon's original, which reads: '*Dans ma maison des champs sans chagrin, sans envie,/Je passais doucement la vie/Avec quelques voisins heureux,/Peu guerriers et fort amoureux,/Ma bergère, mes prés, mes bois et mes fontaines . . /On parlait de l'amour et jamais de la guerre./Je plaignais le roi d'Angleterre/Sans dessein de le soulager . . /Et je me piquais de noblesse/Seulement pour ne pas payer/La taille et les impôts que paie un roturier./Aujourd'hui j'ai regret d'être né gentilhomme;/Ce titre glorieux m'assomme./Hélas! il me contraint dans ce malheureux an/De paraître à l'arrière-ban./O vous, mon bisaïeul de tranquille mémoire.Dont les armes n'étaient que l'aune et l'écritoire,/Qui viviez en bourgeois et poltron et prudent,/Reconnaissez en moi votre vrai descendant./Pourquoi de votre argent votre fils et mon père/A-t-il acquis pour moi ce qui me désespère,/Cette noblesse enfin, qui par nécessité/Me fait être guerrier contre ma volonté? . . . – Tr.*

4. CHAMFORT'S VERDICT ON THE NOBLE 'RACE'
(LATE EIGHTEENTH CENTURY)

The most vaunted claim of the French nobility is their direct descent from some thirty thousand helmeted, breast-plated, cuisse- and brassard-clad men on big armoured horses who trampled eight or ten million ancestors of the present-day nation underfoot. A right well calculated to earn the respect and love of their descendants! And this nobility, to round off its quest for respect, recruits and renews itself by enlisting the selfsame men who have amassed their fortunes by plundering the hovels of those poor wretches who cannot afford to pay their taxes.

CHAMFORT, quoted in TAINE, *L'Ancien Régime* (Hachette, 4th ed., 1877), 420.

5. AN ANONYMOUS PAMPHLETEER
(RENNES, EIGHTEENTH CENTURY)

... always go into people's houses with a rowdy air, open the door with a clatter, and never close it ... don't greet people when they bow to you, but give them a nod to let them know you noticed ... never play games that might be learnt, for play, like love, is all the world's leveller ... be followed wherever you go by a disdainful, numerous retinue, let them insult the bourgeois, let the people reverence them, for the master's greatness is measured by the lackey's insolence ... Have HOSTEL DE ... written on your house in golden letters ... and a Swiss guard with twirling moustache, pleated breeches, big baldrick, long sword and embroidered hat, and let the whole street echo with his raucous whistling ... and never bare your neck, so that people everywhere may see you clad in the badges of your dignity, with a big proud cloak wrapped round you ...

Excerpt from the 'grand et superbe ceremonial du Mortier de Bretagne ...', undated pamphlet quoted in J. MEYER, *La Noblesse bretonne au XVIIIᵉ siècle*, vol. 2, p. 1007, note 3.

6. A BRETON *CURÉ* 1783

The great noblemen who do not live upon their estates ... neither give nor offer the slighest relief to the poor, either in the form of alms or daily work, although they receive the best part of their annual income from our fields; the capital is a pit that swallows everything and gives nothing back ...

Royan, rector of Trébivan, to the Intendant; quoted in J. MEYER, ibid., 861.

FURTHER READING

Feelings run high in this field, and they have produced any number of second-rate works, or worse. Two contemporary historians, François Bluche and Jean Meyer, do stand out head and shoulders from the ruck, and anybody wishing to familiarize himself with the special problems of the nobility will refer to their books and to their extensive bibliographies; but the latest and perhaps the most perceptive venture in analysis and re-examination has undoubtedly been concentrated on Brittany.

BLUCHE, François, *Les Magistrats du Parlement de Paris au* XVIII*^e siècle (1715–1771)* (Belles-Lettres, 1960, 460 pp.).

ibid. *L'Origine des magistrats du Parlement de Paris au* XVIII*^e siècle,* in *Paris et Ile-de-France, Mémoires publiés par la Fédération des Sociétés historiques et archéologiques de Paris et de l'Ile-de-France,* vols V–VI, 1958.

ibid. *Les Honneurs de la Cour* (Les cahiers nobles, 1957, 2 vols).

ibid. (with Pierre DURYE) *L'Anoblissement par charges avant 1789* (Paris, 1962, 2 vols).

MEYER, Jean, *La Noblesse bretonne au* XVIII*^e* (S.E.V.P.E.N., 1966, 2 vols, 1292 pp.) (doctoral thesis at Rennes.).

(All future studies of the nobility will have to make this big fertile thesis their starting-point. It either supersedes most previous work or defines its value and limitations.)

For a first introduction it is worth looking up various works in the 'Que sais-je?' series, such as:

DU PUY DE CLINCHAMPS, Philippe, *La Noblesse* (P.U.F., Que sais-je?, 1959, 128 pp.).

Lastly, the studies of regional history already indicated contain varying amounts of information: they include works by MERLE, LE ROY-LADURIE, GOUBERT, DEYON, etc.

IX · THE TOWNS AND URBAN SOCIETY

Contemporary urban studies contribute nothing towards our understanding of towns under the ancien régime. Here as elsewhere, the historian has to shed the attitudes of his own time.

We have already observed that the urban population was heavily outnumbered by the rural. Paris did not reach the half-million mark until the eighteenth century, and could not muster more than two per cent of the population; there were six towns of sixty to a hundred thousand people; about ten with thirty to forty thousand; fewer than fifty with ten to fifteen thousand, plus a few dozen big market towns and small administrative centres: barely three million inhabitants all told, or fifteen per cent of the population.

But the importance of the towns certainly derives from factors other than population, and they occupy an increasingly commanding position in the realm by skimming off its wealth and talent and becoming the focal points of its power, influence, splendour and culture. France is dominated by an urban minority.

1 THE TOWN, DEFINITION AND ORGANIZATION

TOWNS AND WALLS

All the old dictionaries confirm the general verdict that what makes a town is first of all its walls, which are nearly always flanked by embankments and moats. A town without walls is no town at all, at any rate not until after the seventeenth century, when a great many ramparts fall derelict and are pulled down to make way for public boulevards. This strict definition entails some odd consequences: a huddle of people numbered in the hundreds may retain the title – and privileges – of 'town' if they are or have been walled. Hence the status of sleepy little places such as Gerberoy and especially Bulles, former strongholds in the Beauvais region, which kept their statutes and privileges until the late seventeenth century, having done yeoman service in the twelfth. These relics are quite typical of the ancien régime in its exaggerated veneration for the past.

Quite a few of these towns had built their first walls and moats at the time of the invasions of the Byzantine Empire; others, including new towns, in the course of the ensuing millennium. Many still preserve them, at least as monuments. We know that the fastest-growing towns found themselves having to construct roughly concentric rings of successive fortifications, of which Paris provides the best-known example. These walls served a useful defensive purpose until the mid-seventeenth century, and later still when the town remained or became a frontier outpost. (Here Vauban left his mark.) They did so because as late as Louis xiv's reign war was regarded as a summer pastime of attacking and defending more or less fortified places. The town itself paid to keep the walls in repair and to equip them with artillery, ammunition and defenders, while the government intervened only in emergencies. The town gates were closed every night with all due ceremony, and the citizens could sleep peacefully in their beds, safe from looters, soldiers, vagabonds, thieves – even from enemies. Well into the seventeenth century, the peasants were still taking refuge behind the walls in time of real or imaginary danger, together with their families, wagons and livestock.

It was during the same era that the kings of France learned the lesson of decades of provincial uprisings, set about disarming the walls and the towns, and sometimes had them demolished, but they left a lasting imprint even when derelict and ruined.

First of all, they led to serious overcrowding, and the last outposts of the 'old Paris' – then the most densely populated town in the world – still convey a striking impression of urban conglomeration. In centuries during which the lack of hygiene was worse than in the Middle Ages (when people took pleasure in bathing and steaming), it led to the rapid swarming of parasites and epidemics that spread with lightning speed. It also produced the parochial spirit which marked the attitudes of town-dwellers everywhere and convinced them that theirs was the most important town in the province, if not in the world. Anyone who dared to doubt it would be met with resentment, sometimes animosity, and at least verbal violence.

The main point, however, is that even ancient and crumbling walls demarcated the juridical boundaries. Although the '*ban*' of a town might in some cases extend to '*lieux*' (hence the primary meaning of '*banlieue*' – place of jurisdiction) which enjoyed part of the town's privileges, it was inside the wall that these privileges took on their full force.

TOWNS AND PRIVILEGES

A town without privileges is as unthinkable as a town without walls. Great or small, since well before the sixteenth century they possessed a jumble both of honorific and of altogether concrete privileges and freedoms (the words are almost synonymous), listed, recorded, and confirmed – at a price – with every change of monarch. Many, like Bordeaux, Paris, Rouen, Angers (barring one parish!), Beauvais and many others, were exempt from the *taille,* which gave them a considerable advantage tempered by the long-standing royal practice of levying 'subsidies' or 'subventions', temporary at first, then permanent, but remaining well below what the *taille* would have cost. This takes care of the common misconception that the *taille* was a tax on commoners: this idea is not only wide of the mark for the Midi, it is also inapplicable in the North, the land of the *taille personnelle.* A bewildering number of contradictory financial privileges replaced or reinforced this exemption. They included reductions or special rates for the various taxes on the circulation, import and export of certain goods; partial freedom from the gabelle; facilities for replenishing stocks of timber and wine; and everything which could be devised or conserved by tradition, bargaining, the shifting balance of power, seigneurial patronage and special local conditions and peculiarities. In fact, the town is always more 'free', which means more 'privileged', than the neighbouring countryside.

TOWNS AND MAGISTRACIES

But the most important privilege of the towns was that of appointing their own administration, at least in principle. The medieval 'communes' with their charters and their partial freedom from feudal ties survived into modern times (Henri IV annulled only one, Amiens, and Louis XIII two, Saint-Jean-d'Angély and La Rochelle), despite the gradual and erratic efforts of the central authority to weaken and erode them, mainly during and after the reign of Louis XIV. Every town had its 'council', its *échevinage, consulat* (in the Midi), *jurade* (Bordeaux) or *capitoulat* (Toulouse). These were 'elected' bodies in the old sense, which is to say chosen by procedures which were a far cry from the 'universal suffrage' of later times – usually a system of straightforward co-option from the ranks of the town worthies, with lip-service paid to the old custom whereby the principal of each guild or 'estate' had been entitled to make preliminary nominations. This system was quickly giving way to the powers of governor or Intendant to make their own appointments.

Whatever its origin – and it was never 'democratic' – the *corps échevinal* represents the town, and its considerable power survives even the centralizing, authoritarian policies of Louis XIV and Louis XV.

The magistracy, and in particular its leader – *premier, maire* or *mayeur* – is the embodiment, or at least the symbol, of the town itself. It opens and closes the gates, greets important visitors and presides in ceremonial dress and splendour over the major rituals of high mass, processions, celebrations and mourning.

Often the magistracy still possesses some of its traditional legal rights, more or less overlapping or at odds with those of the seigneur and the king. In Bordeaux, for instance, the *jurats* retained their civil and criminal jurisdiction for some time; it extended to every inhabitant resident in the urban district and a broad suburban region, and applied to foreigners also. In Beauvais, a much smaller town, the 'patrimonial court of the mayor and peers' had trouble in preserving anything more than ordinary supervisory powers in face of the growing strength of the seigneurial bailiwick; and yet Colbert revived the old communal court and transformed it overnight into a mercantile tribunal with jurisdiction over the manufacture of textiles. Long before the establishment of the royal bailiwick, the magistracy of Amiens controlled the first national factory, recorded wills and even ruled on individual successions, and it continued to do so in competition with the bailiwick.

The magistrates were in charge of repairing the walls and defending the town, and they therefore disposed of quite considerable military powers for some time (the old *'milices communales'*), but in the course of the seventeenth century these gradually became more or less ornamental (companies of crossbowmen and arquebusiers whose principal interest was the annual contest). The only exceptions were certain frontier provinces such as Boulonnais and Roussillon, which clung stubbornly to the old traditions. In any case, the military requirements of the towns meant levying contributions from the citizens. (We shall return to these military questions in volume 2.)

In fact, the financial powers of the towns remained extensive, almost excessive, for a long time (much more so than in the twentieth century), even when the central administration managed to keep them under close supervision, as when Colbert attempted to liquidate the huge debts both of the urban and the village communities. Every town possessed land, property and rights, particularly the octroi (a toll on goods brought into it). Every town recruited its own municipal employees, who had to be paid: in 1550, Bordeaux had about fifty officials who dealt with financial and judicial matters, administration and police work (tipstaffs, bailiffs, halberdiers, town criers). Every town had to run an elementary road-repair system and service its pavements and street-lighting; it also had to contribute towards an even more elementary public health department providing drinking-fountains and employing refuse-collectors plus one or two doctors or surgeons for epidemics, all of these paid by the municipality. Every town is responsible for its poor, whose numbers may climb steeply in time of famine, pestilence, political or military emergency, or all three at once: the sudden growth of poverty inside the gates, coupled with the almost inevitable influx of destitute outsiders, gives rise to every kind of problem at once, medical, political and financial. Finally, every important town contributes to the upkeep of a school, and sometimes a university. In addition, the central authority in the person of the intendant keeps a sharp eye on all these activities, but rarely subsidizes them, so that the town continues to have its own budget and to raise taxes on its own account. There are assessors and collectors who compile the tax-records, work out the town's requirements and collect the necessary money. These same municipal employees, often extremely capable men, also assessed and in part collected the royal taxation. Thus the monarchy can call upon the services of a body of experts provided by the urban administration for next to nothing.

Ancien régime towns are distinguishable by their walls, privileges and the still extensive powers of their magistracies: they are also distinguished by their setting, which has so often been obliterated in the passage of time that it is worth recalling some of its prominent features.

THE URBAN LANDSCAPE AND ITS FUNCTIONS

Behind the triple safeguard of moats, embankments and ramparts, the old maps and documents reveal certain unexpected characteristics of town organization under the ancien régime.

The first impression is of the apparent disorder of these direct descendants of the urban Middle Ages. Apart from a few geometrically laid out bastions in the Midi, and various newly built or rebuilt towns, we find an intricate tracery of winding alleyways, slanting crossroads and misshapen squares interwoven with streets, runnels, roods, boundary-stones, churches, cemeteries and cesspits. Closer examination however discloses residential concentrations, organized zones and great open spaces.

Hardly any towns were without their city centre and main square. The city centre – frequently standing on the site chosen by the Romans, and retaining the same towers and stonework – clusters around the cathedral or collegiate church: it will include the episcopal palace, chapter houses, tiny parishes, chapels and the faithful, court-houses and court officials. The city centre is separated by ramparts, gates or at least boundary marks from the market, and here the tradesmen and shopkeepers have settled, with their own parish churches, patron saints, assembly points, institutions and 'maison commune' – civic hall – which rivals the house of the seigneur or bishop. A citadel may constitute a third urban centre. Elsewhere, a less tight-knit pattern of *quartiers* and parishes is inhabited by the indispensable general populace – journeymen, workmen, day-labourers. Yet the past has left an indelible impress on this seeming chaos. Wayward, ancient boundaries mark off the various parishes, which vary from ten to as many as fifty in number in the more ancient and stable towns. Other limits define seigneuries, and con-sequently their jurisdictions; others indicate the '*quartiers*', which correspond to a kind of administrative unit, with their '*quarteniers*' (municipal watchmen), '*dizeniers*' (the head of a *dizaine*, subdivision of a *quartier*) and soon their '*commissaires*'. An eccentric kind of cadastral geometry dating at least from medieval times allocates a 'space' of so many feet to each house, with special reference to the façade, since it enchances both the prestige and the material welfare of the citizen to have frontage on the street: only the wealthy can afford to occupy more than one 'space'. On top of this patchwork of housing planning (strongly reminiscent of the ancient *mansus* encoun-tered in the countryside) and the maze of seigneurial, parishional or other types of boundary, custom or necessity still tend to specialize whole streets and *quartiers*. The tanners and dyers can only set up their workshops and dwellings along rivers or streams, while convenience and tradition have brought the jewellers and furriers together in adjoining houses. The wealthy *quartiers* are often separated from the poor or slum areas by a kind of geographical segregation, but this commonplace observation is not always accurate, for the scheme of horizontal distribution may be com-plicated by various vertical divisions: the bigger towns grow upwards more easily than outwards, with shop, workroom or stall on the ground floor, the wealthier families on the first or 'noble' floor (which has higher ceilings), and poverty rising with the stairs. Elsewhere, families may live one to each room in tiny, quasi rural thatched cottages (slate and tiles are scarce and dear in most areas) grouped around the communal well with its cluster of small gardens manured by the household waste.

The amount of open space (free of houses) is more surprising. As well as public squares and cemeteries (not banished to the outskirts until the royal decree of 1776), there were meadows, vineyards, vast enclosed gardens and sometimes whole fields, all of these maintained for reasons both of convenience and security: a town under siege had to be able to feed itself and provide grazing for the livestock it harboured. Taste, fashion and privilege took over when necessity left off, and continued to give most towns their semi-rural air. Pleasure as well as tradition preserved the flower-beds and kitchen gardens of the many convents, noble *hôtels* and even some burghers' houses. Every citizen living above the bread-line feels the urge to grow cabbages and turnips and if possible to raise three hens and a pig; higher still, he owns a stable, a stall, and perhaps a meadow. Many towns still own communal herds and hire shepherds and swineherds. Butchers too need to have open ground (often in the suburbs) in order to fatten up livestock which has come a long way on the hoof, and launderers and dyers must have broad meadows for hanging and drying, together with big warehouses. Lastly, the magistracy has its own gardens, or its training grounds where the town militia can practise with bow or arquebus, originally in earnest, later on for friendly contests.

The largest spaces are often occupied by the numerous convents established by the Counter Reformation, as well as those built during the Middle Ages. The ten medieval convents at Angers are joined by thirteen new ones between 1596 and 1640, and another five before the century is out. Buildings, gardens and parks usually cover vast areas untouched by urban life, making their own contribution to the intensely ecclesiastical atmosphere of the ancient towns of France – about thirty churches and chapels in Beauvais, sixty-nine in Angers, although some of the more recent stand in the outskirts or suburbs.

Every town normally has its suburbs (*faubourgs*) straggling out along the main roads. Although these lie outside the walls, they often form part of the juridical '*banlieue*' of the city, thereby sharing in its privileges, and frequently enjoying extra privileges such as exemption from the various 'octrois' payable at the town gates. They therefore attract butchers, bleachers and *guinguettes** (where new wine is tax-free, and costs less), quick to cash in on an additional 'freedom'. The rest of the mainly rural suburbs are occupied by

* Popular cafés, usually in the open air, with food and dancing. – Tr.

market-gardens, vineyards and meadows whose produce helps to feed the town. In wartime the suburbs are extremely vulnerable and sometimes destroyed, while their population has to move bag and baggage inside the walls, but this instability tails off in the eighteenth century. With the coming of domestic peace, the suburbs spread outwards and are even absorbed by the bigger or more prosperous towns.

Beyond the suburbs, the last outposts of urban freedoms and privileges, the real countryside lies in economic, seigneurial, financial and mental dependence on the towns, which are often hated by peasants who see the best of their produce being syphoned off with no apparent return in services. The opposition between town and country is no less obvious than their interdependence.

There is no need to dwell on this interdependence. Apart from the markets where people meet, exchange and sometimes dispute, there is a sizeable overlap of labour. Day-labourers and schoolboys stream out into the countryside at harvest and grape-picking time; the rural weaver in the textile regions has frequent contacts with urban workshops and merchants – these are two examples out of many. Nor must we overlook the complex demographic situation: while the towns frequently dispatch nurseling children to the country, they get back a considerable if erratic influx of immigrants who contribute to their wealth and growth as apprentices and domestic servants, but also swell their poorhouses and cemeteries.

But the peasant visiting or moving into town found a more structured, rigid hierarchic society than the one he left behind. This society is well-documented, and will repay a closer examination.

2 URBAN SOCIETY

FROM ITS OWN VIEWPOINT: CORPORATE BODIES

Dozens of ecclesiastics and lawyers attempted to describe their society from their central vantage-point, and they always did so, purposely or otherwise, in relation to ancient schemas, with a view to finding in it those features which they supposed to be sacred and everlasting. Thus Charles Loyseau continually compares the 'orders' of Henry IV's age with those of Rome, or of Heaven, which means that Loyseau and his kind are far better witnesses to their own attitudes than to the realities of their times, although the former are subsumed under the latter, and add to our understanding of them. Again, some of these abstract theorists sometimes manage to be reporters also, although they see in blinkers or through distorting lenses. They too provide a kind of evidence; it is partial and inadequate, but it has to be considered.

They are unanimous in seeing men only as groups. Barring the abstractions of the moralists, essayists and philosophers, which are no more than collective types (the Christian, the sage, the *honnête homme*), man in isolation appears to them both inconceivable and disgraceful, and they barely stop short of suspecting him of sinister plans such as traffic with the Devil (or with God, if he is a hermit). In fact, even those who might today be called 'fringe' or 'asocial' elements – broadly speaking, the 'beggars' of the time – seldom function as individual units and make up highly organized groups with their own leaders, laws (even if unwritten), areas and language, already called *argot*.

All these groups of men were readily accommodated by the very ancient (Indo-European?) juridical classification of the orders: those who pray – *oratores;* those who, in theory, fight – *bellatores;* those whose labour allows the others to pray and fight – *laboratores.* The time-honoured distinction of the 'three orders' lives on, although it is overgrown with annotations and distorted by countless shifts of meaning: while the first order still derives from sacred unction, the second owes its allegiance to 'race' rather than the sword, and the third is nothing more than a vast rubbish tip holding the left-overs. The distinctive quality of the town as compared with the country is that within the three orders the corporate bodies stand out with exceptional clarity and near-perfect definition, and are aware of so doing.

We have seen that the peasant masses are usually differentiated only by their productive role and their standard of living: the groups which the historian can isolate among this amorphous multitude hardly ever equate with any legal or customary standing or even with any precise nomenclature. There is no 'corps' of *laboureurs* or *métayers,* and the meaning of these two terms, if they have one, varies from one province to the next.

In the towns, it is a different story. Each man belongs to a corporate body (*corps*) which has it own legal status sanctioned, and
often taxed, by the legal and administrative authority. The religious
character of each *corps* is often symbolized by its dedication to a
'patron saint' and by communal religious ceremonies. They have
their own admission rites, hierarchy, and leaders with the right to
litigate, draw up a budget or at least to manage funds. Each *corps*
has a state of mind, symbolism and above all a jealously guarded
position in a hierarchy which puts itself on display in the great town
parades and solemn processions. The same precedence operates
in political functions surviving from an older kind of urban life, such
as the elections for the magistracy, which are often carried out
through corporate bodies. Rank in the procession and in the ballot
is a precise ritual expression of the '*corps*' status in relation to those
which march or vote before and after it. Together, they represent
practically all of urban society as visualized in its own time.

But it is only too obvious that some *corps* are more equal than
others, and that there is a considerable discrepancy in dignity,
power and perhaps also in kind between the humble '*mestier*' of the
cobblers and the '*compagnie*' of '*Messieurs du Présidial*'* or of the
still more influential *parlement*.

The strictly professional groups called themselves '*corps et communautés d'arts et mestiers*', or just '*mestiers*'; the modern use of 'corporation' is anachronistic, although ratified by usage.† The
extraordinary diversity of these guilds is often stressed, but does
not obscure their underlying uniformity.

These are professional bodies whose scope ranges from the very
narrow (spurriers, ropemakers, woolcombers) to the fairly wide
(drapers) and whose membership follows the same pattern (eighteenth-
century Paris yields a single helmet-maker and three thousand
haberdashers). What they have in common is clearly their labour,

* The *Présidiaux* were courts of appeal from the bailiwick, established in 1552. They had
authority to judge criminal and lesser civil cases and while their intermediate jurisdiction –
somewhere between bailiwick and *parlement* – seems not to have speeded up the course
of justice, it provided a further fund of venal offices. – Tr.

† 'Corporation' is an English borrowing. The same warning applies to the word 'guild',
used from here on for the sake of simplicity. – Tr.

which is manual, or 'mechanical', to use the contemporary word – but the '*artistes*' such as doctors and apothecaries already feel themselves a cut above the average member of the humbler craft guilds.

The juridical uniformity of the guilds is even more striking. They have the sanction of the urban and seigneurial authorities and of the king himself, by way of the judiciary. When the guild has statutes, they are backed by these authorities, which also exercise supervisory powers, so that no guild may convene, raise funds or render accounts without their specific agreement.

Within this framework the guild does all it can to maintain a work-monopoly; quarrels with rival guilds over the slightest hint of encroachment upon its prerogatives, and keeps a tight rein on its membership. Guild discipline embraces religion (masses, prayers, good works); work (it often, but not always, enforces niggling regulations); finance (subscriptions); and is more or less strictly moral, but also apt to be expressed in charitable provision for orphans and the sick, and funeral expenses, although assistance for the unemployed is very rare.

These legal associations of specialized artisans are nearly always strictly dependent upon a small group of big employers, variously known as '*maîtres*', '*jurés*', '*gardes*', etc. These are close-knit oligarchies, inter-related and perpetuated from one generation to the next. They command both in fact and in law – the law following the fact, in the normal manner.

This handful of powerful men has at least one attitude in common with the mass of journeymen in the guild – a jealous professional pride and secretiveness, a stubborn faith in the 'tricks of the trade', a radical, almost morbid opposition to any kind of change and a naive worship of tradition, whose paramount and sacred nature is hardly ever questioned.

But the '*communautés de mestiers*' constitute only the best-known and most widespread type of corporate body. The scale of prestige extends both higher and lower.

The higher types tended to lay claim to the fairly distinguished title of '*corps*' or the even more desirable '*compagnie*', occupying the most exalted levels of the Third Estate. At their head came the King's legal officers – about ten of them in the average town –

followed by the slightly more numerous royal treasury officers, then the seigneurial magistrates, then, in this order, the essential lesser officials: advocates, *procureurs* (the equivalent of the modern solicitor), clerks of the court, notaries (then quite humble), bailiffs (*huissiers*) and tipstaffs (*sergents*). Each company has its own statutes, accumulated privileges, leaders, rules of assembly, financial structure and corporate mentality – the last so pronounced that, prior to the accession of Louis XIV, it had produced '*syndicats*' well-organized and ambitious enough to play their part in a few insurrections. These sombrely robed men, invested with a fraction of the king's authority, also had to make room for the doctors, who argued precedence with the advocates.

In the early seventeenth century, Loyseau wrote: 'Both in Rome and in France the principal legal practitioners are followed by the merchants . . . the last of the people of honourable rank, being styled honourable men or honest persons and town burghers, titles which are ascribed neither to agricultural workers nor to . . . artisans, and still less to manual labourers, who are all classified as '*viles personnes*'.* Because tradesmen deal in material things, legal luminaries like Loyseau grant them no more than a modicum of respect, and the same grudging recognition applies even to big merchants, although their true role is obviously disproportionate to their given rank. But it must be emphasized that the biggest businessmen seldom form part of any highly-evolved '*corps*': they tend to be sturdy individualists, against state control in favour of total economic liberty, and divided by their own competitiveness, so that their collective organization is often loose or sporadic. They may unite in battle against the claim of rival bodies (drapers against cloth-merchants, for example), or in opposition to those ministers who favour economic planning, but they do so as more or less ad hoc 'societies' whose membership is by election only, with a core of judges sitting on the influential *tribunaux consulaires,* commercial courts created in the sixteenth century on the Lyon pattern, and still surviving in the twentieth.

At the other end of the scale of urban *corps*, the town agriculturists are equally poorly organized, but for different reasons, because

* *Traicté des Ordres et Simples Dignitez . . .,* 1613 edition, VIII, 45.

they embody a kind of compromise between the typical disorganization of the countryside and the 'corporatism' of the towns. Generally speaking, we find one or two ill-coordinated communities of farmers, market-gardeners and vine-growers united only by superficially religious celebrations in honour of various rustic saints, the petitions necessary to prevent trespassing on fields and vineyards, and occasionally a background role in the election of the municipal magistracy. Day-labourers and casual workers occupy the same wretched, insecure position whether they belong to a guild or drift from one employment to another.

Orders, guilds and companies never included the whole of the urban populace. The classical corporate framework does not include the numerous unmarried or widowed women (except for some guild-masters' widows) or domestics (nearly a tenth of the urban population). Almost all of the day-labourers and the whole of the floating population functioned outside this framework, which was virtually non-existent in the countryside and fell well short, even in the towns, of containing all conditions of men, although here there are astonishing local variations which we shall overlook for lack of space.

It need hardly be repeated that this assortment of groups is the expression of a traditional vision rather than of underlying realities. Prior to the eighteenth century in particular, the literate sections of the ancien régime were comfortably off and brought up under the most hide-bound educational system ever. They were incapable of looking social reality in the face, and concerned with recognizing in it only the 'divine' and the 'Roman' orders and with rationalizing the pride of place they themselves occupied, or claimed to.

FROM THE HISTORIAN'S VIEWPOINT:
DEGREES OF CLASS FORMATION

The examples of the clergy and of textile manufacture provide a simple index of the limited, deceptive nature of the traditional vision of society in terms of orders, estates and corporate bodies.

Sacred unction and a strong spiritual and temporal organization are the main unifying factors of the first 'order' of the realm, which contains a partial cross-section of French society, not counting the popular majority. The higher nobility control the bishoprics and abbeys; the upper bourgeoisie (with a sprinkling of lesser nobility) the chapters and most of the convents; what we shall provisionally refer to as the 'middle classes' occupy the rectorships, curacies and lesser convents; the common people hardly make an appearance, except for a few true mendicant monks and unbeneficed priests. The legal decisions of 1695 and 1698 have codified the division of the clergy into two classes, inevitably called the first and second 'orders', thereby sanctioning the subjection of the lower clergy to the bishops.*

Inside the leading 'industry' of the times, it was common (but not general) practice for everybody from the lowliest journeyman to the richest foreman to belong to the same 'guild'. Needless to say, the biggest employers occupied all the key positions and the workers had no effective role. The lowlier members sometimes took badly to this arrangement, and joined the semi-underground *compagnonnages* or journeymen's associations, the archaic forerunners of an as yet unarticulated class struggle. Usually they either contented themselves with murmurings and sporadic disturbances or accepted the inevitable. But corporate unity papered over deep divisions.

Just as in the countryside, it is the basic concept of economic independence which provides the best criterion of the formation of the urban 'classes'.

THE DEPENDENT CLASSES: EARLY CONTOURS OF THE URBAN PROLETARIATS

The urban proletariats – a judicious plural is more accurate here than a sweeping singular – probably made up the most numerous urban category, if not an absolute majority. They can be defined under a few simple headings.

They are practically debarred from ownership of landed property and the means of production, and possess a bare minimum of personal property. In other words, they have no house, no land and no equip-

---

* The reference is to the royal edicts of 21 April 1695 and 15 December 1698, which empowered the bishops to give or withhold authorization to preach and to hear confessions, and to consign recalcitrants to seminaries for a three-month period without benefit of appeal. Louis XIV granted these powers in return for a payment of four million *livres* from the Assembly of the Clergy. – Tr.

ment other than hand-tools. They are always tenants, crowded into one or two rooms, and always in arrears with their rent, with a few sticks of furniture, earthenware crockery, second-hand hempen clothing, little or no money saved and chronic debts. Debts owed to landlord, local money-lender or employer are possibly a dominant feature.

With the exception of the most highly-skilled workers in trades such as building, furniture-making and ironworking, who may earn double the average wage, the run-of-the-mill journeyman has very little to offer by way of professional qualifications, so that there is a great deal of mobility of employment. Many workers go through a whole series of jobs as spinners, builder's labourers, harvesters, grape-pickers, ditchers or navvies, with intervals of 'idleness', which meant unpaid unemployment. With the onset of sickness, old age or economic crisis, this 'idleness' may well become permanent, and the victim relapses into destitution, beggary and vagrancy. The family wages (wives and children above eight years of age work at half- or quarter-pay) cover the basic necessities in normal times, seldom leave any surplus for saving, and carry no prospect of 'promotion': in Louis XIV's time, a man earned ten *sols* a day – about 100-120 *livres tournois* a year – the equivalent of about fifteen pounds of bread a day in 'favourable' times, double that amount if the wife and two children are working. In time of scarcity, and assuming that employment is available, the same wage buys a half or a third less bread. The condition of life in vulnerability, bound up with family health, the number of young children, the state of the market and circumstance.

The intellectual level in these areas of the population further aggravates their vulnerability. Barring a few men who can write their own initials or draw a guild mark, illiteracy is almost universal. Religious practice is riddled with magic and superstitions dating from the distant past, diets are unbalanced (too many cereals, starchy foods and bad wine), hygiene is non-existent, 'fevers' frequent and epidemics rife. Gossip and rumours spread like wildfire and lead to panics and local disturbances which are easily triggered and fairly easily repressed during and after the reign of Louis XIV.

A small fraction of this proletariat are conscious of their situation and try to put up a fight for wages and employment, usually from within various *compagnonnages* which are rivals otherwise, and continually harassed by Church and State. Workers in the skilled trades of wood-, leather- and ironworking and printing are the most active, while the textile workers' militancy amounts to no more than breaking the occasional window-pane. Although the latter are both the most numerous manufacturing group and the most akin to the industrial proletariat of the nineteenth century, they are also the least organized and the least politically conscious. Their low level of skill, poor standard of living and compelling need for work seems to condemn them to apathy or resignation. A fairly sizeable lower stratum with little skill or drive acts as a part-time sub-proletariat, oscillating between mendicancy and casual labour in town or country. At the bottom comes the entire marginal sub-culture living off the society that rejects them or that they themselves have rejected. What little we know about this last group indicates a higher degree of organization. It includes the work-shy, the unfit, outright criminals, prostitutes and cut-purses, and may be stretched to include displaced persons such as soldiers on the run or suddenly released by peace-time. These four probable levels of the urban lower classes have received insufficient attention, although not for lack of documentation.

In spite of these gaps in our knowledge, there is no denying the economic, social, political and mental subservience of these men. Lacking any guarantee of work, they are at the mercy of the employers and of economic fluctuations that they do not understand. Deprived of all participation other than as mute observers, they are prey to all kinds of repressive officialdom, the Church included. They are inherently powerless to improve their situation, because all the guild masterships and all the workshops are practically hereditary. The few known cases of 'advancement' or of rises in the social scale derive from chance occurrences usually involving lucky marriages with masters' widows, but occasionally the result of friendly sponsorships or pious endowments, such as bursaries to schools or seminaries. The higher classes of the State may rest assured of a continuing submission enforced by fear, habit and the perennial 'tranquillizers' (drink, festivities, oral and written escapist literature).

ON THE VERGE OF ECONOMIC INDEPENDENCE: THE 'MÉDIOCRES'

'Mediocre' in the original non-pejorative sense of middling or average was the term applied prior to 1750 to those who were half-way between 'poor' and 'easy' circumstances. They were small employers, foremen, shopkeepers, modest tradesmen and rentiers and lesser officials such as clerks of the court and *procureurs,* with a wide range of possible occupations and status, comparable fortunes and income, and a common degree of independence.

Underlying this teeming professional variety is the essential point that all these men own property, whether it is a shop, a workshop or an entire house. They are also likely to own a suburban garden or vineyard, and sometimes a few acres of ground in the neighbourhood. Usually they have a maidservant and one or more employees, either permanent or temporary. They always have a few *écus* put by in a safe place, together with a little wad of IOUs, and perhaps a few pledges, from their workers, tenant-farmers or neighbours.

They have sufficient education to be able to count and to write, although their reading consists mainly of devotional works if they read at all. They stand out from the common herd because of their correct, sober clothing and their preferential seat at mass, which may take them as far as the quite honoured post of churchwarden. If they are guild-masters or members of a 'company', they may serve as book-keepers or treasurers and participate in the election of the municipal magistrates. They are good customers of the notaries and even of the courts, keeping a close eye on their own interests, arranging their children's marriages like any other business deal, and trying to get one child or another into seminary or convent. As petty local notables in touch with either end of the social scale, they might play their part in local disputes, riots or Frondes, but seldom risked their positions or their necks, although many of them were quicker to come forward at the time of the Revolution. This busy class of modest shopkeepers, lesser employers, minor entrepreneurs and careful investors has a lively sense of its own importance, and every intention of increasing it.

But it is still not immune to chance and circumstance; it is not completely secure in its income, power and independence, and may sometimes lose them. In normal times a shop or workshop can be endangered, even ruined, by a few bad debts, a series of bankruptcies, a change in fashion or techniques, or simply by ill-health. A few ill-advised loans, a stroke of mismanagement or pressure from tougher or cleverer competitors sometimes made short work of small businesses. In the event of war, any kind of blockade, financial or market upsets, political instability or periods when 'old-style' economic crisis alternates with general recession (as in the later seventeenth century), a great many of the '*médiocres*' find their businesses taken over and themselves reduced to manual labour, sometimes to mendicancy. More often they become the 'proud poor' who were the darlings of the religious charities of the time. A certain process of 'proletarianization' can sometimes be discerned in various towns between the Mazarin era and the failure of John Law's 'System'.

Conversely, the shrewder, more intelligent or better-established forged ahead, generally by way of trade, almost always with the assistance of semi-legal moneylending activities, and sometimes through taking a hand in the king's 'business' – tax-farming, military supply, disguised loans – although such activities were rare at this level, just as it was exceptional to achieve high office in bailiwick or *élection* overnight (an intermediate stage was necessary).

Obviously no town could do without its 'masters', lesser merchants and minor entrepreneurs. The *médiocres* were essential to their day-to-day activities, and existed as a sizeable minority which was often well off, occasionally restless, but in the long term stable enough to produce real dynasties of drapers, masons, butchers, tanners, *procureurs* and notaries, whose surnames change slowly, if at all, over long periods. Rises and falls are still unexceptional in this sphere, although it is harder to keep track of the latter.

The fact remains, however, that except for a few periods of general disturbance (the League, the Fronde), they are never the driving force, and certainly never dominant.

THE DOMINANT URBAN CLASSES

Not counting noblemen, a few dozen surnames at most crop up again and again in every important town among the lists of municipal magistrates, cathedral canons, poor-house administrators and magistrates in bailiwick, *élection* or *consulat*. The same names stand out in the notaries' archives, where they settle the largest dowries, leave the biggest legacies, and make the biggest deals and investments.

The fortunes of these interlocking urban oligarchies frequently reach six or seven figures towards 1700. They own the most powerful businesses, belong to the most exalted companies of officials, and make the boldest speculations in land, stocks, taxation and wars. With a few droll exceptions, they also move in the highest cultural circles, and we may as well call them the better bourgeoisie. They therefore deserve special attention, the more so because the old problem of the ancien régime bourgeoisie has become a platform for polemics and confusion, and we need a clear view.

DOCUMENTS

38 A DEFINITION OF THE TOWN IN 1679

Town : Place full of houses, and closed in by earthworks and moats, or by walls and moats.

> *Dictionnaire françois, tiré de l'usage et des meilleurs auteurs de la langue,* by P. RICHELET, published in Geneva by Jean Herman Widerhold, 1679, 20 + 480 + 560 + 88 pp.

39 BORDEAUX IN 1715: THE WALLS

Bordeaux is still an enclosed town, shut in behind the fourteenth-century ramparts which divide it from its *faubourgs* . . . Both on the landward and the seaward side, entrance is always by way of the impractical old gateways of Saint-Julien, Dijeaux, Chapeau-Rouge, Paux . . .

Individuals did not hesitate . . . to open breeches or private passages through the town wall for their own purposes, or to build lean-tos or store materials against it. These abuses were immemorial and self-renewing, like the municipal legislation which attempted to stamp them out by making the offenders wall up illegal entrances and remove unauthorized constructions. Fruitless efforts . . .

The weakened ramparts did at least assist the forces of law and order, and still protected the sleep of the citizens. The restoration of order at home and the remoteness of the enemy abroad had not yet allayed all the old apprehensions. With nightfall – eight o'clock in winter, ten o'clock in summer – the gates are closed. The keys are in the keeping of the aldermen or gate-keepers. Only [five out of a dozen gates] are opened to make way for late arrivals or departures by land or sea, and quickly closed behind them.

Poor upkeep, lack of turrets and the inroads of parasitical building have stripped the ramparts of all military value. They are a relic of the past, overtaken by the expansion of the *faubourgs* and hampering the development of the port, and condemned by economic necessity and the growth of the town as much as by new strides in the art of war . . .

Yet a large section of the population still huddles within these battlements which have a circumference of 5,250 metres (3,050 to landward) . . .

> *Bordeaux de 1453 à 1715*, vol. IV of the *Histoire de Bordeaux* by BOUTRACHE *et al.*, 508–10.

40 THE LAST CONFIRMATION OF THE PRIVILEGES OF DIJON (1781)

Louis, by the grace of God King of France and Navarre, to all those here and in future present, greeting. Our dear and well-beloved viscount mayor, magistrates and citizens of our town of Dijon, capital of our province and duchy of Burgundy, have made most humble petition for the privileges granted by the dukes of Burgundy, their first sovereigns, and confirmed by the kings our predecessors since the juncture of the duchy of Burgundy with our own crown, and last of all by the late king our most honoured lord and forefather subsequent to the letters patent of the month of July seventeen hundred and nineteen. In addition to high, middle and low jurisdiction in matters civil, criminal and municipal in the aforesaid town, *faubourg* and *banlieue,* as by ancient right, they possess all commons, unclaimed property and confiscations, and the right to appoint guardians and to compile inventories at decease in the aforesaid town . . .* the power of sentence and distraint to the value of sixty-five *sols* without benefit of appeal . . . ruling and passing sentence in the first instance upon crimes and misdemeanours . . . gatekeepers and day- and night-watch . . .; the said citizens are also empowered annually to elect the viscount mayor, who may also appoint six magistrates by majority vote† to administer the affairs of the aforesaid town . . . the petitioners are likewise empowered to have and to hold frank-fees and new acquisitions without financial liability, are not subject to the *ban* and *arrière-ban,* and also have the freedom to use bow, crossbow and arquebus in sport . . . permission to hunt and fish, as in the other chief towns of our realm, the right to hold free fairs on the first day of February and July . . . and several other franchises,

---

* The last three rights usually belong to the seigneurial court or to its appointed notary (the seigneur may also be the king).

† In fact, the election has been a sham since the seventeenth century.

exemptions, rights, customs and freedoms . . . which they have always peaceably enjoyed . . . [and they have] petitioned to be granted our letters of confirmation . . . [*all these rights are confirmed in the ensuing text*].

Given at Versailles in the month of December in this year of grace seventeen hundred and eighty-one, and the eighth of our reign. Signed Louis. Countersigned Hue de Miromesnil, and below: For the King, signed Amelot.

> Excerpt from the communal archives of Dijon, printed
> in *La Bourgogne des Lumières, 1715–1789*, published
> by the Académie de Dijon, Centre Régional de
> Documentation Pédagogique, 1968, 87–8.

41 BORDEAUX IN 1715: ASPECTS OF THE *QUARTIERS*

. . . Apart from conventual and private gardens and the Place de l'Ombrière, open spaces and public squares are rare. The cemeteries or '*porges*' take their place . . . [Almost everywhere] the congested buildings prevent massed gatherings. With the exception of the rue d'Albret, no new thoroughfare had been opened through the old *quartiers*, which looked much the same as they had in the fifteenth century. The narrow streets with gutters running down the middle, stagnant waters and smells are the same as ever. Where the rivers Peugue and Devèze have not been bricked over, the same polluted waters can be seen. Ancient houses crumble and sometimes collapse . . . In spite of various parlementary decrees, a rash of chaotic building and encroachments on others' property pays scant heed to planning . . .

In the midst of all this muddle, each *quartier* retains a certain individuality which is the legacy of its past, its traditions, its economic functions and the social standing of its residents. Towards 1715, the *quartiers* still reflect a way of life that dates back to the thirteenth century. The blurred boundaries of these *de facto* communities do not necessarily coincide with those of the fifteen urban parishes, some of them quite small in size . . . Nor are the *quartiers* totally homogeneous units . . . The finest have their eye-sores, while the most decrepit have handsome dwellings to show . . .

> *Bordeaux de 1453 à 1715*, op. cit., 510–11.

42 THE SOCIO-POLITICAL MAKE-UP OF AN AVERAGE TOWN OF THE LATE SEVENTEENTH CENTURY

Analysis of the tax-roll for the 'subvention' (a mild local equivalent of the *taille*) in the town of Beauvais, 1696.

The 'roll' is drawn up house by house along a traditional itinerary that covers the twelve parishes and 13,000 inhabitants of the town. The tax affects all unexempted heads of family; a hearth here roughly corresponds to a family, plus all unmarried persons living alone and above thirty years of age.

1 TAX-EXEMPT (PRIVILEGED) HEARTHS: 1,050 hearths or persons

Ecclesiastics: 460 persons (secular and regular).

Families of gentry: 4 (country nobility resident in town, a rare situation).

Non-noble but exempt officials: 57 hearths (*Présidial* 15; *Election* 16; royal and princely houses 17; others 9).

Privileged workers at the Royal Tapestry Manufacture: about 100 (hearths).

Institutional poor: about 350 persons (Poor Bureau 300; Hôtel-Dieu 50).

Newly-weds: 39 (in Beauvais, they are exempt during their first year of marriage).

Family heads gone to war: 51.

Family heads absent for reasons unknown: 49.

. . . and the man who brought down the popinjay in the annual shooting contest.

2 TAXED HEARTHS: THE TEXTILE WORLD (WOOL AND FLAX): 745 hearths

Merchants: 99

Cloth and serge manufacturers: 104 (middling and lesser employers).

Textile workers: 542 hearths (serge-makers 130; weavers 117; combers 96; nappers 64; shearers 26; reeling-girls designated by name 68; dyers 18, etc.).

3 TAXED HEARTHS: THE EVERYDAY WORLD OF SHOP AND WORKSHOP: 582 hearths

Foodstuffs: 211 (bakers 60; butchers 28; inn-keepers close on 100, etc.).

Clothing: 204 (tailors 21; dressmakers 34; shoemakers 37; cobblers 54, etc.).

Housing, tool-making: 167 (masons 26; joiners 27; locksmiths 11; nailsmiths 14; metal-workers 8; rope-makers 12, etc.).

**4 TAXED HEARTHS: SMALL FRY WHOSE PROFESSION IS
UNSPECIFIED BUT ASSESSED AT LESS THAN 10 LIVRES:**
468 hearths

> 'Widows' taxed at less than 10 *l*.: 230.
> 'Maids': 111.
> 'Poor' designated by name, taxed at a few *sols*: 127 hearths (these three categories are usually wool-spinners).

**5 NON-EXEMPT BOURGEOIS, LEGAL PRACTITIONERS AND
'ARTISTES':** 317 hearths

> *Bourgeois living on income:* 'bourgeois' designated by name 58; widows taxed at over 10 *l*. 49; 'maids' taxed at over 10 *l*. 29.
> *Legal practitioners, court auxiliaries, etc.:* 159 (including 5 notaries, 15 advocates and 24 *procureurs*).
> *Medical practitioners:* 22 (6 doctors, 5 apothecaries, 11 surgeons – the first two groups claim to practise an 'art', not a 'craft').

**6 SEMI-RURAL RESIDENTS OF THE TOWN AND
FAUBOURGS:** 221 hearths
(equivalent to the population of a large village)

> *Tenant-farmers:* 7.
> *Gardeners:* 37.
> *Vine-growers:* 80.
> *Day-labourers:* 24.
> *Semi-agricultural craftsmen:* 69 (including 18 coopers and 15 farriers).
> > Archives of the département of Oise, B 1638, Beauvais tax-rolls, abstract.

NB: the distribution of the total tax-load (14,878 *livres,* an average of 6.60 *livres* per taxable hearth) is also of interest; a short breakdown is appended:

Less than 2 *livres*	1,218 hearths
2–9 *livres*	617 hearths
10–30 *livres*	297 hearths
60–90 *livres*	17 hearths
Over 90 *livres*	4 hearths

(the biggest tax-payer is the 'receiver' of the Diocese, at 400 *livres*)
Total of taxable hearths . . . 2,252

Less than ten per cent of the tax-payers contribute half the town taxes.

> Pierre GOUBERT, *Beauvais et le Beauvaisis . . .,* op. cit.
> 256–61 passim.

43 A FEW GLIMPSES OF THE EARLY URBAN PROLETARIATS

I MAMERS: A WILL OF 1752

(*Jean Launay, a journeyman serge-maker resident in the house of François Le Roy, sieur de l'Auberderie, a Mamers bolting-cloth manufacturer, dictates his will from his sickbed, 31 January 1752*)

'. . . requests and requires that all his linen and clothing, consisting of one pale grey cloth suit, one coat, one pair of maroon plush breeches, one hat, two pairs of shoes, six shirts, two collars, one well-worn suit and coat of drugget, two cotton kerchiefs, three pairs of fair to middling stockings and a copper snuffbox, be sold and their price used to pay his debts, the remainder to defray his funeral expenses and to have masses said and celebrated, declaring that he has no cash in hand and none owing to him.'

Notarial minute from Mamers, Chevalier practice,
printed in François DORNIC, *L'Industrie textile dans le
Maine et ses débouchés internationaux, 1650–1815*
(Éditions Pierre-Belon, Le Mans, 1955), XXVI + 318 pp., 210.

2 BEAUVAIS: SOME FACTS AND FIGURES

Posthumous inventories:

The hundreds of posthumous inventories of wool-workers' assets deposited in the bulging files of the Beauvais seigneurial courts present a number of common characteristics. They are brief and ill-written – the clerk knew that there was little prospect of being paid for this type of work. They end with a renunciation of the estate, which is quite often in deficit. The sale or valuation of the personal effects of the deceased rarely produces a return of more than a hundred *livres tournois,* the price of a good horse . . . Antoine Bara, serge-worker, September 1617, less than twenty *livres;* Jean Comédé, wool-comber, May 1645, 95 *livres* 10 *sols;* Thibault Saulnier . . . weaver, January 1647, 63 *livres* 11 *sols;* Pierre Crestien, wool-comber, June 1650, 62 *livres;* Antoine Régnier, napper, January 1651, 64 *livres* 9 *sols.* Skipping to the following century: Louis Béranger, weaver, February 1722, 86 *livres;* Antoine Lamory, serge-worker, November 1738, 85 *livres* 17 *sols.* The few personal papers noted in the inventories mention only rent outstanding and small debts; never a house, a plot of land or a rood of vines . . .

Pierre GOUBERT, *Beauvais et le Beauvaisis,* op. cit., 304.

Population breakdown, based on the tax-rolls:

In 1696, 1,218 out of 2,252 hearths were taxed at less than two *livres* . . . [say] three or four days' work . . . Who were these tax-collectors' favourites? Textile workers, almost to a man. In the most varied and heavily populated parish in town, Saint-Étienne, forty-six out of fifty-four serge-workers, twenty out of twenty-three weavers, twenty-two out of twenty-six woolcombers and all the reeling-girls could not afford 40 *sols* each in taxes; half of them could not afford ten *sols*. None of the textile journeymen of Saint-Martin paid as much as forty *sols*. In Sainte-Marguerite, fifty out of fifty-six paid no more than twenty *sols*. In the whole town of Beauvais in 1696, 106 out of 117 weavers, 119 out of 130 serge-workers, 88 out of 96 woolcombers and all the reeling-girls stayed below the forty-*sol* mark; 385 out of 481 paid less than twenty *sols* . . .

Not all the minor taxpayers were woolworkers: we find among them most of the journeyman masons, joiners, locksmiths, cobblers, thirty-five of that type of baker who merely provided an oven for other people's dough, the petty haberdashers with small clienteles, nearly all the seamstresses and all of the day-labourers, plus eighty-two over-age spinsters and 178 over-cautious widows, who did not keep themselves by their distaffs. In other words, the social leavings of petty business, the lesser craftsmen and failed family ventures, together with nearly all the wage-earning class: this was the ordinary population of Beauvais . . .

GOUBERT, ibid., 262–3.

The wage of a good able-bodied weaver at the end of the seventeenth century:
It was fifty-five *sols* per week, say about nine *sols* per working day . . . A worker who evaded unemployment drew wages for 270 days a year, so he could average about 7½ *sols* per day . . . In a good year, wholemeal bread cost five or six *deniers* a pound, Beauvais weight . . . say half a *sol* to a Paris pound (489 grammes). In theory, he could afford fifteen pounds. For a bachelor, this was a fairly good living, since he would not consume more than four pounds. For a young household raising one or two children, it practically guaranteed a living, especially if the wife earned two or three *sols* by spinning. A household with any more young children would be hard pressed . . . And yet these are the highest possible standards of living for workers . . . They presuppose a steady job, bread at six *deniers* a pound, moderate family responsibilities, and good health . . . Now the price of bread doubled in 1609, 1618, 1623, 1627, 1631, 1632, 1643, 1647, 1674, 1679, 1699, 1714 and 1720. It tripled in 1649, 1651 and 1661–2, and it quadrupled in 1693–4 and 1710 . . .

GOUBERT, ibid., 298–300.

3 AMIENS: THE 'GREAT CONFINEMENT'
(MID-SEVENTEENTH CENTURY)

[In 1641, a *curé* donates two buildings to house a hospital, and stipulates that they may be used to confine the poor] 'in order to remove them from their bad ways, to spare the people their importunings, and to prevent the disturbances caused by beggars in churches'.

[In 1654, the bishop suggests the internment of all the 'poor', and proposes a by-law]: 'The poor would be instructed in the paths of salvation and the means of earning their living . . . they would be employed in the jobs they knew, such as weaving, tapestry-making, stone-carving and other crafts . . . and if they had no trade, in what they were best fitted to do, like stocking-making, spinning and cement-making.'

[In 1717, the municipal magistracy accuses the poor of spreading infection in the town]: 'The vagrants exhale a stink liable to cause infection in town, and the unfortunate cases of children born with the marks of their mother's imagination, having been struck by the sight of the maimed or sick, ought to make the magistrates take the proper precautions.'

[And the historian concludes]: 'Poverty is no longer sacred, and is becoming sinful. Because charity is unable to relieve distress, and is no longer enough to salve people's conscience, there is a powerful temptation to see vice and improvidence as the root of poverty. The poor must be confined so as to succour them and to protect them against harmful temptations, but also so as to punish them . . .'

Documents and text excerpted from Pierre DEYON,
Amiens capitale provinciale . . ., op. cit., 352–4.

FURTHER READING
General works

An enormous bibliography, but very few first-rate syntheses.

The most recent handbook:

DOLLINGER, Philippe, and WOLFF, Philippe, *Bibliographie des villes de France* (Klincksieck, 1967, 742 pp.).

A good number of older works have not been superseded, such as:

BABEAU, Albert, *La Ville sous l'Ancien Régime* (Paris, 1880), mainly after Champagne sources.

Some very useful works based on the history of institutions:

DOUCET, Roger, *Les Institutions de la France au XVIᵉ siècle* (Picard, 1948, 2 vols), difficult but exceptionally sound.

ESPINAS, Georges, various *Bulletins d'Histoire urbaine* published in the review *Annales d'Histoire Économique et Sociale* from 1929 onwards, and particularly in 1933, 1935, 1937, and 1939 (judicious critiques).

PETIT-DUTAILLIS, Ch., *Les Communes françaises, caractères et évolution des origines au XVIIIᵉ siècle* (Albin Michel, 1947, 400 pp.).

A valuable outline of urban demography:

MOLS, Roger, *Introduction à la démographie historique des villes d'Europe* (Louvain and Gembloux: Recueil des travaux d'histoire et de philologie de l'Université de Louvain, 4th series, 1954–6, 3 vols).

Two recent reinterpretations in the series *Les Grandes Civilisations*:

DELUMEAU, Jean, *La Civilisation de la Renaissance* (Arthaud, 1967); chapter VIII (and IX), first class.

CHAUNU, Pierre, *La Civilisation de l'Europe classique* (ibid., 1966), chapter VIII on the town and the urban setting, and especially chapter X (society) are more hasty and far more arguable.

Probably the soundest approach is to consult some of the better recent urban studies, for example the two theses by ROUPNEL (Dijon) and DEYON (Amiens) already mentioned.

The most outstanding recent achievement is the *Histoire de Bordeaux* (vols. IV and V) under the editorship of Ch. HIGOUNET, frequently used in this and the following chapter.

On urban society, in addition to the above works and the regional theses listed at the end of Chapter 3 (p. 75) the reader is advised to consult the following:

COORNAERT, Émile, *Les Corporations en France avant 1789* (Gallimard, 1941, 306 pp.); the standard, almost the definitive work, as is:

Ibid., *Les Compagnonnages en France du Moyen Age à nos jours* (Les Éditions Ouvrières, 1966, 435 pp.).

HAUSER, Henri, *Ouvriers du temps passé, XVᵉ–XVIᵉ siècles* (Alcan, 5th ed. 1927 XLII + 262 pp.)

Ibid., *Travailleurs et marchands de l'ancienne France* (ibid., 2nd ed. 1930, VIII + 231 pp.)

Ibid., *Les Débuts du capitalisme* (ibid. new ed. 1931, XII + 326 pp.).

(Collected articles, remarkable but for a few outdated general concepts such as the 'capitalism' or 'modernity' of the sixteenth century.)

Of the numerous fairly recent monographs, it is worth consulting:

DAUMARD, Adeline and FURET, François 'Structures et relations sociales à Paris au XVIIIe siècle' in *Cahiers des Annales* No. 18 (A. Colin, 1961, 97 pp.), which raised a storm of criticism, but remains valid.

LEFEBVRE, Georges, *Etudes orléanaises,* vol. 1, *Contribution à l'étude des structures sociales à la fin du* XVIIIe *siècle* (Commission d'Histoire économique et sociale de la Revolution, Mémoires et Documents, XV, Paris, 1962, 276 pp.); the last book by this undisputed master.

X · BOURGEOIS
AND BOURGEOISIES

It would be quite possible to rest content with providing an overall definition of the ancien régime 'bourgeoisie' under the four headings: urban, non-noble, wealthy and power-hungry. The resulting portrait would be without risk and without subtlety. Alternatively, since the words 'bourgeois' and 'bourgeoisie' have accreted layers of confusion and sentiment, it would be possible to advocate the systematic statistical study of their successive or simultaneous meanings. At the cost of a great deal of labour, a few machines and a little insight, such an analysis would no doubt give results.

We shall fall back upon a simple two-stage method: first, to grasp the ancien régime concept of 'bourgeois' by staying close to the documents; second, to attempt to elicit 'structures' by applying the by now almost commonplace formula of going from the 'lived' to the 'real'; in simpler terms, to develop our interpretation by drawing back the veil of appearance which often satisfied the contemporary observer and attempting to restore the various bourgeois groups to their original place in the prevailing system – inside, occasionally on the fringes, and perhaps also outside it.

1 THE CONTEMPORARY VIEW
By referring to dictionaries, literary works and the far more significant evidence of the archives, we can state that the term 'bourgeois' had a good dozen current senses.

THE GENERAL AND EMOTIVE SENSES
The oldest and most widespread amounts to nothing more than a

straightforward statement of residence: the bourgeois lives in a town, the place where a market is held (the first medieval 'burghers' were often connected with markets in very old cities which expanded subsequently), as opposed to the rustic, the countryman; the bourgeois is also seen as distinct from the common urban populace, and the word indicates first a *de facto* then a *de jure* élite.

Yet this sweeping definition is subject to several noteworthy and significant exceptions, particularly in the Midi. In Haut-Languedoc and Bigorre, documents as current and authoritative as the *compoix* (non-pictorial cadastral surveys) bestow the title of 'bourgeois' on the biggest landowners resident upon their own *mas* in the countryside and running them successfully on their own behalf. Coupled with the surname of a wealthy peasant, 'bourgeois' is therefore an expression of respect.

This homage to property, success and power is by no means an isolated instance. Among the working men of the seventeenth century it is common parlance to refer to the employer (not necessarily the owner) as *le bourgeois*: Richelet lists this usage in the 1679 edition of his dictionary.

Towards 1600, the shipowners of La Rochelle and probably of other ports were commonly described in notarized contracts and elsewhere as '*bourgeois de nef*' (ship bourgeois), although these same 'bourgeois' might very well be noblemen.

It seems then that the term if not the title of 'bourgeois', which was used both by its bearers and by their inferiors, expresses a combination of substantial property, affluence and power, usually (but not always) urban, and usually (but again not always) common.

But quite often it also seems that the same term is fairly heavily laden with contempt, where it is spoken – aimed, indeed – by men or groups of men with claims to a far higher station. In this context, 'classical' literature provides an impressive number of known or forgotten examples: the standard parody is Monsieur Jourdain.

The most downright pejorative shades of meaning naturally derive from circles which set an exceptionally high valuation on themselves, very much higher than that of the 'vulgar' herd to which they demote all who are other than themselves, taking good care to stress the gulf that lies between. For soldiers and sailors, the

'civilian' is always fair game for contempt, expressed in the regular
army's description of the provincial militias, mainly of peasant origin,
as '*soldats de bourgeoisie*'. The nobility of self-styled 'ancient extraction' despises the legally better-attested nobility of recent creation –
here the best-known example is Saint-Simon's diatribes against the
'règne de vile bourgeoisie' (remember that all Louis xiv's ministers
were noble). The same sentiment is aired with a kind of sadistic
contrition by the abbé de Choisy in a much-quoted passage in
his memoirs:

> My mother, who was of the house of Hurault de l'Hospital, would often
> say to me: Listen, my son, be not vain, and remember that you are only
> a bourgeois. I know very well that your sires and grandsires were masters
> of requests and counsellors of state; take it from me that France acknow-
> ledges no nobility other than of the sword.
>
> (Francois CHOISY, *Mémoires*, Michaut-Poujoulat ed., 554.)

It is a fair indication of the uneasy position of many 'bourgeois'
(or would-be bourgeois) in the 'good society' of the ancien régime
to hear a woman descended from a long line of political nobility
endorse the most well-worn and deep-rooted schemas of aristocratic racism. Aristocratic and well born, or claiming to be, this
'good society' accuses the bourgeoisie of being small-minded, mean
and vulgar. As early as 1635, Sorel puts the following into the mouth
of one of his heroes harassed by a brawling mob of jeering young
noblemen: 'Bourgeois is the insult given by these hooligans to anybody
they deem slow-witted or out of touch with the court.'* There is a
striking uniformity in the line of contempt reaching from here to the
'Philistines' derided by the young romantics of the *Hernani* controversy, through Flaubert's summary dismissal ('I call anybody who is
small-minded bourgeois') to Gide in his journal ('the bourgeois has
a hatred of the gratuitous, the disinterested') and other more
recent examples.

Earning the deference of those whose wealth and station are
beneath him and the lofty disdain of all who see themselves by birth,
life-style and culture (but not necessarily wealth) as above him, the

---

* Charles SOREL, *Francion*, 1635 edition, p. 286.

ancien régime bourgeois (and any number of his descendants) seems sandwiched between opposing emotive concepts. There are others.

THE JURIDICAL SENSES: THE BOURGEOIS AS MEDIEVAL SURVIVAL, THE PRIVILEGED TOWNSMAN

A statutory, purely urban bourgeoisie came into being during and after the twelfth century. Of course the statutes varied from one town to the next, and the conditions necessary in order to enjoy full legal 'bourgeois' status and privileges were sometimes very stringent, sometimes more lenient. These ancient and variable regulations more or less relaxed in the course of time, but while the title 'bourgeois de —' was sometimes a fairly minor distinction by the seventeenth century, it might also retain a real value: it was still something to be proud of, and the bearer felt that he 'represented' his town.

Whereas all statutory bourgeois, or burghers, are townsmen, not all townsmen are burghers. It is always necessary to be a resident, often a long-term resident, although here and there the traditional 'year and a day' suffice. But residence alone is seldom enough, and often the minimum requirement is that the candidate must be a lease-holder able to contribute to the military and especially the financial needs of the town. Often too, a still more stringent condition is enforced, whereby not only must the burgher own his house but it also has to have frontage on the street, rather than being tucked away off a courtyard, which explains why French towns have so many high narrow façades with long dark back rooms. A still more draconian condition which was more prevalent outside the realm dictated that the true burgher had to have his name entered into the town '*livre de bourgeoisie*', in return both for cash down and the approval of the established burghers (cf. Document 47, p. 255).

Although the old legal sense of the word seemed to be blurring or becoming replaced by other meanings by the early eighteenth century, these statutory burghers certainly continued to benefit from privileges much more substantial than those enjoyed by the general town populace. Here again, extreme variety is the only rule. These privileges were distributed unevenly within the honorific, legal, administrative and financial fields. In some cases and in some towns, the burgher could only be tried before specially appointed courts, and he was partly or wholly exempt from one or more levies, *tailles,* excises, entry dues or frank-fees (which the revenue authorities had roundabout methods of retrieving). Lastly, as long as the assemblies responsible for electing the municipal magistrates retained any powers, the 'statutory burghers' took an official part, usually had the biggest say, and were sometimes the sole eligible candidates.

From the sixteenth century onward, a number of controversial documents held that the name 'bourgeois' referred to 'town citizens in good standing, be they officers of the king, merchants, persons of private means, or others'.* A little later, we know that relatively minor townsmen had the right to this title, especially in Paris, but the fact remains that the above-mentioned trinity constitute a classic, almost casual statement of the approximate juridical composition of the statutory burgher group. In reality the royal officials, vested with a fraction of the king's authority and steeped in their own legal training and dignity, very quickly laid claim to forming a '*corps*' quite separate, superior and distinct from all the rest of the Third Estate. The professional individuality of the merchants (with or without the right to the title of 'burgher') was evident. Lastly, since the sixteenth century the word 'burgher' had also acquired a more ordinary sense designating life-style rather than official status – a life-style which long outlived both the ancien régime and the Revolution.

THE NARROW SOCIAL SENSE: THE BOURGEOISIE AS A WAY OF LIFE, A STABLE TYPE OF RENTIER

'Bourgeois of —', 'bourgeois living on his income without working', '*bourgeois vivant bourgeoisement*': these were common appellations in the seventeenth and eighteenth centuries, and might logically have remained in force until the collapse of the gold franc, after 1914.

This type of man and woman (the many widows and 'old maids' deserve investigation) stand out so vividly from the jumble of the archives that it would be tempting to paint a full picture if Balzac had not intervened just in time.

They themselves do not run shops or workshops, but their forefathers sometimes did. More often, these forefathers had clerked,

---

* Remonstrances of the Parlement of Paris, 1560, quoted in Maurice MARION's *Dictionnaire des Institutions* . . ., *v.* Bourgeois.

pleaded, judged, drafted agreements or collected rents and tithes on behalf of some influential figure – hence the fine house fronting on the street, with its first-floor living room, loft full of grain, court-yards and outbuildings stocked with timber, wool and sometimes poultry, and well-stocked cellar with cheap wine for the maid. For our bourgeois *'vivant bourgeoisement'* always owns property: one house at least, sometimes several, each room with its reliable lodger, and rent in advance if possible when times are hard and accommoda-tion scarce. He also owns a thriving farm or two, partly for the food, fuel, roofing and even clothing, and partly for profit. Plus one or two vineyards with hired managers, producing wine for personal con-sumption and for sale to friends and inn-keepers without paying the octroi.

Their income derives from houses, lands, but above all the kind of 'constituted rent' or annuity described in Chapter 6, more or less long-term loans at more or less legal interest (five per cent after 1665 in most provinces, six and seven per cent, or more, before that time, in spite of a maze of legislation and the easily circumvented canonical prohibitions). This, in fact, was the quintessential type of 'rent' in the provinces and therefore among the majority of the population. Loans made to individuals and secured against real estate with the interest payable at a fixed date are the main occupation of this fairly new type of bourgeois who make their appearance in the sixteenth century, flourish in the seventeenth and live on for cen-turies more. This love of fixed income often stops short of involv-ment with government stocks or the Paris *'rente sur l'Hôtel de Ville'* instituted in the sixteenth century, expanded in dubious circumstances under Louis XIII and Mazarin, paid too irregularly and subject to 'retrenchments' and manipulations, although none of this seems to have dulled the enthusiasm of the speculators, who were mainly Parisians. The more prudent and better-connected bourgeois tended to prefer rents constituted by particularly sound institutions: the estates of Brittany or Languedoc, receivers- and farmers-general and especially the opulent and well-managed clergy. The late seventeenth and still more the eighteenth century saw the development of life annuities and various packages of the tontine type. These were late (but healthy) offshoots of the time-honoured, well-entrenched, legally watertight system of the good old 'constitution', with its regular payments guaranteed by mortgage. A varying dose of discreet usury was an optional extra activity: the bulging coffers of our rentiers often contained sheets, pieces of cloth, jewellery and even gold crucifixes deposited by hard-up working people as pledges against a few *écus*. All based on an efficient system of confidential book-keeping, and thick bundles of debentures, IOUs and court orders.

The most discerning of these men advanced dowries and loans to would-be buyers of office, and made their services available to the provincial nobility, where the latter still owned lands and manors, the ultimate guarantee of a fat return. The boldest of them took on 'receiverships' on behalf of priories, convents or baronies – infallible means to the rise that would rapidly boost their descendants to far greater heights. But the true bourgeois rentier did not have the nerve for this kind of venture, and preferred to sit in his snug, well-stocked house between the hours of mass and evening service, to receive the almost daily visits of the *métayer,* the vine-grower, the weaver's wife, minor official, lesser noblemen and dozens of smaller debtors. He would swell his coffers and carry on lending and speculating while at the same time picking up a plot of land here, a farm or manor there.

Men like these, occupying their quiet niches in a society which could not do without them, had a vested interest in total conformity and stability. What mattered to them was order – political, economic, social, moral and above all financial order, although until 1726 they often suffered from fluctuations in the monetary system. The only active protests came from holders of government stocks, who were exploited when times were bad, and even took to the streets, if only for a few hours, when dividends fell too far in arrears, were cut, or simply cancelled. Possibly some of them might make a vocal contribution during brief violent disturbances or at the time of the League, the Fronde and even in July of 1789.

The 'conquering bourgeois' mentioned by a few impetuous historians will not be found among the conservative, pious, scrimping bourgeoisies; who nevertheless served their purpose, and constituted a distinct and widespread group, typical of a long episode in the social history of France from the sixteenth to twentieth centuries.

Contemporary attitudes, statutory procedure and sources of income are useful indicators of certain facets of that low-born, urban, affluent section of society to which the name 'bourgeoisie' was then applied. But does it include all the bourgeois, and are the really influential ones adequately represented? It seems not. The approach through contemporaries proves either too general, too heated, or too circumscribed; and it does a poor job of sorting out the big game from the small. At this point, we must discard the precious but restricted direct and eye-witness evidence and move on to consider society overall, in an attempt to locate the true position occupied by the big 'bourgeoisie', the men with real power. These are the organizers and managers who make the wheels go round, make long-term plans, accumulate and perhaps invest. On the whole, their fortunes can be measured in at least six figures – possibly seven on a rough conversion into the currency of the Fifth Republic. Most of these people would certainly have been far from flattered in their own day to hear themselves labelled solely as 'bourgeois', because they would have associated the title with the lesser rentiers. But the question of nomenclature is a side-issue, and we shall concentrate on the way they work and live.

2   THE TWENTIETH-CENTURY VIEW
THE BOURGEOIS AS WHEELS OF GOVERNMENT
In this traditional, rentier-dominated rural society, a number of different but interlocking bourgeoisies underpin the administrative services, the collection of ground rent and taxation, transport and exchange.

a) THE BOURGEOIS IN THE ADMINISTRATIVE SYSTEM:
THE OFFICIALS
The world of the administrators, and of the royal officials in particular, will be described at length in volume two, which deals mainly with the State. Meanwhile, it should be borne in mind that although they were separated into various rival '*corps*' and '*compagnies*', the officials saw themselves as making up an 'estate' whose ambition had long been to set itself apart from the other three, and in particular from the Third Estate, towards which their attitude was one of aloofness bordering on disgust, although most of them originated from within it. At best, they considered themselves as the voice, outward expres-

sion and dominant part of an Estate crammed with yokels and legal
ignoramuses whose proper station was walking humbly in the rear.
More often, the officials claimed to constitute a 'fourth estate', and
the most daring ventured to identify all officials with the quasi royal
group of 'those who command',* far outranking the 'obedient populace'* who were the other three 'orders or estates general of France'.

The upholders of these claims saw nothing inconsistent in their
own concerted, systematic opposition to royal envoys, commissaries
and intendants in the time of Richelieu and Mazarin – not that this
opposition was ever prolonged, still less heroic. With a few brief
exceptions, this bourgeoisie of the robe felt very much at home in the
bailiwicks and provinces which were the seat of their power. They
were the voice and instrument of a political system, and it rewarded
them with very substantial privileges, such as exemption from a wide
range of taxes. Their dissident leanings were mainly vocal in any
case, and after declining under Louis xiv they never seriously revived;
in spite of a few grouses in the eighteenth century, the bailiwicks and
élections seldom became hotbeds of the new thinking, even if some
officials backed it in their personal capacity.

The official world was always subdivided into several levels; the
lesser level of the clerks and minor officials was no higher up the
scale than the '*médiocres*' encountered in the previous chapter; the
upper 'level', that of the sovereign courts, belonged not to the
bourgeoisie but to the nobility, whether modern or very ancient
(cf. Chapter 8).

The intermediate level of the bailiwick comprised comfortable
landowners, all of them interrelated, the fathers and brothers of
canons, with surnames endlessly embroidered with the names of
seigneuries acquired. These were the pillars of the urban community,
usually ensconced in the town hall, able to take on the occasional
profitable receivership, and likely to be well-read. Nobility was their
common ideal, and many of them would be saving up in order to buy
it, or to enable their sons to do so.

Despite a few rash but bygone interludes, these low-born officials
were utterly subservient to the régime and well entrenched in its legal,

* Charles LOYSEAU, *Traicté des Ordres* . . . Foreword.

administrative, political, social and even psychological systems, since their dream was nobility, the crucial bourgeois aspiration of the age.

b) THE BOURGEOIS IN THE BASIC ECONOMIC SYSTEM:
COLLECTORS OF REVENUE

Hardly any of the big seigneurial, lay or ecclesiastical landowners found either the time or the inclination to supervise their own estates, tithes, 'feudal' rights and all the types of rent described in Chapter 6. They were always replaced by astute commoners, who did not usually lose on the transaction. There were quick fortunes to be made by men who were already well off, bold, intelligent and versed in law; we know that some wealthy *laboureurs* played the same role and so were classified among the 'rural bourgeoisie'. It is no overstatement to say that a fair number of the higher bourgeoisie of the ancien régime were collectors as well as managers, collecting corn, wine, timber, cloth, cash and also taxes. Collection, transport, exchange, taxation, conversion and circulation of money: these were perhaps the essential functions of the old bourgeoisie.

Barring accidents, the resulting accumulation of capital was often considerable. What became of it?

Any number of monographs have been produced on this subject, but no general studies are available and it would be no easy task to produce one; we are consequently forced to theorize from insufficient evidence.

It is well known that the big '*receveurs*' for dioceses, chapters or baronies often set out by acquiring a town house and a country farm, for security as well as for show. This was only one stage. The shrewdest of the big collectors could choose between two courses, and sometimes adopted both. Some embarked upon the king's 'affairs', which meant collecting his taxes and lending him money: we shall revert to these in the next paragraph. The rest diverged into the influential offices, and their descendants acceded to the Parlement, then to the great governmental posts, after a more or less rapid 'cleansing'. Two typical examples are the Dreux family, who became marquis de Brézé after 'receiving' for the bishoprics of Poitou, and the famous parlementary and ministerial family of the Lamoignons, who did the same job for the house of Nevers. We return to the con-

clusion of Chapter 8: sooner or later, the wealth amassed in the course
of big receiverships leads unerringly to nobility, and to power also.

c) THE BOURGEOIS IN THE FINANCIAL SYSTEM:
TAX-COLLECTORS AND BANKERS TO THE KING

The monarchic financial system under the ancien régime will be sur-
veyed in Volume Two, but it is common knowledge that it was one
of the weak points of that régime. Taxation was complicated, inconsistent, variable, difficult to collect and subject to delays in delivery.
The king's staff was too small, and sometimes too incompetent, to
take care of collecting and transferring every kind of tax throughout
the length and breadth of the realm. He therefore had no choice but
to delegate, and most of what today would be called indirect taxation
was collected by companies of '*traitants*' (he made '*traités*', or agreements, with them). These *financiers,* as they were also called, were
nearly always shrewd, powerful bourgeois, and it was not unusual for
them to be officers of the king's own treasury in addition to contracting with him in their private capacity, and to holding receiverships
on behalf of great seigneuries, provincial Estates and sometimes big
merchants. Their profits were exaggerated by the pamphleteers and
a hostile public, but there is no doubt that they were considerable,
and generally legal. Partly as a sop to public opinion, the State therefore announced from time to time that it would 'make the *traitants*
disgorge' by setting up ad hoc tribunals which recouped quite considerable sums, in particular under Colbert and in 1716.

Unless they went bankrupt or wound up in jail, the *traitants* had a
brilliant future ahead. As F. Bluche has shown, the wealthiest parlementary families of eighteenth-century Paris were all descended in
the male or female line from *financiers*: finance even provided a kind
of queen, in the person of Jeanne Poisson, who became marquise
de Pompadour.

Some of these financial subordinates to the monarchy played a
further part, one in which they were not alone. The kings of France
often needed large sums of cash in a hurry, mainly in war-time, and
it could well be the *traitants* themselves who advanced the money.
At other times the lenders were big merchants like Magon of Saint-
Malo, or Le Gendre of Rouen, during the last years of Louis XIV.

More often, they were businessmen of international rank and prestige, who tend to be known as 'bankers', a quite inappropriate term in view of the fact that the bankers of the time (who change money and keep bills of trade in circulation) are not necessarily large-scale operators.

Between the sixteenth and eighteenth centuries these big lenders were often foreign. The kings of the sixteenth century could not afford to go to war without the help of the bankers of Lyon, who were mainly Italians from Florence, Siena or Lucca. Richelieu added a few Dutchmen and Germans after their banker predecessors had become prelates (Gondi, Zamet, Bonzi, etc.). Mazarin naturally reverted to Italians: the Cenami, Airoli and Cantarini, with one foot in Lyon and the other in Paris, represented him and the State at once. He was partly to blame when they finally came to grief. Now the German Hervarth came to the fore, by way of Switzerland and Lyon: it was to him that the young Louis XIV wrote for a few quick millions just after the death of Mazarin; he also maintained a salon, and his wife patronized La Fontaine. After 1685, the monarchy turned to an almost unbroken series of great merchant/shipowner/tax-collectors, businessmen (all at once) – men like Le Gendre, Bernard, Demeuves, Crozat and the brothers Pâris – then a quick succession of Protestant bankers of Swiss, often Genevan origin, again by way of Lyon. These included Tourton, Saladin, Mallet, Perrégaux and Hottinguer, the series ending (temporarily) with the famous Necker. Herbert Lüthy has already explored the complex international activities of these and many other families; other important discoveries remain to be made, but their relationship to the régime is clear enough prior to 1750.

The monarchy needs them, and pays generously for their services by mortgaging as much of the future national income as possible. They in their turn need the monarchy, since it affords them a great many opportunities for profitable deals – farming the taxes of a wealthy region, provisioning the military and, less directly, speculation in stocks and property. It also affords them nobility, at least in the persons of their sons, who will become counts, marquises and parlementary presidents while the old nobility wrangles over their daughters, frequents their brilliant eclectic salons and admits them to its own, when it has any. Their success may have given offence to a few purists and crotchety gentry – a La Bruyère or a Saint-Simon – but the fact is that at these levels there is no longer any distinction of birth, caste, order or vanity. Anyone who is successful belongs to the same milieu, where background defers to opulence, chicanery, extravagance, taste, patronage, wit, and on occasion the most daring philosophies of the Enlightenment. The putative opposition between the nobility and this particular 'bourgeoisie' now makes only fitful or superficial appearances. The barriers are down at the top: the financial, political and cultural élites are one and the same.

d) THE BOURGEOIS IN THE COMMERCIAL SYSTEM: THE MERCANTILE BOURGEOISIE

The entire shopkeeper group can be left among the '*médiocres*', where they were assigned in the previous chapter. The word '*négociant*', meaning merchant or businessman, did not really come into prominence until the time of Louis XIV, reaching a kind of consecration with the publication of Jacques Savary's *Parfait Négociant* in 1675, but the phenomenon far predates the term.

The biggest bourgeois fortunes in all towns of any importance belonged to the big merchants, who tended to remain unspecialized through most of the duration of the ancien régime, and dabbled in almost everything. Specialization certainly set in eventually, but never completely. A good merchant would have struck up close relationships with his counterparts in other towns, including foreign towns. He had accredited agents in Antwerp in the sixteenth century, in Amsterdam in the seventeenth, and in other key points before long. Willy-nilly, he had to develop an interest in international transport, and therefore in shipping; in the conversion and transfer of cash and bills of exchange, and therefore in international banking, at first working with the Italians, then with German, Dutch, Swiss and English agencies operating out of Lyon, then intermittently from Rouen and finally from Paris. The 'perfect merchant' was inevitably involved with the source-countries of gold and silver specie, the 'Indes de Castille' (Spanish America), funnelling their wealth through Seville, then Cadiz, and with the countries which afford the most tempting profits – again the Indies, then the 'Isles' (of the

Caribbean, particularly San Domingo), and lastly the South Seas. This means that the sea was a necessary part of his horizon, even if he lived in Grenoble.

This kind of connection and activity dictate a way of life quite different from that of the bourgeois rentier or official. They put a premium on technical education (which the French were late in developing, despite the Italian, Dutch and English models), quick-wittedness, copious, organized correspondence, rigorous book-keeping (here again the French were late developers), and the capacity to move cash and credit far outside the narrow orbits of town and family (but the 'associations' set up for this purpose were often tentative, restricted and short-lived). Above all, they necessitate the ability to maintain credit for months and years, since the slow turnover of convoys, cash and bills of exchange meant that it was by no means unusual for most of a big merchant's wealth to be 'in transit' and on paper. Even a big merchant could be quite a small landowner (one or two houses, a few plots of land, a seigneury), while it was entirely possible for the merchant to go through cycles of fantastic success (the slave trade could more than double the original investment) and near-ruin (loss of cargoes, bad payers, the bankruptcy of an important client, war-time blockades, monetary upheavals, etc.). It is difficult to keep track of the capital of the great merchants because it is mobile, fluctuating and uncertain. In addition, and in spite of books and decrees aimed at establishing large-scale commerce as honourable and non-derogatory, the profession is not always respected either by the 'race'-obsessed nobility or by the *dévots* and the Jansenists, who verge upon seeing moneymaking as a sin. The mainstream of French thinking on this subject is far removed from that of the Italians, the Dutch and especially the English.

The behaviour, sources of income and venturesome mentality of this type of wealthy bourgeois (what else can we call him?) locate him at the opposite pole to the 'good bourgeois living on his income without working', and at quite a distance from the official, and even the big tax-collector. His offspring, not always willing to submit to the vagaries of commerce and the more or less contemptuous attitudes of high society, frequently tend to opt for security or for a more prestigious 'estate'. The children buy official posts, or become canons; the grandchildren acquire nobility and dress it up with military service. For some time, most of the mercantile families felt out of place in the régime, and their eventual response was to ingratiate themselves by adopting the status normally associated with the ownership of seigneuries, office and the title of *écuyer*.

All the same there were exceptions, and they proliferated with the decline of the régime. Savary and a few others initiated a kind of public relations exercise aimed at glamorizing large-scale trade, and the government weighed in by awarding well-deserved letters of nobility to big merchants from time to time. We have already cited the example of the big shipowners (and slave-traders) of Nantes, whose new-found nobility did not prevent them from continuing to sell sugar and slaves until the outbreak of the Revolution (in which they were never on the 'progressive' side); but without the Revolution, would their descendants have persisted? Others, including some recent noblemen, broadened their scope, passing from trade to the '*affaires du roi*', companies of *traitants* and loan associations (in any case, the king left them no choice, for instance when he appropriated part of the hard currency imported from America and gave paper in its stead). The Atlantic coast shipowners and the businessmen of Lyon and Paris knew enough to diversify their operations, combining finance with long-distance ventures and wholesale commerce; in this manner they joined those companies of financial supporters of the régime which have already been discussed.

And yet it was these mercantile circles which gave rise to certain forms of opposition to the economic and hence the political régime, based on a critique of the protectionist, authoritarian policy personified by Colbert. As long as that minister lived, opposition was bland and muted, although he still ran into difficulties in attracting investors for the trading companies he founded. Once he was out of the way, open warfare broke out against his 'system'. The heart of the matter is that the merchants of the realm saw themselves as free agents. On several occasions, mainly after 1700, their chambers of commerce and 'deputies of commerce' made their position abundantly clear; in practice, the irksome, impracticable regulations were often breached, and the representatives of the central authority sometimes turned a blind eye. The usual outcome was fraud, but not active revolt. But these appeals to liberty tied in with others which denounced certain kinds of 'despotism' yet did not exactly derive from bourgeois circles: the Fénelon group and great deputies of commerce such as Descazeaux of Nantes were contemporaries.

For the most part, and in spite of exceptions like the above, the assorted bourgeois groups which have just been reviewed – administrators, receivers, *traitants,* businessmen – were pillars of the régime, and felt at home inside it. Those who were moderately well off or careful led peaceful family lives in the provinces, secure in their property and guaranteed incomes, and busy with good matches, handsome inheritances and parish gossip. Those who had the ambition and the wherewithal found that in the long run the doors of the nobility always opened either to themselves or their descendants, and this was the great objective of most of these bourgeois. Those with a mite more wit or luck went very much higher, and became integrated into that élite of money, success, pomp, extravagance, and often of culture and intelligence, in which all past family origins merged or were courteously overlooked. It ran ever more complex enterprises, subsidized philosophers and artists, and intrigued at court in a ferment of pleasure, gold and ideas. As for the failures, they relapsed into the 'mediocrity' of the lesser bourgeoisies, or sank into the massive lower depths, and oblivion.

Individual circumstances aside, there are no antagonisms between these bourgeoisies and this regime, at any rate prior to 1750.

Does this generalization always apply to all the bourgeoisie?

FRINGE BOURGEOISIES?

There were some groups of influential men – usually towndwellers, and either wealthy or intelligent – who felt more and more at odds with the régime either because of the nature of their activities or upon intellectual grounds. The 'ideologues' (to borrow a term from Napoleon, who knew them well), international businessmen and perhaps the new capitalists dedicated to industrialization were to some extent able to criticize or obstruct this régime, either from within or without. Although their 'contestation' has to do mainly with the second half of the eighteenth century, it is necessary to raise the problem of its character: how 'bourgeois' was this disaffection and opposition?

a) THE IDEOLOGUES

There had always been criticism of the government – rather than of the régime – in books, pamphlets and broadsides, and from time to time this criticism culminated in plots, disturbances and more or less dangerous developments. But it is no easy matter to discover their social significance, which is never clear-cut, and nearly always disputed among historians. It is well known today that the Huguenot opposition of the sixteenth century had no particular social colouring, and was certainly not 'bourgeois' at any rate. Nor is there anything patently 'bourgeois' about the opposition encountered by Richelieu, still less by Mazarin. Some interpretations talk in terms of 'popular uprisings', others of aristocratic revolt; certain crown officers may have played their part, but their daring was tempered by prudence and never went all the way, with a few individual exceptions. As for the 'ideologues' who may have pioneered, supported or defended these movements, where do they stand in the social scale? The writers are either salaried household staff or men of independent means whose only common feature is culture; to call them 'bourgeois' throws no further light on their character, and often they are not even juridically members of the Third Estate.

Similarly, the 'bourgeois' character of the 'enlightenment' is open to question. Looking at it in terms of the writers involved – from Fénelon to Montesquieu and Baron d'Holbach – it is the nobility who lead the way. On the other hand, among the readers and disciples more and more attention is being paid to the emergence of a new group, the *gens à talents*. These men are the sons of lesser officials or of merchants turned rentier, or nephews of canons. They have been well educated by clerical teachers, are widely read and argumentative, and have received an early initiation into the bar, the *feudiste*'s profession, the *sociétés de pensée,* and gracious salons. Does this class of bold young intellectuals constitute a new fraction, and soon a faction, of the bourgeoisie? Yet it seems to contain a fair number of young noblemen, and especially of the *noblesse de robe*. Does this gifted élite not transcend the usual subdivisions? Is it not the 'political class' of the future, blurring the distinctions of birth and caste? The Revolution and its aftermath will show.

b) INTERNATIONAL BUSINESSMEN

It is common knowledge that the immediate trigger of the Revolution was a protracted financial crisis. On top of the very deep-seated shortcomings of the financial system, the cumulative defection of the monarchy's traditional backers probably had a decisive effect. Even the intervention of Necker did not restore the confidence of international finance and its agents. The first signs of disenchantment had appeared long before the American War of Independence, but became more pronounced during and after it. In the same period, the great shipowners of the Atlantic coast preferred to insure or reinsure with London. In spite of Lüthy's findings we would need to know even more about these financial consortia, with their preponderance of Swiss and Protestants, before venturing to assert that after some particular date a key group of big bourgeois financiers was actively betting against the régime. In any case these groups of financiers and bankers would turn out to be a fine blend of noblemen and commoners, clergy and laymen, Frenchmen and foreigners – the dying eighteenth century heralding the nineteenth. Such an assertion would necessitate proving what already seems abundantly clear: that the big banking interests assumed to have thrown their weight against the crumbling rule of the feeble Louis XVI were soon supporting the strong men who ultimately replaced him. Did not the younger banking generation of the Mallets, Delesserts, Perrégaux, Hottinguers, Lecoulteux and Périers, the contemporaries of Louis XVI, come together again to found and 'govern' the Bank of France?

After serving and being served by the ancien régime, it might be said that these bourgeoisies outgrew it.

c) A 'CAPITALIST' INDUSTRIAL BOURGEOISIE

Economists and historians have tried to discover the origins and early stages of a new industrially based economy preparing to launch itself in the course of the eighteenth century. Crossing this threshold presupposes harnessing the kind of expertise and capital which only a 'new bourgeoisie' would have been capable of bringing together. The adoption of new techniques, often of English origin; the industrial development of coal, iron and the new textiles; the modernization of agriculture to produce higher yields; the wider and faster cir-

culation of capital and goods – these are familiar enough developments. But what sort of men took part in the preparatory phases, in
the beginning of that split with the traditional seigneurial and rentier
economy of the countryside – if split there was?

As regards the early beginnings of the 'transport revolution', the
driving force was unquestionably the Corps des Ponts et Chaussées
(set up in its original form under the Regency). The brothers
Trudaine, Perronet and all the engineers seem to belong to that
intellectual élite created by contact between the technological bourgeoisie and the best of the aristocracy: they were usually backed
up by the great progressive administrators, most of them noble for
several generations back, who staffed the intendancies, the services
of the *Contrôleur général* and the government ministries themselves.
The fiercest opposition to the 'highway revolution' came from the
peasants, who saw it absorbing their sweat and money without
appreciating its utility.

As regards the major improvements advocated (and more rarely
implemented) in agriculture, nothing important emerged prior to
1750, the year in which Duhamel du Monceau published a trans-
lation of the English agronomist Jethro Tull. Now it was the turn
of the physiocrats, who drew their strength from several sources, but
were championed and heralded by some of the very highest nobility –
names such as Mirabeau and La Rochefoucauld. The rare applications
of the ideas developed in Anglophile salons were the work of the
nobility much more than of the bourgeoisie. Are we to say that they
were contracting a 'bourgeois' attitude because they were finally
buckling down to putting their vast estates to more profitable use?
Quesnay knew what he was about when he referred to the '*classe
propriétaire*' and cut loose from the old distinctions.

We are left with the big enterprise of an 'industrial' character. Many
of the longest-lived were run by big commoner entrepreneurs: drapers,
dyers, finishers and bleachers, but more usually traders who coor-
dinated orders, stockpiled both the raw materials and the finished
articles produced in dispersed workshops, and took over to their
own profit (and at their own risk) the distribution and sale of
commodities at home and abroad. Some of them covered a very
wide area, and linen goods were reaching Spain and Spanish America

at a very early date. While some of the descendants of these big entrepreneurs carried on the family tradition, others branched out into investment, sometimes coupled with office, preferably of the ennobling variety, while others went into shipping and ventures to the 'Isles', again departing from industry. Except for the misfits and the incompetents, all of them entered the nobility in the normal course of events.

In the wake of a few earlier ventures often subsidized by the state for military purposes, the eighteenth century saw a series of large-scale developments in coalmining, metallurgy, glassmaking, cotton goods and printed fabrics, involving a heavy concentration of capital, labour and skill. For some time now, historians of every school have been almost unanimous in awarding to 'the bourgeoisie' the credit for these fortunate and crucial innovations – or else they label all these hustlers 'bourgeois', whatever their origins.

Recent detailed studies enable us to be more discriminating. For example, Pierre Léon has pointed out that out of 603 ironmasters recorded in 1771 and 1788, 308 were noblemen, often of the most exalted kind, and 57 were churchmen. He goes on to show that this industrial honours list is headed by the dukes of Penthièvre and Béthune-Charost, the prince de Croy and the marquis de Cernay, maréchal de Lorges and the comte d'Orsay, and that Saint-Gobain, the first French enterprise, was dominated by the Ségur and Montmorency families. Some genuine sprigs of the bourgeoisie did of course move into the new enterprises and distinguish themselves; the best of them snapped up their titles very fast, like the Wendels of Lorraine and the Gradis of Bordeaux, to give only two instances. A sizeable fraction of the nobility ancient and modern thus wasted no time in converting to the economy of the future and paved the way for its expansion. Even economic progress was not the exclusive province of a class older than itself, and at most that class was able to make its contribution to the formation of a new one whose growth was to be a little unsettled by the onslaughts of the Revolution.

There is no evidence of conflict between a 'feudal' aristocracy and a 'capitalist' bourgeoisie within or around the confines of the *manufactures* and the first modern mechanized factories; the 'feudalists' are elsewhere, or come to light only under the pressure of coming events. Important groups of the so-called aristocracy and the so-called bourgeoisie are firmly cemented by wealth, way of life, culture, a modernizing outlook and even a common desire for political reform. Barring a few crusty backward provinces, the true rift lay not between the big bourgeoisie and the old nobility, both of them experienced in business, but between this composite élite and the rest of the nation, whom it basically despised.

Study of the cultural factors of the ancien régime will confirm this elementary observation, which has not always received its due recognition.

DOCUMENTS
44 DEFINITIONS OF 'BOURGEOIS' AND 'BOURGEOISIE': A SEVENTEENTH-CENTURY DICTIONARY

BOURGEOIS, *n.* A town-dweller . . .

Among working men, this word indicates the man in charge (working for the bourgeois. The bourgeois wants that.)

(*Familiar*): *Cela est du dernier bourgeois* [the ultimate in bourgeois], meaning crude, ungallant.

BOURGEOIS, BOURGEOISE, *adj.* that which is of or for the bourgeois (bourgeois bread, bourgeois caution).

(*Familiar*): Lacking in Court graces, not altogether polite, over-familiar, insufficiently respectful.

BOURGEOISIE, *n.* The bourgeois as a body, all or nearly all the bourgeois of a town.

Dictionnaire françois tiré de l'usage et des meilleurs auteurs
de la langue, by P. Richelet, Geneva, 1679, 88–9

45 THE *CAPITATION* OF 1695 AND THE 'BOURGEOIS': A NARROW RENTIER DEFINITION

For the collection of this new tax, the French people were summarily divided into twenty-two 'classes'; the 'bourgeois' are mentioned by name in three of these:

13th class (taxed at 60 *livres*): King's lieutenants and town mayors, presidents and *lieutenants criminels* of the *élections* and salt-storehouses, mayors of second-order towns, bourgeois of big towns living on their income.

1 5th class (40 *livres*): Chief constables, gentry having fiefs and châteaux, treasury officers of the Paris Hôtel de Ville, bourgeois of second-order towns living on their income.

19th class (6 *livres*): Infantry officers and adjutants, gentry having neither fief nor château, notaries and small-town bourgeois, publicans . . .

> Schedule of the *capitation,* published in Marcel MARION,
> *Les Impôts directs sous l'Ancien Régime principalement au*
> XVIII*ᵉ siècle* (Editions Cornély, 1910, 434 pp.), 245.

46 DEFINITIONS OF THE BOURGEOISIE
I ERNEST LABROUSSE: A BROAD DEFINITION

Define bourgeois? We would not agree. Instead, let us seek out this urban species *in situ,* in its haunts and its towns, and put it under observation. This is only a first step, a provisional, conservatory procedure. The danger lies in setting our sights too low and stopping short of possible limits. From now on, the task will be to include the maximum number of cases in the inquiry, proceeding from a summary description in terms principally of profession and social level . . . First, the inquiry. The definition comes later.

. . . Attention will fall upon . . . the group of officials . . . and civil servants in executive capacities . . . retaining all those not absorbed by the nobility. It will also fall upon the proprietor, the rentier '*vivant bourgeoisement*' not to be confused with some 'bourgeois' on the burgher-rolls who may owe their position only to a certain period of residence in the town, and may be nothing more than journeymen. Bourgeois too, of course, are the liberal professions in the usual sense of the term.

All these higher varieties developed from the teeming family of self-made businessmen who make up the numerical bulk of the class and who, either as owners or managers of independent means of production operated by paid labour, derive their main livelihood therefrom, and in particular get the lion's share of the commercial and industrial profits. It is a many-sided family, ranging from financiers, shipowners, manufacturers, merchants and tradesmen down to the bottom levels of the lesser categories, shopkeepers and workshop masters, and the independent craftsmen who work the raw material using paid labour, and market the finished article direct to the consumer . . .

No class is ever a self-contained, homogeneous group, but in this case the class as a whole can still see itself as the repository of certain common values, originating as it does out of the profits of business, and in comparison with other classes and other social groupings in that ancien régime society which does not disappear in western and central Europe until somewhere between 1789 and the mid-nineteenth century.

> Ernest LABROUSSE, *Voies nouvelles vers une histoire de la bourgeoisie occidentale aux* XVIIIe *et* XIXe *siècles, 1700–1850,* in x *Congresso Internazionale di Scienze storiche,* Rome, 1955, *Relazioni,* vol. IV (Florence, Sansoni), 367–9.

2 PIERRE VILAR: THE PRELIMINARY MARXIST DEFINITION

. . . I am aware that our history has no vocabulary. Its 'bourgeois' – Eustache de Saint-Pierre or Henry Ford, President Molé or the black-marketeer in *Le Bon Beurre** – has as yet been brought into relief only by the descriptive powers of the historians, a stage which was passed by the other sciences four centuries ago. All the same, when E. Labrousse asks today for the time of definitions to be postponed until after the investigation, I wonder if he is not being unduly cautious . . . Any analysis of the real proceeds out of a minimum of systematization, which provides the scholars with a common language . . . We already have a first approximation of the matter of history. It only has to be used. Furthermore, its actual, practical successes are not unrelated to the historical fate of the word 'bourgeois'. Let me add that this approximation is just about the only one we have. Its opponents set it not against an alternative, but against a refusal to systematize, to consider history as thinkable. When it came to locating the bourgeois both at source and in the statistical mass, E. Labrousse did so in Marxist terms: those 'who, either as owners or managers of independent means of production . . .' [etc., see above] . . .

Here we are then, with some real criteria:

1. Free availability of the means of production. 2. Their operation, under free contract, by a working force lacking any resources but its own manpower. 3. The consequent appropriation of the difference between the price realized by the merchandise and the wages of the working force used.

Anybody who does not live directly or indirectly off the social levy as defined above is not a bourgeois . . . We should therefore be wary of too 'citified' a conception of the bourgeois . . . Because they provide certain services financed by the upper classes, it does not seem to me that the liberal professions are specifically 'bourgeois'. And as for the bourgeois

---

* A famous post-war novel condemning black-market profiteering under the German occupation.

officials, bourgeois civil servants and (in certain conditions) bourgeois rentiers, they are only provisionally bourgeois. A successful career will convert them into noblemen. A devaluation will ruin them . . .

Even the typical medieval bourgeois, the merchant, is in a sense the antithesis of our own version. Given that his wealth came from risk, monopoly and usury, capitalism only expanded by destroying these (in any case limited) opportunities for getting rich, as the market grew. Certainly the last ventures of merchant capital laid the basis for the 'primitive accumulation' of modern capital. But right away investment changes its nature.

Definition therefore becomes all the more necessary because the same word denotes contradictory types which mutually destroyed each other. The product of the capital-salary structure dominates our own social dynamic . . . In the absence of definition and theory, no amount of description will create a science.

Pierre VILAR in *Atti del Congresso internazionale . . .*,
Rome, 1955, 518–20.

47 STATUTORY BOURGEOISIE: THE LILLE
EXAMPLE

Juridically the Lillois were divided into two categories: bourgeois (burghers) and *manants* (citizenry). Burgher status was obtainable from the town magistracy, which had the right of refusal, for the sum of fifteen *livres parisis* in the seventeenth century, and was hereditary provided that the sons 'renewed' it a year after their marriage [*probably by paying a further tax at the reduced rate of ten livres*]. It was incompatible with holy orders, but a nobleman could be a burgher of Lille. The principal political and civil privileges conferred by the title were eligibility to the Magistrat [*the town magistracy*], the right to trial by the town magistrates alone, both in civil and criminal cases, and immunity from arrest for debt, and from distrainder upon goods and chattels. These privileges were a powerful attraction in the Middle Ages but were not much in demand by the end of the seventeenth century, except by outsiders . . . The number of burghers at that date has been estimated at around one twentieth of the population. The *manants* were the rest of the inhabitants, and had no special rights.

Alain LOTTIN, *Vie et mentalité d'un Lillois sous Louis* XIV
(Lille, Raoust, 1968), 13.

(The passages in square brackets are abridged from the original.)

48 THE FORTUNES OF TWO NORMAN OFFICIALS

... *Noble homme* Jean de Houtretot, president of the *élection* of Caudebec, had 36,615 *livres* or man-days* by his marriage contract of 25 November 1618: his office – say 8,000 *livres;* a house at Caudebec, the gift of his father – the equivalent say of 300 *livres* of income, 6,600 of capital; and about seventy acres of land farmed out at 9 *livres* 15 *sols* per acre, or 682 *livres* 10 *sols* per annum, making 15,015 *livres* of capital. His future father-in-law provided 7,000 *livres* [of which] ... 3,500 *livres* were to be invested in a constituted rent of 250 *livres* ... Jean's income could there-fore be put at 2,082 *livres:* at least 800 for the office, 682 *livres* 10 *sols* for the land, 300 *livres* for the house and 500 *livres* for the sums received from his farm. A handsome start for the young man ...

In 1619, *noble homme* Charles Mayne, *lieutenant général aux eaux-et-forêts* of Normandy, bequeathed something like 103,631 *livres* to his daughters, consisting of 67,490 *livres* in landed property (65 per cent) – a house in Rouen, vavasory at Guenouville, and four farms of 177 acres in all (value unknown) – 12,131 *livres* in rents (12 per cent), and his office, which may be estimated at 24,000 *livres* (24 per cent). His income would thus have amounted to 6,978 *livres* or man-days: 3,385 *livres* (50 per cent) in land; 1,013 *livres* (15 per cent) in rents; say 2,400 *livres* (35 per cent) for the office.

Roland MOUSNIER, *La Vénalité des offices sous Henry* IV *et Louis* XIII (Rouen, Maugard, n.d., XXXII + 690 pp.), 451–4.

49 A BOURGEOIS MARRIAGE CONTRACT IN 1648 (SUMMARY)

The husband-to-be: Jean Borel, age thirty, receiver general of the diocese of Beauvais from 1650 onward, later 'pantler in chief of the King's Household'.

His father: Pierre Borel, cloth merchant, mayor of Beauvais, gives him 16,000 *livres,* 6,868 in gold and silver.

His four uncles: Toussaint Foy, member of the *élection,* receiver of the diocese of Beauvais since 1635, and of the abbeys of Saint-Quentin and

---

* This is the man-day of a journeyman builder of Rouen at the same date; this wage is among the highest earned by working men (op. cit., 341).

Saint-Symphorien since 1629 and 1638 respectively; Nicolas Gaudoin, member of the *élection:* Germer Brocard and Toussaint Gueullart, officers of the *Grenier à Sel.* *

The bride-to-be: Marguerite Pocquelin, age eighteen [no relation of Molière]. Her late father, Louis, was a merchant, burgher of Beauvais, municipal magistrate and *juge-consul;* her mother, Claire Flouret, settles on her daughter a dowry of 14,000 *livres* (6,000 in ready cash).

Her four uncles: Pierre Gavois, merchant, future municipal magistrate and *juge-consul;* Guy Pocquelin, merchant and burgher of Paris; Eustache Flouret, cathedral canon; Romaun Flouret, *écuyer,* officer exempt of the Queen's Guard.

> 'Marriage articles' of 11 October 1648, André Hanyn
> records, Archives of the département of Oise, Maître
> Jouan deposit.

50 BORDEAUX MERCHANTS ON THE WAY UP
SIXTEENTH CENTURY: THE PONTACS

. . . An Estève de Pontac was a pewterer in the late fifteenth century, but the true founder of the dynasty is Arnaud de Pontac, burgher and merchant of Bordeaux, charterer of a Breton vessel in 1496, importer of wine and woad, as well as honey and vine-plants, and exporter of cloth. He had acquired an excellent vineyard at Le Taillan, and its produce was highly popular with the English. The seigneur of Escassefort en Agenais, the '*honneste homme*' then the '*honorable homme*' of the turn of the century was the '*noble homme*' of 1504, and mayor of Bordeaux in 1505. A single lifetime had spanned the progression from trade to titles.

. . . The day-book of one of his sons, Jean, . . . *fermier de la Grande Coutume,* mentions a host of land returns, some of them tiny, scattered from Belin to Entre-Deux-Mers, as well as three noble houses or sei-gneuries; [among them] Haut-Brion, purchased in 1533 . . . for the sum of 2,650 Bordeaux francs . . . He is the true creator of Haut-Brion . . .

At the end of the sixteenth century, the far-flung possessions of the Pontacs stretched from Angenais and the banks of the Ciron to the pine forests of Buch and the vineyards of Saint-Estèphe. They had brought [twelve] seigneuries and noble houses into their patrimony . . . They were

---

* Literally the salt-store, hence the administration of the royal monopoly on the sale and taxation of salt. – Tr.

equally rich in profitable and ennobling posts: tax-farmers . . . receivers of the *tailles* . . . notaries, a clerk of the court . . . several counsellors in the Parlement, the first [dating from] 1543 . . . two presidents, paving the way for the parlementary apotheosis of Arnaud de Pontac, who became First President in 1653. The family also gave the Church two canons and one learned prelate, Arnaud, bishop of Bazas.

J. BERNARD in *Bordeaux de 1453 à 1715*, vol. IV of the *Histoire de Bordeaux* (Bordeaux, 1966, 562 pp.), 177–9.

SEVENTEENTH CENTURY: THE DARRIBAU-DALONS

Raymond Darribau the elder was still nothing more than a merchant of La Rousselle, and had not obtained his *lettres de bourgeoisie* until 1616: an affluent merchant, however, since he gave his two sons twenty thousand *livres* each on the occasion of their marriages. Raymond Darribau the younger, 'burgher and banker', consolidated this fortune by means of successful ventures into bottomry and other operations. He gave his only daughter a dowry of sixty thousand *livres* in cash and property, and married her to Raymond Dalon, *conseiller du roi* in the Bordeaux Parlement. Some months later, in April 1662, he received his letters of ennoblement in recognition of his loyalty during the Fronde . . . His grandson Romain Dalon became First President of the Bordeaux Parlement.

Françoise GITEAU, in *Bordeaux de 1453 à 1715*,
op. cit., 496.

EIGHTEENTH CENTURY: THE GRADIS

. . . The grandfather, Diego Rodrigues, was just an ordinary merchant who had settled in Toulouse but was turned out in 1685 and returned to Bordeaux, where he was born. He bequeathed his sons a fortune of less than ten thousand *livres* when he died in 1695. David received 5,100 *livres,* much more than his brothers, to carry on the business. In spite* of the war of the Spanish Succession he made a quick fortune in wine, spirits, cloth and other merchandise. In 1715 he easily survived a trading loss of 150,000 *livres,* and after 1717 he had no hesitation in turning to trade with the Isles, fitting out three vessels for that purpose. The 'System' cost him 115,800 *livres* without hampering his activities or damaging his credit. In 1723 he sent his son Abraham to the Low Countries to further his commercial education and extend his contacts, and he took him into partnership in 1728 . . . In 1731, David Gradis

---

* Or because . . .

became a burgher of Bordeaux: only two others of his fellow-believers had achieved this distinction since 1679. He died in 1751, at the age of eighty-six, leaving a personal fortune of 400,000 *livres,* some property, and a flourishing business.

Abraham had been the real head of the business for some time. He was an expert maker of influential friends: baron de Rochechouart, M. de la Porte, head of the colonial service in 1738; M. de Rostan, paymaster-general of the Navy; the d'Harcourts, the Berryers . . . The maréchal de Richelieu, the duc de Lorges and the maréchal de Conflans were in his debt . . . During the war of the Austrian Succession, Abraham Gradis became a supplier to the king's navy, a business whose many advantages included a considerable reduction in the risks of loss, the certainty of very sizeable returns, and above all the entrenchment and growth of his commercial reputation, since he naturally did not abandon his other interests. This line of business required big financial resources to offset long delays in settlement. In 1755 . . . for example . . . he received the contract to supply the magazines of Quebec, which meant dispatching fourteen ships in 1758; only one vessel returned, and it took several years to recoup his enormous outlay of 2,700,000 *livres.* He must have been worth over ten million *livres* at his death in 1780 . . . During his last illness, 'the *jurats* put a ban on ringing the bell and firing the cannon . . . so that he would not be disturbed by the noise, for his house stood close by the Hôtel de Ville'. He had remained a practising Jew . . . He maintained a high standard of living, with a considerable staff of black servants, making frequent visits to the spa of Bagnères and to Paris, where he put in his appearance at the Oeil-de-Boeuf.*

> J.-P. POUSSOU, in *Bordeaux au* XVIIIᵉ *siècle* (Bordeaux, 1968, 723 pp.), 348–9.

FURTHER READING

The texts and studies bearing upon the bourgeoisie often form part of general urban studies of the type listed at the end of Chapter 9; the reader is referred principally to the relevant chapters of various books already mentioned, dealing with Amiens, Beauvais, Bordeaux, Dijon, Orléans, etc.

The problems, which are mainly theoretical, often formal but oftener still polemical (and polemics have no place in this book), have

---

* The ante-room to the King's Bedchamber at Versailles – Tr.

been tackled by almost every historian with a systematic temperament. Two differing but sober viewpoints are quoted in the preceding Documents, those of E. LABROUSSE and P. VILAR (at the Tenth International Congress of the Historical Sciences held at Rome in 1955). We can pass over the much overrated study by Werner SOMBART, but not the perceptive essay by GROETHUYSEN already quoted, *Origines de l'esprit bourgeois en France, l'Eglise et la bourgeoisie*. A summary view of the historico-sociological concept advanced by R. MOUSNIER and his colleagues is available in a number of ideological and polemical articles, the most accessible of which is the Introduction (pp. 9–49) to:

MOUSNIER, R., LABATUT, J.-P., and DURAND, Y., *Problèmes de stratification sociale. Deux cahiers de la noblesse pour les États Généraux de 1649–1651* (P.U.F., 1965).

A large number mainly of Norman and Parisian examples of the bourgeois sector of the official world are provided in the cited thesis by:

MOUSNIER, Roland, *La Vénalité des offices . . .* (Rouen, Maugard, n.d.).

A remarkable little (European) conspectus of the merchant world is:

JEANNIN, Pierre, *Les Marchands au XVIe siècle* (Le Seuil, 1957, 192 pp.).

Two local examples, among others, in:

GOUBERT, Pierre, *Familles marchandes sous l'Ancien Régime, les Danse et les Motte, de Beauvais* (S.E.V.P.E.N., 1959, 192 pp.).

Three books on the world of finance and banking:

BOUVIER, Jean and GERMAIN-MARTIN, Henry, *Finances et financiers de l'Ancien Régime* (P.U.F., Que sais-je?, No. 1109, 1964, 128 pp.) A brief outline.

GERMAIN-MARTIN, Louis and BEZANÇON, Marcel, *L'Histoire du crédit en France sous le règne de Louis XIV*, vol. 1 *Le Crédit public* (Sirey, 1913, 244 pp.). Not up to date, but vivid, if not rigorous.

LÜTHY, Herbert, *La Banque protestante en France, de la révocation de l'édit de Nantes à la Révolution* (S.E.V.P.E.N., 2 vols, 1959–61). A difficult but first-rate summary.

Lastly, the reader is referred to the recent findings of:

LÉON, Pierre, on the 'new élites' in the coming P.U.F. publication, *Histoire économique et sociale de la France moderne*, vol. II, *1660–1789*.

XI · ATTITUDES AND CULTURES: THE LEVELS AND THE BARRIERS

The most difficult, fascinating and therefore dangerous terrain to be opened up in the centuries-long history of the ancien régime is the history of cultures, not culture, the history of sensibility, imagination and dream, commonly subsumed under the inelegant title of the history of 'mentalities', or attitudes. Apart from the lucubrations of a Michelet and the efforts of a few precursors, the pioneer in this field was Lucien Febvre, who exerted a powerful influence on Robert Mandrou, the authority to whom this chapter owes almost everything. Two pitfalls await the historian in what is still a youthful discipline: the meagreness of the sources, and the subjectivity of the observer. But a few general outlines seem to be established.

The French people were divided into three highly unequal groups by the two barriers of cursive handwriting and Latin, and these cultural divisions may go deeper than any other factors. We shall pay particular attention to the largest of the three groups.

1 THE CULTURE OF THE ILLITERATES

THE EXTENT OF ILLITERACY

Involuntary sociologists, inquisitive individuals and professional educationists have been trying for some time to estimate the distribution of what has come to be known as primary education. The method used was fairly conclusive, and consisted of studying and counting the obligatory signatures which married couples had to append to parish marriage certificates from the reign of Louis XIV onward (the *curé* had to make a note of any who could not sign their name). Although the investigation conducted by Maggiolo, a scholarly parish priest, in the days of Gambetta and Jules Ferry, was not entirely satisfactory, it did cover almost sixteen thousand communes, and his main findings may be summarized in the following simple statements:

1. Four fifths of the population in 1685 were completely illiterate (the exact figure is 78.7 per cent of 219,047 cases studied).

2. The women were a lot more ignorant than the men (86 per cent of wives, as against 71 per cent of husbands).

3. The West, Centre and Midi were in far worse case than the North and East, with the exception of the Protestant regions, where the literacy-rate equalled or exceeded that of Picardy or Champagne: Protestantism never found total ignorance to its advantage.

4. There was definite progress between 1685 and 1785 (illiteracy fell from 79 to 63 per cent), but it was concentrated almost completely on those regions – from Normandy to Lorraine – which were already more highly developed.

The interpretation of these facts poses even more problems than the investigation itself. Everything seems to hinge upon the existence or absence of village schools. These function (on a voluntary basis) in nearly all the parishes in the 'educated' dioceses, for boys at least; elsewhere they are three to ten times as rare. Since the individual or collective users of these schools provide a lot more finance than the clergy, we are driven to conclusions about the wealth of the educated provinces and their inhabitants' readiness to give their children (during the winter pause) at least the rudiments and if possible the practice of reading and writing.

It hardly needs adding that the social distribution of illiteracy corresponds to the major limits of what we have called the 'dominated groups', and is heavily weighted against the countryside. Generally speaking, and at comparable social levels, the town is less ignorant than the country: the small shopkeeper and the artisan on the fringes of independence cannot do without the rudiments which only a few well-to-do rural *laboureurs* or '*ménagers*' possess.

The historian has to understand rather than deplore this widespread illiteracy. The first point to consider is that except when he is backed by reliable advisers who come up at least to the level of the public scrivener (rare in the country), the illiterate falls easy prey to the shrewd literates who collaborate in his subjection – employer, landlord, moneylender, agents of seigneur and tithe-owner, tax-collector, and sometimes *curé*. Like it or not, he has to 'sign' (with an X, a scrawled initial or an emblematic pitchfork or hammer) what they put in front of him. In confrontations with businessmen, lawyers or magistrates, he is disarmed in advance, beaten before he starts. Sharp practice may not be the rule, but it is only too prevalent. The illiterate small fry are the appointed victims of the lawcourts, whose principle is to 'make the punishment fit the rank', which means that the humble and the wretched are always penalized more severely.

Apart from a few charitable individuals and some pious souls anxious to enrol future priests, the current of opinion in cultured or merely literate circles runs utterly counter to the education of the people: Voltaire himself wants scullery-maids and day-labourers. The educational ventures recorded here ar.d there in the eighteenth century are only aimed either at the well-to-do classes or potential clergymen – with a few exceptions and a few hopes of 'advancement' through education in northern France. It is a necessity for the people to be ignorant.

But it is obvious that illiteracy does not mean stupidity or mental blankness. All these illiterates are Christians, if unaware of the controversies over the nature of grace; they live and move within a regional and social mentality whose roots are sunk deep in a very distant past; all of them receive an oral culture and even a bookish culture, by way of a reader or story-teller, since there is a whole printed literature designed specially for them. This literature is far more important than anything else published under the ancien régime: pedlars sell it for two *sous* apiece, and it is printed in editions of hundreds of thousands.

THE CHRISTIANITY OF THE ILLITERATE

The 'faith of centuries past' has been and remains a fine text for sermonizing. It is certainly appropriate to stress the fact that all these people lived under the sign of the cross from baptism to the last sacrament – under the cross of the belfry, between the boundary-crosses of the village. At the least, all able-bodied adults were united by Sunday mass and Easter communion, the universal as well as compulsory meeting points of a Christian nation. Anybody who fails to attend without a good excuse runs the risk of severe reprimand or worse. But Sunday is also the day of the parish meeting, the exchange of news (the most serious is communicated to the priest by the civil authority, and dutifully passed on to the congregation), the assemblies of community and church council, and also the day of the tavern, *boule, paume,* quoits – and dancing, when it is allowed.

Church attendance continues to preserve its atmosphere of ribald familiarity, showing off, gossip, and interruptions whenever the preacher gets into a muddle or talks out of ignorance – about marriage, for instance. A man may spit on the ground, or bring his dog to church. Priggish reformers were later to make a clumsy success of suppressing this rough and ready familiarity.

Christianity is rudimentary but fervent: it barely goes further than the Creed, and does not always entail conscientious payment of tithes and church expenses. Above all, and in spite of the laudable efforts of clergy and laymen sympathetic to reform (which does not reach the villages until the late seventeenth century), Christianity is combined with practices eventually considered as 'superstitious', or at any rate questionable. A host of saints, Lucifer and his minions, and the worlds of sorcery and magic partner one another in an ill-assorted but long-lived union.

It would not be difficult to sift through both the most naive and the most learned sources and collect an anthology or cautionary miscellany on the worship of dubious saints with improbable relics and unlikely virtues, invoked during processions involving strange rites, the sequel to interminable pilgrimages which sometimes end in great carousals. Until the end of the seventeenth century, the Church had willy-nilly to make room for the last stirrings of rural paganism and give the odour of sanctity to some spring, tree or wishing stone. Statues of St Medard were dipped into fountains to bring on rain, and wasps went on being excommunicated until the time of Voltaire.

The presence of the Devil is everywhere proclaimed and attested, and the monks who preach against him have no doubt that he is master of part of the universe. It is a well-known fact that some men bear his 'mark': these must be unearthed and denounced, and their influence exorcized. All witchcraft is associated with Lucifer, and burnings are occasions for revelry until the middle of the seventeenth century. Witches' sabbaths do take place. What villager has not met and secretly consulted the local witch, who has the power not only to cast lots and spells but also to provide medicines for a ricked back, baldness or sterility? Every shepherd, living as he does among animals, far from settlements and gazing at the stars, is supposed to have esoteric knowledge and to be able to 'read' the 'book' of nature. Everything is meaningful and portentous – the configurations of the heavens, the hues of the sky, the forms of the clouds, where strange beasts lurk, and sometimes armies, and the changing faces of the moon. The life of plants, beasts and men is ordained from on high (under God's will, the prudent will add).

The underlying influence of astrology is present even at court (at least until the time of Louis XIII, who was called 'the Just' because he was born under the sign of Libra), and governs the destiny of men. Each month on the calendar is surmounted by its sign of the Zodiac. The stars of birth dispose, while the patron saints protect and save. In spite of the rather belated emergence of a new priesthood from the Jansenist seminaries, all these beliefs rub shoulders together. The illiterate world has no real sense of the contradictions, and the same man who believes in Jesus and Mary will believe in the Devil and witches, quacks and diviners, Nostradamus and showers of blood. The world is a frightening, mysterious place, beyond the will of man. Fear reigns supreme.

The age-old fears of natural scourges, barbarian conquerors, armed tax-collectors, plagues and famines naturally had a tight grip on these complex, earthy men who were more sensitive to rumour and hearsay than to the evidence of their eyes and the voice of reason. They are hardy creatures, toughened by experience, their diet alternating between privation and full bellies, their nerves stretched sometimes to breaking point by extremes of tension and relaxation. Only a hair's breadth separates fear from violence.

VIOLENCE AND THE ILLITERATE

Insults, fistfights and cracked skulls are a common feature of the country Sunday (and the town Monday) after the taverns close, and of market Saturdays. Drunken brawls and disputes between neighbours (a party wall, a stray cow) fill the records of the seigneurial courts and sometimes reach bailiwick level. It is not unusual for a man to lose a limb or an ear, in town and country alike; duels may culminate in free-for-alls, pitting one clan, village, *quartier,* gang of youths, craft or journeymen's association against another, and this went on well into the nineteenth century. Calabrian villages cut each other to pieces in the last century in disputes over the merits of their respective patron saints. It would not be very surprising if the same happened in eighteenth-century France.

Far more serious are the eruptions of savage rage, the '*fureurs*', which may overwhelm whole regions upon the announcement of reports (even false ones) of a heavy increase in the *taille* or a new tax, like the surchage on new-born children which was rumoured on several occasions during the reign of Louis XIV. These brutal outbursts may end in murder, ritual mutilation and even cannibalism, and become springboards for the great uprisings of the seventeenth century, mainly in the West and the Midi, although the longest-lived of them needed organization and leadership and had various other starting points – agitators or exploiters make their appearance, and these are literate men. There are *fureurs* of urban workers against their bosses; women reacting against sudden rises in market prices; mobs driven more by fear of famine than by actual starvation, who prevented wagons and grain-barges leaving to supply nearby provinces. Calm was usually restored by a show of strength from the watch, a 'bourgeois militia' or a few companies of the regular army, but real force was often necessary. A few quick hangings would settle the matter, as the State could seldom brook the 'rabble' taking to the streets or marauding the countryside for longer than a few weeks. The effects of this primarily popular violence often shook provinces or fractions of provinces, never the whole realm at once. Outbreaks were frequent until about 1675, then harshly suppressed under Louis xiv, and apart from a few brief clashes it looked as if they had had their day in the eighteenth century. Hardly anybody anticipated the belated resurgence which was to alter the course of the incipient Revolution.

THE LITERATURE OF THE ILLITERATE

Historians of minority literature – the 'great' literature, which had the smaller readership – have tended to overlook the popular literature published by a few shrewd businessmen, best exemplified by the booksellers of Troyes, whose products reflect a fairly lifelike image of their intended public.

Pedlars flooded the countryside with tens of thousands of thin, roughly printed booklets selling for a few *sous* apiece, probably read aloud at evening gatherings by some exceptionally educated person, and passed on by the garrulous, faithful memory of the illiterate.

The themes remain surprisingly consistent from the sixteenth to the twentieth century, in the age-old and rather obnoxious tradition of escapist literature, calculated to intensify the debasement of a subjected and therefore alienated majority.

First of all, 'Superman': the Paladin who splits Saracen skulls with a single blow; the crusader knight on his way to liberate Jerusalem and pausing to do the same for 'Babylon'; the saint who performs amazing miracles while carrying his or her head in one hand and a palm-branch in the other; the good giant Gargantua, coolly removing the bells of Notre-Dame; the artful righters of wrongs, straight or comic, Lancelot or Scaramouche; the invincible good enchanters and powerful fairies whose miracles almost outshine the saints'; and the champion of champions, the unconquerable king, Charlemagne or Louis.

After the giants and the mighty of this world and the next, the inevitable lore of the 'occult'. Calendars and almanacs abounded with signs of the Zodiac. 'Prognostications' and horoscopes were rife, whether prescribing the time for love, grafting, litigation or war: some of them claimed to cover periods of seven, twelve, fifteen or nineteen years, and vied with each other in cleverly balanced, deliberately hermetic contradictions and complications. Cabalistic signs and magic numbers deciphered the future, just as the curve of a nose and the colour of the hair made it possible to decipher character, vices and virtues, lucky and unlucky days, lineage and destiny. And if the omens were too dark, there was always the exorcizer, the spell-remover, and even the good Lord. Generally speaking, stars and wizards decided everything, God permitting.

And if this world is a vale of tears, the 'oral-written' literature which the people lapped up has to provide them with all their escape-routes – into the past, space, the 'certain lore' and the equally enticing world of crime and scandal. History boils down to the legend of Charlemagne, the Crusade against the terrible Infidel, good Saint Louis, good King Henry, and for background the legendary Pharamond* and that Clovis who reigned as a pagan king for fifteen years until the Holy Ampulla came down from Heaven especially for him. Geography is reduced to garbled old lists of ancient provinces, augmented by medieval names, lists which remained unchanged for centuries, so that in the reign of Louis xiv nineteen out of twenty took no account of the existence of America! The main thing was to daydream about outlandish names and strange tribes who always slept in the shade of their own feet. Then there was the flight into pseudo-science, a mixture of Pliny, Aristarchus, the Cabbala and Tycho Brahe, with echoes of the philosopher's stone – and not a hint of Galileo, Pascal, Harvey and Newton. Another escape route lay through the realm of the sensational news report: juicy crimes sung in interminable lays, one *sou* per sheet, incendiarism, maned stars, weird, contagious ailments – useful employment for the bemused minds of the common poor, taking their thoughts off their troubles or any attempt to understand the world.

THE 'ALIENATION' OF THE ILLITERATE

It is not merely a gesture towards any particular doctrines of the later twentieth century to emphasize the fact that this ignorance

* Supposed to be an ancestor of the Merovingian kings, but not reliably documented – Tr.

and this kind of literature and superstition were (and still are) actually, objectively (and purposely?) conducive to the continued peace of mind of the dominant groups. Ignorance and supernaturalism make the 'vile populace' toe the line of work and obedience, and the printers and the constabulary keep them cordoned off within the confines of outward respect and harmless fantasy. Now that it has secured regular payment of the tithes (which had begun to break down before the intervention of Henri IV in the sixteenth century), and has isolated and theoretically cast out 'heresy', the Church contents itself with explaining that the stars are controlled by God, and that many 'superstitions' and nearly all witches are 'false'. Steps were taken to abolish astrology from the almanacs and to introduce various decorous prescriptions to keep the congregation quiet and the church tidy during mass. Perhaps it was a mistake to react so strongly against popular superstition. The peasantry and lesser citizenry did not always take kindly to these reforms, which made the expression of faith into a stiff, sober exercise, devoid of deep emotion and communal feeling. This ill-timed regimentation may have disaffected some of the urban and rural masses, and created fertile ground for subversion, or so it has been suggested.

Many other developments point to a growing standardization in the 'conditioning' of the general populace: systematized rents and taxes, more and more efficiently collected; the habitually harsh treatment meted out to the common people by the courts, which were still passing death sentences for theft by servants in the reign of Louis XVI; debasing literature; continual disdain, barring a few worthy exceptions. In this alienated world, the clever looked to education for a way out, given the assistance of some relative or god-parent, while the more impatient had no recourse but to resume the collective uprisings of earlier times in the less blinkered circumstances of the years prior to 1789.

2   FROM LITERATE TO EDUCATED: THE STRATA AND THE CONFLICTS

Above the threshold of cursive handwriting, extensive research and great discrimination would be necessary to disentangle the varying levels, evolution and stresses acting over a period of three hundred

years on some hundreds of thousands of men, nearly all of whom
belonged to the dominant classes. It would need a thorough examination of the output of books, pamphlets and broadsides, concentrating
on numbers printed and the nature of the market rather than on
literary merit; coverage of the contents of the various libraries, including the less well-known; analysis of educational methods at all
levels, integrating the many separate monographs; a review of the
surviving correspondence, down to the most tedious; further scrutiny
of all types of family records; careful research into the various kinds
of public entertainment, venturing beyond dissertations on the
'classical' theatre to include the travelling circuses and Tabarin; a
descent into the '*Enfer*'* of the Bibliothèque Nationale and some
other libraries to bring to light those publications kept from the
public eye by outworn concepts of decency. Any amount of additional
work remains to be done to clarify the attitudes and cultures of the
occasional or habitual reading public. This is one aspect of the ancien
régime which will be explored and brought to light in the near future.
Meanwhile we can pick out some of the more demonstrable features.

LEVELS OF LITERACY
a)   THE LEARNED MILIEU
Anybody whose schooling or tuition has equipped him with fluency
in Latin belongs in effect to a privileged milieu with its own cultural
code of references, tags and allusions; a mixture of secular and canonical Latin was the usual practice, with a smattering of Greek for
the more venturesome. This conditioning also explains why so many
men of immense learning should have understood their nation and
visualized the future by continual reference to the Ancients. It is
second nature to them to cram their tracts and correspondence with
classical references lovingly larded with pedantic commentaries. The
theologians, jurists, and 'political' writers, would-be commentators on
their own times, only observe them through the eyes of Saint
Augustine and Ulpian, and much the same can be said of the doctors,

---

* Oxford Companion to French Literature: 'the section reserved for books that for
various reasons (obscenity, blasphemy, etc.) are *enfermés* (and shelf-marked '*enfer*') and
cannot be issued generally.' – Tr.

who heal by Hippocrates and Galen and deny the circulation of the blood.

Fortunately, a few independent minds surface from time to time among these societies of retrograde thinkers; Montaigne, Descartes and Bayle did find disciples eventually.

The disputes endemic in these circles of aspiring scholars have given rise to so many traditionalist tracts that their spiritual heirs are referred to them direct.

b) THE UTILITARIAN LEVEL

Jacques Savary scandalized the traditionalists in 1675 when he suggested that the *'parfait négociant'* had no need of Latin, but in fact the men of action paid it scant attention. All they needed was good arithmetic, ready reckoners and conversion tables, texts of royal decrees and customary law and perhaps a devotional work or two. When trade horizons widened there was a ready market for 'descriptions' of foreign countries and travellers' tales which mixed a little fantasy with a great deal of practical information, such as what kind of products were in demand in 'Honduras' or 'Mississipi'; Savary's nephew gratified their curiosity from 1723 onward with the publication of his *Dictionnaire du commerce,* an excellent handbook. It was essential, of course, for a competent merchant to have a working knowledge of contemporary commercial correspondence, in an age when writing was the principal means of communication.

In other fields, the work of a great many lesser magistrates, notaries and bourgeois rentiers did not necessitate any great number or variety of works of reference – the common law of the locality and the surrounding area, a *'conférence'* (comparative guide) to common law, a collection of key legal decisions, 'opinions' by famous lawyers, a few case-studies, plus a few mementoes of school and devotional works. Yet it is in this milieu that it is common to find non-professional curiosities, mainly religious in character, and whole shelves are very often devoted to the basic Jansenist texts.

c) THE ELEMENTARY LEVEL: TOWN AND COUNTRY

The ability to read, write and count is practically a daily necessity for a workshop owner, master mason or seigneurial *fermier*, if not a continual activity. Men like these had to know enough to check a lease, invoice or order. They read slowly and write awkwardly, but their arithmetic is more accurate than most. Their efforts to master these working tools make little difference to their social attitudes. The big *fermiers* reflect the traditional rural mentality, while the residential position of the town-dwellers exposes them to an entire literature of gossip, fly-sheets, 'canards' and lampoons, not to mention the songs, rumours, tall stories and jokes which were orally transmitted and have seldom survived. Some of these were instrumental in the street rioting which was a feature of difficult times, like the thousands of *mazarinades* which went the rounds during the Fronde.

In these spheres, the town once again outstripped the country because of the volume, diversity and liveliness of oral and written information, which became a driving force first for mob action and later for revolution.

SOCIAL CONFLICTS AND NATIONAL DISPUTES

The field of social conflict is broader than that of the conflict of ideas, but whereas the second seems reasonably well explored, the history of the first remains to be written. It would involve studying distinctions of sensibility, imagination, and the collective conscious and unconscious, not all of which are necessarily reflected in the socio-political superstructure. We shall recapitulate some of the more elementary conflicts, which are no less acute for being commonplace.

a) THE TOWN-COUNTRY CONFLICT

Roughly speaking, we find the privileged pitted against the under-privileged, rich against poor, the location of most of the 'dominant' against that of the bulk of the 'dominated'. There is great awareness of the process whereby money, production and manpower drift towards the towns and seldom return. A number of collective urban attitudes only make matters worse: the townsman tends to despise the peasant, who is worse dressed, more vulgar, more ignorant, slower-moving and more traditionally minded, and he makes no bones about saying so. This feeling, and its country counterpart, certainly did not disappear with the ancien régime: it was partly responsible for the various counter-revolutionary movements, including the Vendée, and for the bitter clashes arising out of price-fixing legislation and dechristianization.

The antagonism of these different worlds survives until the progressive absorption of country by town in our own age.

b)   THE PARIS-PROVINCIAL CONFLICT

France was always a profoundly federalist realm, for reasons which include linguistic and sometimes ethnic differences, the survival or remembrance (and partial resurgence under Louis XVI) of separate and fairly independent provincial institutions (the *États*), variations in common law and the staying power of class élites in a few leading regional capitals. Now whereas the king himself is above controversy, his administrators and tax-collectors command varying degrees of respect, and are often resented bitterly, and not just because of their function but because they really are outsiders – foreigners speaking a harsh, shrill language that spread only slowly; 'nordic barbarians' according to their more exalted antagonists. Many of the outbursts against the royal representatives and intendants were exacerbated because they were Parisians either by birth or adoption. There could even be misunderstandings from one province to the next, and no great desire to smooth them over: pride and traditional enmities collided and went on colliding for a long time. Unity, first of the realm and later of the republic, was consequently an imperative ideal obstinately pursued by the kings and revolutionary assemblies of the nation, and still more by the Empire.

The clash with the Midi was among the most deep-seated, and derived from the basic nature of things – climate, language, customs, laws (we have kept encountering these differences even in the rural world), and a certain independence of mind that combined with bitter and tenacious memories (of too many spurious crusades against the land of the Cathars, the Huguenots and the habit of freedom) to sustain a temperamental incompatibility whose traces still remain. The geography of resistance and revolt often coincided with that of the *langue d'oc* or of Roman law.

c)   AUTHORITY VERSUS LIBERTY

From the point of view of some historians obsessed with originality at any price it has become almost ludicrous to refer to those traditional accounts that glorify the birth of the critical spirit and methodical doubt and the growth of the complex feelings and aspirations of liberty, which were not the exclusive province of the intellectual élites. It is not the business of the historian to glorify these developments – still less to overlook them. Their main targets were the authority of the Church and of a would-be absolute monarchy.

It takes some nerve in what is still a Catholic country to insist that the Roman Catholic church of France was the unshakeable champion of a certain conception of the world – nature, mankind, knowledge, education – in which everything was intractably predetermined. It was an unbending concept, and had been seen as the one true picture since the time of Aquinas, compelling the Church to deny, persecute and if possible exterminate all others by every available means. It is a routine task for the historian to recall these facts. From the pro-Spanish league to Tartuffe, the excesses of the *dévots* were combatted by some remarkable men who had either to conceal their beliefs or go to ground as a precaution against informers, but who were protected by great lords and briefly by the young Louis XIV. They were an educated minority, and we do not know what echoes they may have roused among the common people, but we do know that among the urban populace the journeymen's associations were hounded by the Church and the secular arm in tandem, who were also anxious to 'purge' the more naive manifestations of faith, possibly with the usual results. A great many cultured and upright individuals went over to the side of Bayle and his followers because of the persecution of the Huguenots, and their numbers were swelled by the treatment of the Jansenists. There was an improvement in the training of the lesser clergy after the long-delayed creation of the seminaries (after 1650), but for over a hundred years the Church insisted on making them sign a 'formulary' condemning Jansenius in the most clumsy and erroneous manner for 'propositions' not present in his writings, which they were forbidden to read in any case. The entire minor priesthood were at the mercy of the bishops after 1695, and many of them were under no illusion about their masters; many *curés* who lived in close contact with the people were turning to the Encyclopédie, preparing to fight their superiors in the elections of Spring 1789, and so cementing that common cause with the Third Estate in June which alone enabled the Revolution to go forward. It was the inactivity, extravagance and pretensions of the Church which crystallized these oppositions, fostered the decay of the faith in several towns and provinces, and account for certain profound divisions. Voltaire and his disciples were given every opportunity.

The brunt of criticism has fallen upon the other despotism, that of the State, with its absolutist ambitions. In the next volume we shall take the opportunity to show that this 'absolutism' was more a tendency than a reality and that the occasional accusations of 'despotism' overlook its weaknesses and failures of nerve. All the same, a number of the individuals and social groups which we have already encountered felt that they were labouring under the blinkered authoritarianism of the 'bureaux' and the 'administration', and criticized the latter for being centralized, choked with red tape and, yet again, too 'Parisian'. Patches of liberalism appeared in many fields, and were not always interlinked. We have already met the traders and shipowners, those champions of commercial 'freedom', who claimed that they were tied down by niggling regulations and in fact circumvented them with or without the tacit cooperation of the administration. Then there was the older aristocracy, clinging to its 'race' and wedded to genealogies and escutcheons, which claimed the right to advise the king in every eventuality, and lived in hopes of a second Golden Age of aristocratic rule which would revive their image of a distant Merovingian or 'Carlovingian' past (the *champs de mai* or *champs de mars,* the peers . . .). Jurists and travellers like Montesquieu, who were working towards the creation of a political science, reported on the wisdom of the English solution and advocated the inclusion in the government of the 'intermediary bodies' – themselves. Add to these the rare republicans of the Rousseau type, whose many descendants were to come to the brink of power; those who dreamed of a kind of Virgilian agrarianism, and who metamorphosed into latter-day champions of a 'new agriculture' when the future belonged to the steam engine; and those towns- and sometimes countrymen who were influenced by proverbs, pictures and tales into identifying themselves with the beggars or with '*bonhomme Misère*' and looked to the good King, the sacred healer, to deliver them into good fortune in the teeth of his own representatives. Although they came from many walks of life, all these people thought, wrote, hoped or dreamed of a bygone liberty which they themselves had lost but which their ancestors had supposedly enjoyed (in the days of the so-called provincial, communal and village 'liberties') and which their descendants would enjoy again. Whatever we may feel about this kind of simplemindedness, wishful thinking or delusion, or about dressing up simple material aspirations in idealism, the fact remains that most of these men believed that they were fighting or yearning for a great struggle against 'despotism'.

These ideas and struggles clearly come to light in the eighteenth century, after their semi-underground existence in the time of Louis xiv. The most prominent sectors of the dominant classes – ancient, parlementary and 'political' nobility, financiers, bankers, government officials, judges, lawyers and even the priesthood – took sides at a very early stage and were mainly in favour, although with any number of gradations of opinion and coteries. The story of those salons, academies and '*sociétés de pensée*' has been told and retold a hundred times over and from every angle, down to the most distorted. The loudest voices and strongest convictions belonged to the numerous groups of young men who had benefited from clerical educations and were insatiable readers and talkers, kicking their heels in the outer corridors of power. These were impatient men, whose numbers grew with the demographic rise and economic and educational progress, and who fretted under the firm, kindly conservatism of an entrenched establishment. If it is true that they took over the major roles in the final years of the ancien régime, with the backing of a few members of the 'older generation', should the Revolution be reinterpreted in terms of clashes of generations?

Any account must certainly include social conflicts, tensions between collective attitudes, the force of ancestral brutalities and grudges and the power of hopes thwarted for too long, and a whole unconscious – several, rather – repressed for centuries. It is no longer possible to petrify the Revolution into the victory of a notional 'capitalist bourgeoisie' gaining ascendancy over an equally notional 'feudalist aristocracy' doomed by industrialization. The reality is far more complex, far more differentiated and far more unknown. To reject the stock formulas and to apply themselves to rediscovering it will be the work of the younger generation of historians of mental attitudes who will welcome the best contributions of sociology, psychology, psychiatry and linguistics before immersing themselves again in the tide of evidence and sources and trying to plumb them in all their variety, to elicit even the unexpressed.

To be truly known and understood, ancien régime society now stands more in need of enthusiastic inter-disciplinary research than of prefabricated theories of whatever stamp.

DOCUMENTS

51 THE FRENCH LANGUAGE

When Louis XIV died, French had long since become the language of the king, the state, the law, the court, high society, the academies and the world of letters, and might have appeared to be the language of France, but such was not yet the case. Even in Paris, there were some fields left to conquer: it had not fully converted learned circles and was only just beginning to attract the consideration of professors and students and to seem worthy of their station and learning. Furthermore, anybody who moved away from his home region found that the country dwellers and even the inhabitants of the smaller towns either knew no French or understood it without speaking it. While it was meeting next to no resistance in its conquest of Europe, its invasion of France was proceeding painfully slowly, province by province. It still had competitors, and in some places near-rivals, inside the realm . . . The ancien régime came to an end before the French language had made itself the undisputed master of the whole country, and even before its official establishment in the role of principal language.

. . . the glamour of the 'great King's' court has dazzled its observers to such a degree that their eyes are rendered almost incapable of discerning the realities, wretched enough, of the rest of the kingdom. The talk at Versailles was so fine that we assume it must have been so everywhere else, and tend to forget that you needed an interpreter in Marseille, or that Racine on his travels was unable to request a chamber-pot.

In any case, Louis XIV was not particularly perturbed at being harangued in Picard patois a few leagues out of Paris, and his successors hardly gave a moment's consideration to such a trifling detail, which in no way diminished the obedience of their subjects or the powers of the monarchy. Not one eighteenth-century administrator imagined that there could be any moral advantage in unifying the French under the language of their king. A few set phrases in royal decrees paid lip-service to the idea, but it was a matter of form, leading to no conclusion . . .

Ferdinand BRUNOT, *Histoire de la langue française des origines à 1900,* vol. VII, *La propagation du français en France jusqu'à la fin de l'Ancien Régime* (Colin, 1926), Introduction, pp. 1–2.

52 MAGGIOLO'S INQUIRY INTO 'THE NUMBER OF MARRIED COUPLES WHO SIGNED THEIR OWN MARRIAGE-CERTIFICATES' (*c.* 1877–9)

Overall findings

Years investigated	Number of cases	Percentage of non-signatories	
		Men	Women
1686–90	219,047	71.26	86.03
1786–90	344,220	52.55	73.12
1816–20	381,504	45.63	65.53
1872–6	500,836	23.05	33.00

Some regional figures (by present-day départements) for 1686–90

Figures for men, départements with the lowest illiteracy-rate (to the nearest whole number)

Hautes-Alpes: 36 % (special case of a mountain region which 'mass-produces' schoolmasters)

Marne: 39 %

Calvados: 50 %

Meuse: 49 %

Aisne, Ardennes, Oise: about 45 %

50–59% Aube, Eure, Meurthe-et-Moselle, Moselle, Seine-et-Oise, Seine-et-Marne.

Départements with a male illiteracy-rate of over 90 %:

Ain, Ariège, Haute-Garonne, Landes, Lot-et-Garonne, Morbihan, Nièvre, Pyrénées-Orientales, Haute-Vienne.

After the *État récapitulatif et comparatif . . .* published by the Ministère de l'Instruction publique, 8 pp., *s.l.,* n.d., Bibliothèque Nationale classification no. 4° Lf 242–196.

For distribution maps, see Michel FLEURY and Pierre VALMAR, 'Les Progrès de l'instruction élémentaire de Louis XIV à Napoléon III', in *Population*, 1957, No. 1, 71–92.

53 POPULAR BELIEFS

1. THE INFLUENCE OF THE MOON

The Moon is foster-mother, regent and ruler of all that is wet in terrestrial bodies. For which reason . . . the prudent farmer will never slaughter pigs, sheep, oxen, cattle and other livestock for the consumption of his family in the last quarter of the Moon, for meat killed under a waning moon shrinks from one day to the next . . . Will not buy equine and other beasts born when the Moon is on the wane and aging, forasmuch as they are more stupid and weaker than the rest . . . Will geld his boars, rams and bull calves when the Moon is on the wane . . .

Will take care to observe what power the Moon exerts each day not only over beasts and plants but also over the disposition of the government of men, in order to use it when necessary in due time and place, following the sure and continued observations of our forefathers . . .

On the first day of the Moon, Adam was created; if a man fall sick on this day, then will his sickness be long, yet the patient will recover; dreams will fall out joyful; the child born on this day will be long-lived.

On the second day, Eve was created; this is a good day to begin a voyage, either by land or sea, and the traveller will be well pleased with all his lodgings and hospices; this same day is good for procreation . . .

Cain was born on the third day. No task should be undertaken on this day . . .

> Charles ESTIENNE and Jean LIEBAULT, *L'Agriculture et maison rustique*, 1st ed., 1564, 1, 9 (frequently reprinted until the eighteenth century).

2. AGRARIAN EXCOMMUNICATION

In June 1681, the parishioners of La Madeleine obtain a monitory *contra vermes* and walk in procession to fulminate it; in the month of August the vicar-general is asked for an order of excommunication against the wasps which were causing a lot of damage at the time; in June 1684 the order excommunicating earthworms is renewed; these cases are as common as the entreaties for rain or fine weather on the relics of Saint Prothade.

> Claude FOHLEN and colleagues, *Histoire de Besançon*, vol. II, 108.

3. THE DEVIL AT LARGE

[After the chronicle of Pierre-Ignace Chavatte of Lille, basic source of

Alain LOTTIN's book *Vie et mentalité d'un Lillois sous Louis* XIV (Lille, Raoust, 1968, 444 pp.)]

The werewolf (1683)

'The talk turned only on a certain werewolf on the Notre-Dame de Grâce road, which attacked several people, even priests. It spared no man, and brought with it a certain beast on a short leash . . . and this little beast was like a mole. People thought that it was a devil, and it was taken at Messine, three leagues from here, on the sixth day of August.'

The devil and the young maid (1664)

'A young maid bewailed her lack of suitors to one of her friends, and she made a mischievous remark, which was that she cared not whether it be a devil or a devil of a lover . . . she would walk out with him . . . That very day came a fair fine suitor, marvellously attired . . . [*They fall to talking, and the gallant suggests a stroll.*] . . . she goes with him readily, all unsuspecting, talking of this and that as behoves a suitor with his beloved; and when they were near a place by the little thicket, she looks at his feet and swoons clean away . . . [*The creature was*] a devil, and vanished away behind her . . . '

Witches outside Lille (1679)

'The leaves fell from the trees and shrivelled and the fruit remained upon them, and creatures like mice were seen running up the trees . . . only they had no ears and it was thought to be witchcraft . . . On the twentieth day of September the peasants stoned three witches out of the village of Épinay and drove them toward Seclin, where one was killed . . . and then chased the others as far as the mills of Lille at the Porte des Malades, half-dead, and so broken by stoning that they could barely move . . . '

Execution of six witches at Lille (1683)

' . . . And these are the cruelties they did . . . I am told that they were held responsible for two or three hundred murders, and then they confessed to having eaten the hearts of children to quench their blood-lust, and having taken cruel actions which may not be told . . . Three were hanged, two went to the gibbet to be strangled, and the other to a wheel nearby the gibbet, and all the market place was thronged with soldiers . . . '

LOTTIN, op. cit., 265–71.

4. WEATHER 'FORECASTS'

He will forecast rain if the horns of the new moon are obscured . . . He will foretell a long winter if he sees the oaks laden with fruit, or the ducks with reddish breasts, or if there is hail before October is out . . . He will expect a hot summer if he sees the rams and old ewes coupling often during the spring . . .

ESTIENNE and LIEBAULT, op. cit ., I, 10.

5. 'NATURAL' REMEDIES

. . . For tooth-ache, some deem it a secret that to wear a man's tooth wrapped in taffeta or a pierced bean containing a louse round one's neck removes the most unendurable tooth-ache.

For stomach-ache, nothing more sovereign than to wear a silver ring or box on one's person, containing a piece of the navel-string of a new-born child . . .

For dysentery . . . take the dung of a dog which has gnawed nothing but bones for three days, dry and powder it, and give the powder to the patient twice a day, together with milk in which you have quenched several river pebbles heated up in a blazing fire . . .

To prevent smelly feet, put iron dross in your shoes.

To make a barren woman fertile, take a doe big with her fawn, kill her, remove the womb from her belly, pull out the fawn and, without washing it, dry it in the oven . . . [*the rest is easy to guess: the process is a kind of magical 'transfer'*]

ESTIENNE and LIEBAULT, ibid., I, 12.

54 PEASANT ATTITUDES IN EIGHTEENTH-CENTURY AUVERGNE: SUPERSTITION AND BRUTALITY

The peasants of Auvergne remain susceptible to a broad spectrum of heterodox beliefs with a taint of witchcraft or magic: in most of the province, like it or not, the *curé* has to allow his parishioners to set the bells pealing when storms come, to ward off hail; red cattle are in greater demand than the rest because they are supposed to be easier to fatten; there is a deep-seated faith in dowsing, which is used to search for hidden treasure; the *curés* themselves hardly seem gladdened when the peasants bring them a dangerous grimoire to baptize so as to enhance its power. The widespread loathing of 'casters of lots' need not surprise us then, whether in the case of the geographers who came to make surveys for Cassini's map and were driven off by the peasants of the Maringues region under suspicion of being warlocks calling down thunder and hail, or in the matter of that inhabitant of the parish of Marsac, already detested as an incorrigible womanizer, who also ties the lace* for newly-weds and blankets the country with his spells.

There seems to be a great deal of tolerance towards violence, and brutality is an everyday occurrence: scuffles and brawls, under the generic name of '*carillon*', are extremely common between members of rival parishes, in drunken bouts after fairs . . . In war-time, there is an excellent expedient for getting rid of the biggest nuisances, which is to press them into the militia . . . Recourse to out-and-out ruffianism, murder or assault and battery . . . seems to incur a lot less public resentment and to be less likely to put a man beyond the pale of rural society than crimes against property and damage to another man's estate. Ordinary household theft is always a hanging offence in eighteenth-century Auvergne†, and complicity in armed robbery also incurs the death penalty, whereas assaults on individuals are usually indemnified by notarized transactions stipulating damages based on the surgeons' bills . . . Research into the criminal records of the bailiwick of Pont-de-l'Arche, in Normandy . . . has suggested possible changes in the pattern of offences in the eighteenth century, with direct or indirect crimes against property coming to the fore. In Auvergne, on the other hand, similar research into the dossiers provided by the *subdélégués* to the intendancies after 1760 shows the persistence of an archaic pattern characterized by the continuing preponderance of acts of corporal violence, blows and wounds, brawls, ambushes or murders.

Abel POITRINEAU, *La Vie rurale en Basse-Auvergne au* XVIIIᵉ *siècle* (P.U.F., 1965), 617–19.

55 WARLOCK IN THE VENDÉE

A farmer from La T--- had lost a dozen pigs and several cows in the space of a few weeks . . . He sent for a dowser to find out who had cast this spell on him, and she explored the nooks and corners of the farm, pendulum in hand. After drawing a blank, she spread out a map of the commune on the table and dangled it over each house, speaking the owner's name at the same time. When the name of Abel F--- was called, the pendulum began to spin . . . Abel F--- promptly became the warlock.

His wheelwright's shop and cafe were boycotted, and the peasant breathed again. His stock was safe . . .

---

* A very widespread magical ceremony carried out during the wedding benediction to prevent the bride and groom from consummating their marriage.

† Likewise in Paris, according to research carried out by a group of students from Nanterre and Paris into the Châtelet archives.

Some time later, there was a funeral. When the hearse was outside the F--- café . . . it stopped and could not be moved. The mourners had to push it all the way to the cemetery . . . On the way back, the vehicle broke down once again.

The resulting situation proved disastrous for Mr and Mrs F--- . . . The mayor advised them to sue . . .

The gossip has continued, and a small boy caught up in the general climate of feeling is quoted as saying: 'The warlock dresses up like an animal and walks through town with a skin over his head. My daddy says so.'

> This throwback to the attitudes of the ancien régime comes from the year 1966. *Le Monde*, 17 March 1966.

FURTHER READING
This is a fairly young field of study, and covers a number of extremely elusive and controversial topics. Only the foremost or most stimulating works are therefore mentioned.

BASIC WORKS
BRUNOT, Ferdinand, *Histoire de la langue française des origines à 1900* (A. Colin, new ed. in preparation). The standard work.

FEBVRE, Lucien, *Le Problème de l'incroyance au* XVIe *siècle, la religion de Rabelais* (Albin Michel, 2nd ed. 1947).

FEBVRE, Lucien and MARTIN, Henri-Jean, *L'Apparition du livre* (Albin Michel, 1958, 557 pp.).

MANDROU, Robert (in addition to those works already cited):

Introduction à la France moderne, essai de psychologie collective, 1500–1640 (Albin Michel, 1961, 400 pp.)

De la Culture populaire en France aux XVIIe *et* XVIIIe *siècles* (Stock, 1964, 223 pp.).

Magistrats et sorciers en France au XVIIe *siècle* (Plon, 1968, 532 pp.).

(These works, with their bibliographies, lead the field for the time being.)

DUPRONT, Alphonse, et al., *Livre et société dans la France du* XVIIIe (Paris and The Hague, Mouton, 1965, 240 pp.).

INTERESTING OR USEFUL WORKS
(In addition to those cited in the 'Documents'.)

AGULHON, Maurice, *Pénitents et francs-maçons de l'ancienne Provence* (Fayard, 1968, 452 pp.).

BLOCH, Marc, *Les Rois thaumaturges, étude sur le caractère surnaturel attribué à la puissance royale, particulièrement en France et en Angleterre* (A. Colin 2nd ed., 542 pp.).

CHAUNU, Pierre, *La Civilisation de l'Europe classique* (Arthaud, 1966, 706 pp.). Lively, absorbing, lyrical rather than historical, but overflowing with ideas, to say nothing of hypotheses.

DAINVILLE, François de, 'Effectif des collèges et scolarité aux XVIIᵉ et XVIIIᵉ siècles dans le Nord-Est de la France', in *Population*, 1955, pp. 455–88.

Ibid., 'Collèges et fréquentation scolaire au XVIIᵉ siècle', ibid., 1957, pp. 467–95.

ESTIVALS, Robert, *Le Dépôt légal sous l'Ancien Régime* (Rivière, 1961, 141 pp.).

Ibid., *La Statistique bibliographique de la France sous la monarchie au XVIIIᵉ siècle* (Paris and The Hague, Mouton, 1965, 460 pp.).

FERTÉ, Jeanne, *La Vie religieuse dans les campagnes parisiennes, 1622–1695* (Vrin, 1962, 454 pp.). Very thorough.

FOUCAULT, Michel, *Histoire de la folie à l'âge classique* (Plon, 1961, 673 pp.). Stimulating and often profound, if slightly hasty here and there.

GRAND-MESNIL, Marie-Noelle, *Mazarin, la Fronde et la presse, 1647-1649* (A. Colin, coll. Kiosque, 1967, 308 pp.). Intelligent and evocative.

GROETHUYSEN, B., *Origines de l'esprit bourgeois en France : l'Église et la bourgeoisie* (Paris, 4th ed., 1956, 301 pp.). Extremely intelligent.

HAZARD, Paul, *La Crise de la conscience européenne, 1680–1715* (Fayard, new ed. 1961, 430 pp.) Brilliant rather than profound, but evocative.

LOTTIN, Alain, *Vie et mentalité d'un Lillois sous Louis XIV* (Lille, Raoust, 1968, 444 pp.). Excellent monograph.

MAGGIOLO (cf. Document 52).

MOUSNIER, Roland, *Fureurs paysannes* (Calmann-Lévy, 1967, 354 pp.). Part One in particular.

PLATELLE, Henri, *Journal d'un curé de campagne au* XVII*ᵉ siècle* (Éd. du Cerf. 1965, 208 pp.). Excellent monograph.

ROTHKRUG, Lionel, *Opposition to Louis* XIV (Princeton University Press, 1965, 533 pp.). Some quite original chapters.

SÉGUIN, Jean-Pierre, *L'Information en France avant le périodique, 517 canards imprimés entre 1529 et 1631* (Larose, 1961, 132 pp.).

SAINTYVES, Pierre, *L'Astrologie populaire* (Paris, 1937, 470 pp.). Useful popularization.

Brief articles may sometimes be much better than hasty syntheses. For example:

BILLACOIS, François, 'Pour une Enquête sur la criminalité dans la France d'Ancien Régime', in *Annales E.S.C.,* March–April 1967, pp. 340–9.

FURET, François, 'Pour une définition des classes inférieures à l'époque moderne', in *Annales E.S.C.,* May–June 1963, pp. 459–74.

Index of names and French terms

Abbeville 184
aides 69n
Aix 174
allivrement 91
allodia 84–5, 95–6, 101
Alsace 13, 45, 114, 192
Amiens 55, 57, 66, 72–3, 110, 206, 229
amodiateurs 169
Amsterdam 63, 67, 68, 244
Angers 184, 205, 210
Angoulême 184
Anjou 11–12, 159
Antwerp 72
Anvers 244
Anzin 192
apprécis, the 131
Armagnac 190
arpent 112 & n, 177
arrière-ban, the 195, 199 & n, 200, 223
Artois 134n
Auvergne 84–5, 92, 96–7, 128, 176 & n,
    194, 281–2
auxilium 163; *et consilium* 166
aveu 95 & n
Avignon 79
Aymeret de Gazeau family 190
Azay-le-Rideau, château 169

Baehrel, René 140
Balzac 175n, 236
ban 83, 205, 223
banalités 13, 83n, 126, 141, 165, 174
banlieue 205, 210
banvin, right of 84
Basque region 79
Baulant, Micheline 74, 75
baux à rentes 129
bas peuple 118–19
Bayle 271, 274
Béarn 134n, 155, 156
Beauce 14

Beaufort 171
Beaujolais 9n, 82
Beaumarchais 183
Beaune 99–100
Beauvais 55, 56, 57, 130, 144, 145, 154,
    164, 189, 195, 206, 207, 224–6, 227–8
Beauvaisis, the 177, 105, 204
Bernard, J. 257–8
Besançon 279
Besse, château of 13
Beuvron, duc de 169
Béziers 73–4
bichet 100 & n
Bigorre 233
billon 62, 64, 65
Bloch, Jean Richard 180
Bloch, Marc 16, 79
Bluche, François 188, 189, 190, 242
bocages 81
Boileau 183
bon laboureur 110 & n
bon ménager 68, 69, 114, 132, 177–8
Bonzi 243
Bordeaux 58, 197, 205, 206, 207, 222–3,
    224, 251, 257–9
bordier 129, 146, 147
Bossuet 41
Bouhier 86
Boulainvilliers 160, 171
Boulonnais 207
Bourdaloue 131
bourg 33, 53, 59, 110, 116
Bourges 32, 184
bourgeois 114, 155, 232–60
Branges, marquis de 86
Brézé, marquis de 190, 241
Briare canal 58
Brittany 13, 16, 33, 39, 41, 78, 82, 85, 88,
    102, 110, 111, 124, 125, 127, 134n,
    135, 163, 165, 166, 167, 169, 172–4,
    175–6, 177, 181, 189, 190, 192, 201, 237